# as i remember them

# as i remember them

## childhood in quebec and why we came west

**Jeanne-Élise Olsen**

Edited by

G. Lorraine Ouellette

&

Ian Adam

UNIVERSITY OF CALGARY PRESS

University of Calgary Press
2500 University Dr. NW
Calgary, AB T2N 1N4
www.uofcpress.com

**National Library of Canada Cataloguing in Publication**
Olsen, Jeanne-Elise, 1899-1976
As I remember them : childhood in Quebec and why we came west /
Jeanne-Elise Olsen ; [edited by] G. Lorraine Ouellette, Ian Adam.

(Legacies shared book series, 1498-2358 ; 7)
Includes bibliographical references.
ISBN 1-55238-068-8

1. Olsen, Jeanne-Elise, 1899-1976. 2. Country life—Quebec (Province)—Laurentian Mountains Region. I. Adam, Ian. II. Ouellette, G. Lorraine (Grace Lorraine), 1923- III. Title. IV. Series.
FC2945.L387Z49 2002 971.4'4 C2002-911224-9
F1054.S3O47 2002

Canada Council for the Arts Conseil des Arts du Canada

Canada

We gratefully acknowledge the financial support of the Government of Canada through the Book Publishing Industry Development Program (BPIDP) for our publishing activities.



Printed and bound in Canada by AGMV Marquis.
♾ This book is printed on acid free paper.

Cover design and typesetting by Sona Khosla.
Cover photo by Don Tremain/Getty Images.

# contents

## Notes

# about the author

*by G. Lorraine Ouellette, née Olsen*

Jeanne Richer was born at the end of the nineteenth century in Val-des-Bois, a tiny settlement in Québec. In 1918, young, enthusiastic, full of dreams, she came to Saskatchewan in response to a call for a bilingual teacher. In Saskatoon, she met another recent immigrant: young, energetic, full of grand plans for the future.

Chris Olsen had come to Saskatchewan from Scandinavia by way of the U.S.A. Between these two were enormous differences of background and culture. English was for each of them a second language. His considerable talents, unfortunately, did not include a facility for courtoisie. One day, he approached her with a suggestion:

> "How would you like a job? Would you like to keep house for me?"

> "But," she replied, surprised: "I have a job; I am employed by the School District of Zenon Park."

It took minutes for her to recognize his proposal of marriage.

In the French-Canadian settlement of Zenon Park, Jeanne and her younger sister Damienne did not lack admirers; they were not, however, easily impressed, and Jeanne felt stirrings of an urge to escape from the limitations of the ethnically limited society in which she had been brought up.

In spite of the heavy punishment inflicted upon her parents (for her father, as will appear in the text, had, before his marriage, served for ten full years as a Roman Catholic priest and the Church looked with abhorrence upon his defection), her parents never deviated in any particular from their exemplary Roman Catholic life style: daily prayer; acceptance of all of the church's tenets; French punctiliously spoken in the home – these things formed the basis of their routine. Jeanne, in spite of her love for her parents and her people, yearned to escape from this tribal rigidity. She longed for intellectual freedom of which she felt the lack. She believed she would find it in marriage with a foreigner.

On the 24th of August, 1920, in Saskatoon, Saskatchewan, Marie-Jeanne Élise Eugénie Richer (dît Louveteau) became Jeanne-Élise Olsen, and the pattern of her life was altered forever.

If she kept a diary in those first years I have not been able to find it, but there are letters, photographs, and notes for a planned account of those busy times. She intended yet another memoir. She meant to call it *The Olsen Saga*: the story of how Kristian

Lauritz Olsen (now called 'Christian L.') made a place for himself in Canada. Her notes suggest the story of their adjustment to a new country and to one another.

In 1923, she was delivered of me, her first child. Since she took an active part in her husband's financial enterprises – general stores – hotels – she had little strength or energy for parenting: especially since, I am told, I was unusually demanding, requiring to be sung to and entertained. My grandmother undertook my care, and I was with her for extended periods throughout my babyhood and, indeed, until I was sent to school at a convent in Prince Albert.

Papa had tried farming, but though he loved life on the land he found the living much too precarious, and so he sought and obtained employment with the Western Empire Life Assurance Company. Papa was no gambler. He was prepared to work very hard, but he wanted assurance of a solid future. He never borrowed money in his life.

In 1930, Papa was offered the managership of the Edmonton branch of his company. That very year, my little sister Leila was born, and we moved to Edmonton for the winter months, retaining the farm in Saskatchewan for the long summer holidays.

And now, Mama was living in a city in which there was a university. She very much wanted to study. Papa saw no reason why she should not, and so, with the help of Grandmother to care for little Leila and with me in boarding school, Mama was able to fulfil her dearest ambition. She enrolled in the University of Alberta in the Faculty of Arts.

Sometimes, in the years that followed, Mama would entertain her college friends to dinner at our house. More than once, a guest inquired of Papa:

> "And did you go to the university, Mr. Olsen?"
> To which Papa would unblushingly reply: – "Oh, yes; yes, indeed. I went to the university for ten years!"
> "And what did you take?"
> "My wife."

These were the years of the Great Depression. No one had much money, but there was lots to eat on the farm. We had meat, vegetables, cream, eggs – and because Papa did not depend for his livelihood on the produce of the farm, we lived very, very well. In the summer, Mama canned meat, chicken, vegetables, and fruit. She made jam and pickles. We had more food than we could use.

It was hot in Canwood in the summer, and I remember that often she would wait until night to fire up the big stove in the summer kitchen, for meat had to be processed for a full four hours at a rolling boil. It was cool and quiet, then. I can see her now, sitting at the rough table by the light of a coal-oil lamp, her German grammar in her hand or, with eyes closed, listening intently to the music of her little wind-up gramophone.

In the fall, we would go back: I to convent, Leila to Grandmother, and Mama to her beloved university.

The photograph on the next page is my favourite picture of Mama. She is seated in her laboratory, and behind her can be seen some of her botanical drawings. (She majored in German and minored in Botany). This picture, in her album, bears the title *The Happy Time.* Her ten years of study were for her the happiest of her life. In 1940, she submitted her thesis, *The Scientific Work of Goethe* and received the degree of Master of Arts.

Afterwards, she taught Art, Botany, and French. Her vision was never limited, either by her time or by her circumstances. She was a citizen of the world, and she ranged far and wide in space and in time, exploring, in her reading. And though she wandered far from her home to seek her future, she retained for her family a deep and abiding respect, love, and loyalty. She felt the need to leave to her children this little book of memories so that those who should come after should know a little about her parents and should do them justice.

She knew how to listen. She attracted young people seeking a confidante of absolute discretion. My cousin Mary-Josephine once said: "*When I visit Mrs. N ... I do so to please her. When I visit Aunt Jeanne, I do so to please myself.*"

*Jeanne-Élise Olsen, née Richer* (dît *Louveteau*), *in botany laboratory at the University of Alberta, circa 1940.*

# foreword

This is not intended as a book or anything resembling one. I have always preferred to read them and have often thought that there are too many already, especially poor ones.

However, when I looked over some papers, manuscripts, and others which Father had preserved, I thought that he must have wanted us and our children to know more about him and his life than he had discussed with us.

Much has changed since we were children in the beautiful Laurentian country. A way of life has practically ceased to exist, and, since distance as well as time separates our children from those scenes, I have tried to set down as faithfully as I could my recollections of our parents and our childhood in Val-des-Bois.

Memory is very selective and imperfect, especially in early years. Being the oldest in the family, my souvenirs go back further than those of the others, but I hope my brothers and my sister will some day add to these recollections for the benefit of their children.

Jeanne-E. Olsen
Edmonton, February 25th, 1973

*To some child yet to come within our family who will look upon our kin and our people — accepting them with a curiosity not unmixed with affection....*

*To this future little Jean or Jeanne, I dedicate this imperfect account of our early lives. It was written in part for my own pleasure and also because it may be of interest to other members of the family.*

*Let my limited audience excuse me if I offer no apology for its literary quality. As the philosopher's wife said, "If I had anything better you should have it."*

# prologue: the literary context

by Ian Adam

Jeanne Olsen has stated in her 'Foreword' that her work is not "a book or anything resembling one" and I think she may have meant that it would resist the pigeon-holing appropriate for most published volumes. It is certainly true that hers is not an easy work to classify. It is at once autobiography and biography, social anatomy, family history, and apologia. Broadly, it begins as memoir but concludes as settlement narrative. And, while it is in many ways a scholarly study, it is not one in a conventional sense. The author has provided illuminating footnotes, illustrations, maps, original correspondence, and other apparatus to supplement, clarify, and sustain information and arguments given and points made; later, her daughter Lorraine Ouellette is to add to these. However, the work remains largely based on personal recall: it is a primary source, of the raw material that formal history must draw on to carry out its tasks. Its action unfolds leisurely and with intimately realized detail through rural Quebec at the turn of the last century before its final stages recording a family's precipitous transport to Western Canada. Throughout, it explores a major cultural force in the Franco-Canadian community: religious faith in its doctrines and dogmas, its hierarchy and eschatology. It is a document that charms, but it also engages with its moral and intellectual integrity.

Of course, the above account is shaded and shaped by personal associations. I was privileged to know the author, my aunt and my mother's sister, over many years. In addition to numerous memories of her through everyday events, from the bottling of home-made root beer to evening readings of Thackeray's *The Rose and the Ring* at a cottage in Alberta's Lac St. Anne, there are many others that had direct bearing on my own life: in particular, gifts of books from a well-stocked library that challenged me to rise to their levels of thought and expression, and provocative conversations that, long past the years when I was a little boy, I still vividly recall. A remarkable person, coming, as this book will indicate, from a remarkable context.

That context begins with an enclosure, a dwelling, a nest. It is '*le hangar*' or '*la remise,*' the first family home, a one-room structure with a loft. From it emerge the earliest recollections in this narrative of the remembered and recreated. These are few, but vivid, sometimes tender, but more often traumatic. The child absorbs the world of the attic with its sundry treasures, but even more vividly recalls a scalding, the bite of a dog, or a fire quickly extinguished. There are glories in the world that match desire, but there is also the pain of alienation.

A larger dwelling soon replaces *le hangar*, and in it glories preponderate over pain. Each of its components — attic, bedroom, library, kitchen — has its own character. The kitchen, source of savoury and sweet, odours and taste, has a large window from which the young ones may look out and see the arrival of visitors or the passage of others along the road. The dining room recalls not the culinary pleasures but aesthetic ones: the cherry-wood cabinet and its glass and china or the house plants: "a fuschia covered with graceful, bell-lake flowers — so tall that it almost reached the top of the window" (15). In the master bedroom, engaging pictures, *The Soul's Awakening* and a print of Landseer's *The Stag at Eve*, leave a deep impression. Awesome is *le bureau de Papa*, father's office, where matters legal, commercial, and dental are carried out, and a wolfskin rug guards entry. Upstairs are two special areas. First, the attic, with access restricted to rainy days. Through its hazardous trap-door opening lie contents linked to history, not only familial but also political in relics from the 1837 Papineau Rebellion. Just below, on the second floor, lies the library, a room central both literally and figuratively. Its contents engage the author for more than two full pages: reading and the acquisition of knowledge are themes to which this book and this life are to return again and again. The rounds of chores and household and farmyard duties help fill the days, not without pleasures, in which animals — domestic, wild — play a large role.

The context gradually expands beyond the house and immediate surroundings. An early emergence is a winter at the James McLaren lumber camp where the father is employed. It is estranging, though a kindly cook helps lighten the days. Later, there are visits to neighbours and family, often with young people present. This is a community with many large families and companionship with other children is not lacking. The young Jeanne's keen eye defines particularly the older inhabitants, at times with the taxonomic thoroughness of the bestiary. The pompous or cruel do not escape, the kindly and generous are noted, and such telling details as a drink of water from a patriarchal cup are meticulously highlighted (49). The widening spirals of experience loop again as the outside world comes to the small community. Visitors from afar come and go: a Scotsman who, to the children's dismay, persuades the father of the virtues of oatmeal; peddlers packing suitcases full of goods; tradesmen such as a shoemaker claiming descent from the third dynasty of French kings of the tenth century. They bring to the child awareness of outside areas to which she imaginatively ventures and to the like of which she is later to actually go.

But that is to come. The world that absorbs her, that absorbs much of the passion of the prose, is the world of sister and brother. The tether to the centre, the house and family, remains, but it is extended, largely within a community of two, in a sensitive exploration of a tender sibling bond. Christian and his older sister have so much in common: humour, intelligence, and curiosity, and these shared endowments bloom in shared activities: picking berries, fishing for carp, participating in games, exploring bog, meadow, and forest. The two younger siblings, Damienne and

Serge, are generally outside this relation, the first through temperament, the second through being too young. But the older children treat them with affection, though teasing may go too far, as when sister Damienne finds her Eaton Beauty doll hanged by the neck from the top of the attic stairs, victim of some demon in Christian's imagination.

There is one element which threatens this orderly expansion of horizons. It is something buried in the past, a kind of time bomb. There are few hints of its nature before the end of Chapter 6,[1] but there it explodes. Its origin lies in the history of the author's parents. In 1897, Wilfrid Daniel (a.k.a. Damien) Richer, parish priest at Val-des-Bois, weds his eighteen-year-old parishioner, Eliza Côté, in a Protestant ceremony in Ottawa, an action which leads to their excommunication. Nevertheless, the couple continue to live in the community for over twenty years, during which time their children are born and raised. Throughout, these children remain almost entirely ignorant of what to other community members is the scandal of their begetting. In 1918–19, through an extended process, an arrangement is concluded with the Church which lifts the ban from Damien and Eliza, but only on specific conditions, one of which is exile to places west. This process begins in a 1911 visit by a Father Côté to the mother, gravely ill in an Ottawa hospital. That visit leads to the astonishing 1917 letter of pages 166–168 and to some twelve pages of discussion opening Chapter 7.





1 Though one notes mother Eliza's tears on being queried about her certificate of first communion (16).

At this point in the narrative, a remarkable thing happens. In what turns out to be an aesthetically potent decision, the author turns away from these events, not to return to them for over twenty pages. In her university studies and teaching years, Jeanne Olsen worked a great deal in the life sciences, particularly botany (a background which shows in the detailed representation of vegetative life in this volume). She would probably have been familiar with Haeckel's[2] dictum "Ontogeny recapitulates phylogeny": certainly the principle of recapitulation is evident here. The leisurely progress of the young Jeanne and Christian through childhood is re-enacted, but with differences, and the source of those differences can only be seen as knowledge. There is more depth, less glow, more resonance, less magic. Many of the scenes of the earlier chapters are revisited, but with more sombre perspective. Again books are invoked, but with new information, or they are other books. Again the family calls on relatives and neighbours, but with new or greater detail. And the father, a major but somewhat shadowy presence in the previous chapters, emerges here as a source of lore anecdotal and encyclopedic. Here is summer in the two visions. From Chapter 4 we read:

> Summer was the best time.... Random walks along the road or through the fields would generally turn up something of interest. Grass stems were tasty bits,

2 Ernest Haeckel (1834–1919) was a prominent Darwinian. The capsule phrase cited argues that the stages in the evolution of mankind (phylogeny) are replicated in the development of the human embryo (ontogeny).

> the soft, juicy part above the node. Gum could be carved out the bark of venerable spruce trees; thimbleberries were more or less everywhere; blackberries lined the ditches along the road in some places; dewberries favoured shady spots, strawberries the sunny places, though the best and largest were among tall grasses. Pincherries were fairly common along the road to the lake; the *amélanchiers* had few fruit, but were tasty. If we were out early, we might come across spider webs still unmarred by the wriggling of some unwary prey, the morning sun making each bedewed thread of these incredible structures a row of scintillating crystal beads. (75–76).



While from Chapter 7 the following:

> Summer holidays were good times.... On one occasion, though, our isolation was brought home to us: Christian and I accompanied Father to La Salette to do some haying on a farm he had just sold, reserving the hay crop for himself. Uncle Omer and his sons Antonio and Nilphas were helping with the haying, and I did the cooking while the men worked in the field.... While we were there, the neighbours happened to have a party: there was music and dancing — the usual country entertainment. Christian and I did not know how to dance and so we were mere

> observers. It seemed to me such innocent fun that I felt resentful that we would certainly never be allowed to join in this frivolous sort of activity. It was the first time that the narrow boundaries of our puritanical way of life stood revealed, and I resolved that I would, some day, be free of meaningless restrictions. (202–03).

Note the changing contexts: the younger children in companionship with themselves and nature, almost absorbed into it; the older engaged in tasks, observing social events, and in Jeanne here, feeling the stirrings of possibilities beyond what is allowed. Such moments make the transition to the West recorded at the end of Chapter 7 and in Chapter 8 and the Epilogue seem not so much an enforced relocation as a psychically inevitable one. Perhaps the analogy to invoke should not be from Haeckel but from William Blake, Bard of Innocence and Experience.

There is one other aspect to this book on which I wish to comment. To do so, I will again draw on the botanical science in which Jeanne Olsen was so knowledgeable. I speak of its rhizomic, or multi-rooted qualities. I have already indicated something of these: there are many narrative threads supplementing major ones: anecdotes of family and community, reaches into contexts of written history and fiction. There are other threads (tendrils?) that are scarcely narrative, if we think of narrative as tracing a progress through time. These are rather less linear than vertical, explorations of wonders — often humble ones — the gathering of raspberries (93) or the making of paper flowers (113) as well as such events as a train trip to Ste. Anne de Beaupré, its Basilica and surroundings (135–36). There is further rooting that takes shape in the appendices, in the story of a teacher's failed romantic ventures or in a neighbour's visit to the metropolis, Montreal. And one must make special note of the story of the lumber mill so often alluded to in the text, which is fully presented in Notes 8 and 8a, particularly in 8a, where it is given in the voice of the author's brother Christian, speaking here in 1994 at the age of 92 in a nursing home in Nipawin.

The rootedness also is found in the strong presence of some family members. This is, of course, a narrative with a proclaimed hero in the remarkable figure of Damien Richer. His innocence in certain areas, his omni-competence (both practical and theoretical) in most others, and his steadfast adherence to the tenets of a faith that had made him and his outcast: these inspire affection and admiration. But there are also potential heroes. While their story is more subordinated and less complete, their presence nevertheless evokes in the thoughtful an awareness of *latency*: what they might be, in another context, another telling. My perception in this narrative is that such roles are not played by Richers (other than the children, of course) but by Côtés, and among the Côtés it is particularly the women who are notable. This preponderance is not surprising: the men of the village, and perhaps especially Damien, are at work away from home and hearth by day and often for longer periods. Those that remain behind will remain there in memory as well. In the Epilogue Lorraine Ouellette has provided much information on Eliza Côté supplementary to that given by her mother. Among the other women, grandmother Marie is an immensely powerful presence whose "books were ever ready for the final audit" (125). And Aunts Arthémise and Eugénie also stand out: the former with her raconteurish skill and wicked humour, the latter somewhat more quiet, but also droll, telling the laughing children with mock gravity to "Respect my black hairs!" A city dweller and the godmother, she hosts her young niece on early visits, and heralds modernity.

There are others of note not mentioned, particularly the classroom teachers from the school years. But I now leave the reader to the pleasure of the text itself.

# *a note on family relations*

Jeanne-Élise Olsen's father and mother, Damien and Eliza, have between them thirteen siblings, several of whom are discussed in the text, often along with their parents, spouses, and children. While these are considered most thoroughly in Chapter 5, "Relatives, Household Crafts," they also are referred to elsewhere. As a guide to the uninitiated reader, I highlight the most prominent of these.

Of the four grandparents, only grandmother Marie Côté (née Tremblay) is a major subject. Her husband, Phidime Côté, died sometime during the author's earliest years. The reasons behind the absence of the Richer grandparents in the life of the family may be easily inferred from the text.

The Côté grandparents had eight children. In descending order of age, they are Joseph, Rose-Anna, Alice, Charles, Eliza, Eugénie,

Arthémise, and Émilienne. They all marry, some rather later in life than others; their spouses are respectively Alexina, Charles Lemieux, Marcel Charbonneau, Rose-Alba, Damien Richer, Joseph Tremblay, Nazaire Lemieux, and Pierre Beauchamps. Parents Eliza and Damien apart, these are the uncles and aunts, by descent or marriage, on the Côté side of the family for the four children, Jeanne, Christian, Damienne, and Serge.

Prominent among them (as noted in "The Literary Context," above) are Eliza's younger sisters Arthémise and Eugénie (the author's godmother): mention should also be made of the vivid presences of brother Joseph and his wife Alexina.

Eliza's elder sisters Rose-Anna and Alice, along with their husbands Charles Lemieux and Marcel Charbonneau, receive more cursory treatment. Uncle Charles Côté, the author's godfather, works itinerantly and often outside the community: his profile is also relatively low. I have designated him "Uncle Charles" to distinguish him from "Uncle Charles Lemieux."

Cousins are featured less than their parents; but notable among them are Jeanne Côté (the eldest of Joseph's children and of an age with the author), the Charbonneau children Margot, Arthur and Joseph, and the Lemieux children Edmond, Emmanuel, Rose and Laurence.

The Richer grandparents had nine children, six of whom account for some thirty-eight grandchildren, thirty-four of whom would be cousins to Damien and Eliza's four offspring. But only three of Damien's siblings figure with any substance in the narrative per se: Uncles Omer and Oscar and Aunt Amelia (Sister

Antoine Marie). The Richer cousins scarcely appear except for Omer's sons Antonio and Nilphas and daughter Alzire, the latter to be seen with her parents in the visit captured in the photo on page 100.

Not surprisingly, most of the people noted above live in close proximity in three villages in the southern Lièvre River country, north of Ottawa–Hull. Val-des-Bois is at the northern tip of a narrow triangle whose base is formed by Poltimore to the southwest and Notre-Dame-de-la-Salette to the southeast. Approximately fifteen miles separate Val-des-Bois from its sister villages, which themselves are about ten miles apart. Damien Richer and family live about two and a half miles from Val-des-Bois proper, where the Joseph Côté's reside; in Poltimore dwell Grandmother Côté with daughters Arthémise and Émilienne; very nearby are elder daughters Rose-Anna Lemieux and Alice Charbonneau and families. The family of Damien's brother Omer lives in Notre-Dame-de-la-Salette. Brother Oscar lives nearby.

The home village of the other Richers, St. André-Avellin, lies well to the east of the area.

Ian Adam

# introduction

As is so often the case in human undertakings, I am deeply conscious of the shortcomings of the work I have done. It ought to have been sooner begun while the best sources of information were not yet lost. As I have indicated in the Foreword, I did not seriously contemplate this project until I went over Father's small store of papers and manuscripts. But regrets are idle. What matters now is not to delay any longer lest more opportunities disappear and further changes obscure the picture of the past which we would preserve, for whatever interest it may have for us and for our children.

The first time I saw home again was in 1959. Our cousin Ivan Lemieux was kind enough to drive us, Aunt Eugénie and me, to Val-des-Bois and to Poltimore. It was startling to reach both places in such a short time; we had been used to thinking them so far apart in the horse and buggy days. Many changes had taken place in the village in consequence of the hydroelectric development at High Falls. None of the dwellings are left which bordered the Lièvre and which in our time constituted most of what was little more than a hamlet. The church, replacing the one we knew, had been moved up the slope which was formerly behind it. It stands now on a new level, that of the new main street. The old cemetery which was behind the church is now below it, close to the river bank.

New features include a little grotto in the church grounds, a 'Calvary' by the road intersection, a modern school, a hotel, a restaurant with windows looking out on Lac Vert, which I had not known of, though it must have been there all along, hidden by the thick forest growth that bordered the road. The covered bridge was there still in 1959, but it has since been demolished and replaced by a modern concrete structure. There used to be several of these picturesque sheltered crossings. I took a snapshot of ours and of one already condemned at La Salette. There was a third one on the way to Poltimore which I heard is to be preserved.

The alterations in the region bordering the river were begun soon after our departure, as we knew from letters from Uncle Omer and from Father's friend Isidore LaRocque.

Further away from the river, the level of Pelletier Creek and also of the lake which bears the same name, is much altered. Below the mill, the creek or little river is higher by reason of the water level in the Lièvre; above, the lake is lower because the old dams no longer exist.

Vegetation now fills a section of the creek which was made by the dams into an artificial lake. We called it Lac de la Carpe (carp were very numerous there). Some fields which sustained sparse grass meadows are now forested with pine. Land has been subdivided into smaller units along the stream. People live there and work in the village or further afield. A tourist lodge (White Deer) is not far from where we used to cross to go and pick raspberries.

The house where we lived is still standing, apparently as solid as ever. The interior has been altered so I declined to go in, though we were invited to do so. Only the main building remains. The woodshed has gone, as have the smaller house or '*hangar*' and the ice house. Three of the four elms Mother planted have gone because they interfered with power and telephone wires. The stables and the hog pen have disappeared.



The road to the mill still follows the outline of the *montagnon*: such a mass of granite is not easily budged. A tall maple which every fall made a large dark blood-red patch at the base of the mountain near the corner is no more to be seen. Neither are, I am sure, the wild strawberries we picked there and in the ditch on each side of the road. Gone are the fine tall cedars near the road towards the dam. The walnut tree which was near the spot where we used to wade across the creek to go and fetch the cows must be drowned by the raised level of the water.



The mill has grown older, greyer, but while it remains standing the change will not be too noticeable. Its walls of vertical boards were already weathered when we were young. In 1959, the water wheel no longer turned, a gasoline motor provided power for what machinery was still used. Now all life has departed from it, all activity has stopped, and the owner, Edouard Plante, still living near it, has been retired for some time.

But the years have passed lightly over our dear mountains — the Hills of Home — like unto no other hills — the familiar landscape bordered by the lofty horizon line reaching down to the top of the lovely tree-clad Laurentians. The very stones themselves seem to have a look of glad recognition for me. I found myself swept as on an overwhelming wave of emotion. I have never been given to homesickness, even as a child, but all at once I wanted to cry out: "*this is home: the centre of the world is here!*"

Yes, the everlasting hills are still there, their ancient slopes richly clothed with the tapestried beauty of the successive seasons. Perhaps in the remote hollows between their summits lakes are still crystal clear as they were, and the loons still may be heard to utter their weird, lonely cry.

# 1

# out of babyhood

The first building I remember is the little house in which we spent some years before the larger one was constructed. It was used in later years as a storage place, and it was termed '*le hangar*' or '*la remise*.'

The ground floor was originally divided into a kitchen-cum-living-room and one bedroom. When Mother took a course in photography, a part of the space, the northwest corner, was partitioned off and felted to make a darkroom lit only by a small red lantern for photographic work, while the remainder was furnished as a studio.

The upstairs or attic was filled with bins and shelves with pieces of harness and sundry articles. When in use, the bins contained green peas and yellow peas for soup, field peas and oats in mixture for the chickens, and buckwheat which was ground at the mill for pancakes. Peas and buckwheat were threshed with a flail. Sometimes we explored the attic. It might hold some long-forgotten toy, or a new mouse nest in the sawdust which trickled out through cracks in the wall.

I can still see myself in the main room, very small indeed, leaning against Mother's knee as she held a baby — presumably my first little sister who died at two and a half of whooping cough. I very much wanted to be picked up and felt rather forlorn.

After Christian was born, I was occasionally sent to get a container of milk from the people who lived at the mill. Being just over three, I yielded to temptation one day and drank a few mouthfuls off the top. Mother's eagle eye noted at once the lowered level of the liquid. "*Jeanne, did you drink some of the milk?*" — "*Oh, no! That's all they gave me.*" — But it was not very long before I came back, shamefaced, to confess my dereliction. I really had little talent for deceit.

Time went by and I was allowed, on occasion, to play with the Paquettes' little girl Ti-fille. How I envied her blonde, curly hair! I also envied her the elegant name of Paquette and found mine undistinguished and unmusical.

Eva, the older daughter, had a dog that was fiercely loyal to her. One day, she was playing with me as people will with small children: holding my hands as I was climbing up the front of her with much giggling and screaming. The dog had no sense of humour where Eva was concerned. He misunderstood the purpose of the exercise and bit me severely on the leg. It has been difficult for me to trust dogs since, but I like to think that it is chiefly that I find cats more congenial.

A couple of incidents happened in the little house, one of which nearly put an end to me. Mother had filled a large bucket or small tub with scalding water from the stove and set it down near the stairs. Somehow I stumbled backwards into the bucket. Mother, as she told me about it many years later, still shuddered at the horror of that moment. She had just turned her back on me when my cry of fright and distress made her look around. As she told it, she snatched me up and quickly loosened my lower garments — and the skin came off with the little panties, leaving me with thighs completely 'scalped' on the inside. The nightmare of the succeeding months is so engraved on my memory that I need no help to recall it. I lay on a heap of pillows near the stove — it was early Spring — wrapped lightly, thighs thickly coated with vaseline, dreading the twice-a-day bath and dressing because, in spite of everything, the flesh of one thigh would come into contact with the flesh of the other and stick. My screams must have awakened the echoes in the hills about. Mother would soothe me but, when soothing was ineffective, she would threaten to "call the wolves," who did duty for the bogeyman. (I'm sure Farley Mowat would have disapproved). By then, I would staunchly cry right back: "*Let them come!*" That, of course, was the recklessness of despair. I was never admirable for stoicism under physical pain. One gets away with such cowardice nowadays, thanks to the mercy of anaesthetics and painkillers.

Father was in Wabassee at the time, a lumber camp based on a timbered area or farm owned by the McLarens. Some well-intentioned neighbour informed him of my misadventure, and he started for home, walking all the way, a matter of some forty miles,

*Wilfrid Daniel Richer, 1865–1941*

*Madame W. D. Richer (née Eliza Adèle Côté) 1878–1953*

with never a stop. Judging from his swollen face when he arrived, he must have been crying most of the way.

The same room was the scene of another happening, one time when Aunt Arthémise was visiting us. She and Mother were peeling boiled beets for pickling, and I was sitting under the table pretending that the tablecloth, which hung quite far down, was a tent. I was very fond of fresh, still warm cooked beets and sat contentedly eating a fat piece while they chatted and worked by the light of a coal-oil lamp. Now, I decided it was time for another piece. I started to get up, faltered a little, and, reaching for support, took hold of the table-cloth. Before I realized what I was doing, tablecloth, beets, lamp, and all were down, and the spilled oil was flaming all over the floor. Aunt Arthémise rushed into the bedroom like a flash and came back with a grey blanket. She soon smothered the flames. Mother had quickly snatched me out of danger. I was so startled that I don't know whether I was scolded or not. All I can remember is a cold numbness settling over me at the sight of my latest exploit.

We must have moved into the larger house soon after this. My next memory picture is of Mother sitting near the wash-stand in the kitchen peeling potatoes, and me lying on the floor flat on my back *les quatres fers en l'air* (arms and legs in the air), holding a primer and laboriously deciphering the letters of the alphabet. The next step was assembling them into syllables. I would get up and run to Mother with each new combination. The whole thing was put into a little ditty which I cheerfully sang, a new verse for each consonant:

*Un B avec un A fait BA;*
*Un B avec un E fait BE;*
*Un B avec un I fait BA, BE, BI*

and so to the end. My life-long love affair with the printed word had begun.

Father loved the land, but best of all he loved the forest. Though he was fond of our little farm, tilling the soil was not for him. Our few acres could not in any case have yielded us a living since, as with most other holdings in that part of the country, mountains, lakes, and streams covered a good deal of the ground and most farmers spent their winters in lumber camps. Father had always been interested in map making, and soon he was engaged in surveying and mapping timber limits for the James McLaren company. This was a life to his liking: walking through the splendid hardwoods mixed with pines, fir, and cedar: camping; visits with the Indians; dealing with the jobbers and at times acting as game warden, accompanied always with some of his favourite books. I think he must have been a happy man in those years. There was certainly little to worry him at home where Mother always had the situation well in hand, though possibly somewhat under protest.

There were two of us now: Christian crawling much of the time on all fours, sometimes sitting with me under the table — a very good cover for two small children who do not like to be sent to bed while anything interesting is going on. The dark comes early during our Canadian winters. I remember us two huddled together in the deep shadows of the tablecloth when the dismal howling of timber wolves would sound frightfully near on cold clear nights. We would sit very still, hardly breathing, as the mournful notes would rise slowly to the skies and end in a soft, tenuous wail. In later years, we were to hear them again on evening walks, calling to each other from mountain top to mountain top, knowing there was no danger, but still with that cold thrill along the spine.

When Christian was nine or ten months old, we went to Wabassee to spend a winter at the McLaren Camp.

There was a store at the camp, and a cookhouse. The cook, a fat, jolly woman (name of Docherty) was very nice to me and most generous with cookies and doughnuts. Of course, I was not permitted to wander away from our house and (in Mother's opinion) 'make a nuisance of myself.' Mother would come and look for me, and Mrs. Docherty would hold her huge snow-white apron spread out to hide me while she blandly told Mother "*No, I have not seen your little girl today.*" That little comedy delighted me, of course, but Mother showed a deplorable lack of humour and took to tying me to the leg of the table with store string. Obviously, I could have broken the string, but I was so furious that I scorned to escape and sulked instead.

Occasionally, I was despatched to the store on errands. On one proud occasion, I was sent to go and purchase my new Reader. It was a larger book than the dog-eared old primer, with more pictures, and, of course, much bigger words. On the way back, I had to brace myself against the wind with all my strength to keep from being blown off my feet, hugging the while my brand new treasure.

We had left my toys at home, and Mother had made me a rag doll out of a long stocking. She was dressed in an ankle-length skirt, like an adult, and I thought of her as a 'grand'mère' doll. I remember watching over her anxiously when we packed our things to return to Val-des-Bois in the spring.

Somewhere on our way, we met Aunt Arthémise. I was overjoyed to see her: threw my arms around her neck and burst into tears, repeating over and over, between sobs: "*I thought I'd never see you again!*" It must have seemed a long winter. Souvenirs of those early years are vignettes scattered through a forgotten text. Few incidents were sufficiently fixed in the mind to endure.

Two years after the birth of Christian, Damienne was born, and approximately two years later Serge joined our number. We were all involved more or less in the various activities which filled our lives, in degree according to our ages, in part also according to our various temperaments.

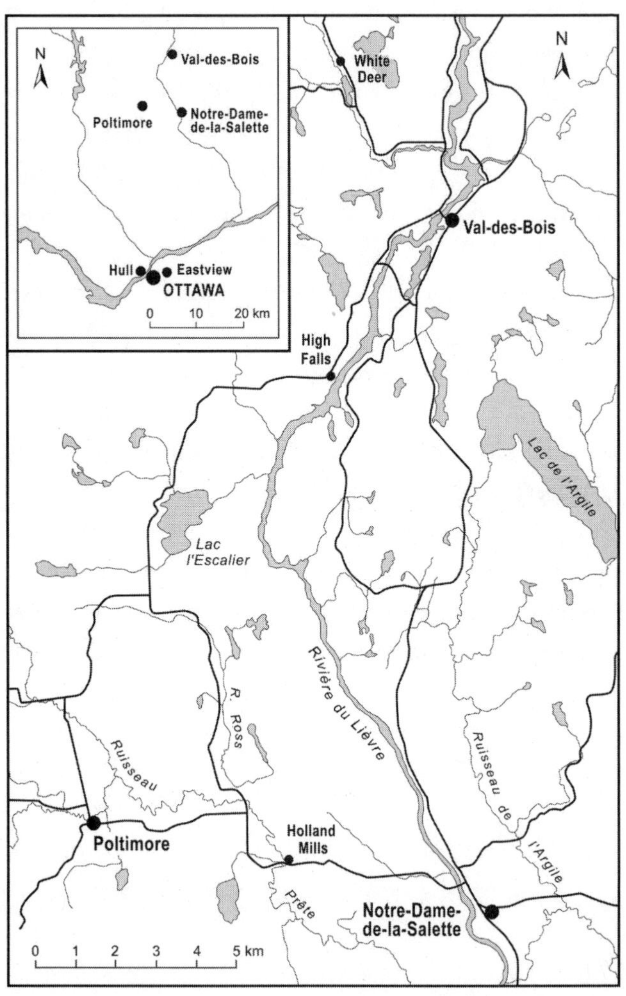


*Map of Lièvre River area, including Ottawa.*

2

# home, lessons, chores

I'd like to describe our house as I recall it. The building, as the photograph shows, was a squarish structure with the kitchen at the back. From the kitchen extended a porch which continued out to the woodshed, filled with wood for the winter and serving as a summer kitchen in warm weather.

Seen, then, from the inside, the kitchen opened onto the back porch on the west and into the dining room on the north side. On the east wall was a largish window through which we used to watch for expected guests to round the corner; here a huge rock extended like a staunch buttress from the base of the mountain, causing a sharp turn in the road. Sometimes we were allowed to go and do our sentinel turn on the very rock itself, where Mother could see us but where we could command a view of the road as far as J. B.

*The Richer house, circa 1906, still without the balcony and porch. Seated on the steps, Jeanne, Christian and Damienne. Father stands beside Mother's house plants.*

David's place. A smaller window in the south wall looked down the slope over a cultivated area to the creek. A path along the porch and house led to a covered outside entrance to the cellar. Beside the path was a trellis supporting a luxuriant growth of hop vines.

This entrance to the cellar was used for carrying in bulky things such as vegetables — potatoes, turnips, carrots, cabbages (hung from the ceiling in winter) and crocks or barrels containing salt pork, salt cucumbers or green beans, or salt fish (herring, mostly). There was always an abundance of canned fruit. The cellar had an earthen floor, and it was cool and dry. The narrow stairs led up to the kitchen through a trap-door located under the attic stairs along the north wall.

Furniture in the kitchen, as well as I can remember, was: a good-sized table, a bench and some chairs, cupboards, upper and lower — the latter with sugar and flour bins, a stove with a warming oven and warm water reservoir; (this stove had replaced one of heavier metal, highly embossed and without the warming oven); a low cabinet, enclosed, on which rested a pail of drinking water with the traditional dipper, and a hand basin and a soap dish. To the right of this last, on the wall, was a holder for a roller towel. Between the cabinet and the door, during the winter there stood a barrel of water daily replenished (by us) with snow.

There were changes through the years. A wash stand had first occupied the space later filled by the more spacious cabinet. My little pink rocker had its day and disappeared. There was at one time one of those rocking cradles which are to be found now in museums. This was made by Father, as were a number of other articles such as a chest of drawers in the dining room, my rocker, and my first bed.

Beyond the door, in the northwest corner of the kitchen were the attic stairs. A square platform about a quarter of the way up the stairs and the upper steps of those stairs provided a favourite listening and observation post when we had visitors. We could be out of the way and yet miss nothing. It was there, too, that I would amuse younger guests by reading them stories. It was a cosy sort of corner: warm with the heat rising to the ceiling from the crackling fire in the kitchen stove.[1] Outdoor clothing hung on pegs above the platform and lower steps.

Access to the attic was not too often granted, but we were sometimes, on rainy days, allowed to go there. There was no railing along the trap-door opening and Mother was very conscious of the danger this presented. We enjoyed our excursions to the attic. There was a barrel of discarded clothing and the like, including old

1 It was pleasant in the winter to sit by the kitchen stove when the weather was very cold. In the evening, a mixture of green and dry wood was used to make a long-lasting fire. The sap produced a soft hissing sound as it boiled, and that mingled with the crackling of the more seasoned logs. If among the green sticks there was some cherry wood (*merisier*), we would peel off the inner bark (*phloem*) and chew it. It had an agreeable slightly sweet cherry taste. Cedar was our favourite wood. It was easy to split, the fibres ran so straight. Ideal for kindling, we also used it to make a species of shooting toy. A strip of wood could be split partly down its length, and a match-like stick inserted at the tip could be propelled to a distance of several feet by pressing on the two 'arms' of the 'gun.' Naturally, it was a contest, and the boys always won. The trick was the correct placing of the 'bullet.'

lace curtains and such furbelows as frilled and laced and tucked petticoats, which wonderful materials were available to Damienne and me for dressing up and making dolls' clothes. There were boxes filled with old letters, papers and various miscellany, and older treasures under the eaves. Father had some old guns, one with a bayonet, and a cannonball cracked by contact with the stone walls of the church of St. Eustache during the Rebellion. We never tired of admiring these and examined thoughtfully these real-life links with history.

The dining room was often used for sewing, and it provided a thoroughfare between the various parts of the house. It contained a table and chairs, a chest of drawers, a stand by the window with house plants practically filling the space. There were geraniums of various hues, richly coloured coleus, begonias, shamrock, and others, but most memorable of all, a fuschia covered with graceful, bell-like flowers — so tall that it reached almost to the top of the window. I remember also a lovely heliotrope, delicate alike of hue and of fragrance: one of the only two occasions on which I have met this uncommon plant. There was a cherry-wood china cabinet between the window and the kitchen door. The dishes I remember best are a set of blue willow of the deepest, richest blue. There was also a carafe of coloured Bohemian glass and wine glasses. On the wall at one time, there was a representation of the Holy Family; later on, a picture in sepia entitled *The Soul's Awakening*. I thought this inexpressibly beautiful. On the south wall, a large print of Landseer's *The Stag at Eve*. The majesty of the magnificent animal impressed me deeply.

In the master bedroom, there was a bed with a tall headboard of carved mahogany with dresser and chest of drawers to match. I think a linen chest, too. At one time, a crib stood at the foot of the bed. On the wall was a framed, illuminated document: Mother's certificate of first communion. I needs must, of course, climb on a chair and decipher the signature and ask Mother about it. Her only answer was silent tears.[2]

From the dining room, one entered *le bureau de papa*; that is, Father's office. Father kept his papers there and attended to his correspondence. Father was a Notary Public, and it was there that people were received who came to see him for a variety of reasons: to ask advice, to have deeds and contracts drawn up, and wills, and that peculiar arrangement of succession called *la donaison.*[3] One of these involved a piece of land which Father later purchased from the heir, a young man by the name of Ruet.

People even came to him (and that comes of being self-sufficient and obliging, both) to have teeth extracted. Father had a most business-like pair of forceps and, though they had been intended for family use only, many an aching jaw in the neighbourhood

2 The signature was W. D. Richer, and I asked Mother if it was that of a relative.

3 Mother did not explain this in her text and I must do so, for the benefit of the uninitiated. In Québec, the farms were small and the families large. Family lands were insufficient in extent to be divided among the sons. A father arriving at the end of his active years, by the custom of '*donaison*' — (literally: 'gift') would turn over to one of the sons, usually the eldest, the farm in its entirety with the understanding that the parents would remain upon the land, guests of the new owner, until their time should come to die. Later on in this story, the custom appears again. (Lorraine)

found relief by means of them. We generally kept out of the room when people came strictly on business, but on these occasions we had leave from Mother to retreat as far from the house as necessary to spare our sensibilities. Without anaesthetic, some of these four-point molars were not easy to extricate from an equally solid jaw. Having read and heard a good deal about Canadian natives, we tended to share their contempt for men who give way to pain in sound or gesture. The loudest groans to offend our ears issued from one very fat man whose name I have forgotten. However, I am sure the least stoic of Father's 'clients' could do better than I did. One day, he held me on his knee to pull a back tooth, and I fainted dead away in his arms, though the tooth came easily enough. As for Father, he even pulled his own teeth. Any tribe would have been proud of him.





Father's desk was in a small alcove formed by the staircase which led from the dining room to the second floor. It had been made from a small organ, furnished with all manner of pigeonholes and small compartments, even to a 'secret' space behind the tier of larger drawers on the left side. It was much carved and highly polished mahogany and treated with respect by us. Even Mother was not allowed to do more than dust surfaces that happened to be bare. Her unique attempt at 'tidying' it had been no more welcome than the soap-and-water treatment she had ventured to apply to some of Father's well-seasoned pipes.

The chair was one of those round arm chairs, and there was another chair beside the desk by the window. Against the stairs partition, a horsehair sofa stood. Above this hung a large framed charcoal drawing of the original buildings of the Collegium Bourget at Rigaud from which Father had graduated: a simple structure indeed compared to the extensive establishment of today. An archway joined the office to the parlour on the left and a heater stood in the corner on the office side of the partition.

A wolf-skin rug lay in front of the heater. This wolf had come into our lives one winter night that Father had arrived home after we children had gone to bed. Someone had caught the poor beast in a trap, and it had frozen — all stretched out to its full length of six feet (including the tail). Father had brought it in and leaned the rigid carcass against the wall to thaw it in order to skin it. Christian had meanwhile been disturbed by the sound of the goings-on, no matter how muted, and he came down to investigate. Mother said that when he pushed the swinging door and came practically face to face with Red Riding Hood's old acquaintance — large as life and twice as threatening — he turned as white as a sheet with the shock and caused her no little concern. I followed him downstairs, but by that time there was talk, and explanations made the animal a source of interest and wonder. It was a beautiful specimen and the rug made from its fur lasted many long years and was much admired.

In the parlour there were two windows: one looking north like the front door, to the road and the mountain just beyond, one looking towards the '*hangar*' and the road to the mill. Of furniture, a piano (a *John Raper*) above which hung a large oil painting, several chairs, a table, and a shelf for knick-knacks (*étagère*) are what I remember best. One of my weekly chores was to dust and polish these.

There was a rather elegant brass lamp with a decorated shade in the parlour, in contrast with the plainer glass ones used in the other rooms. Serge, who has an enviable memory, recalls that there was a blue heron (stuffed) standing in the parlour, and I now remember making a drawing of a stuffed woodpecker because of its interesting markings. Father's baritone horn stood there, too, on the piano: and he used it, but not very frequently. I recall well my daily practice here: (Mother taught us music as she did all the rest) — counting the beats: 'one; two; three.' Mother had to be able to hear me from the kitchen because she was occupied with her many tasks. It did not endear the exercises to me, but I must say it gave me a well-developed sense of rhythm (or something). Damienne recalls that she, too, hated to have to audibly count the beats as she practised her piano lessons.

There were times when I played for fun: that is when the others would sing. Mother had a book of songs in English, and we were fond of it. No doubt Christian will remember such old favourites as *Long, Long Ago*, *Just Before the Battle Mother*, *The Prisoner's Song*, *The Vacant Chair*, and others. The French songs were sometimes sung without accompaniment, for we had learned them by heart, mostly from Mother, the aunts or Grandmother ('*mémère*') Côté. Exceptions to this were the songs of Botrel,[4] which soon became a prime favourite.

4 A Breton folk singer whose songs won instant popularity with the people of his province and of most Francophone circles. His work was rich with the sentiment and the robust humour typical of Brittany, and we were sufficiently familiar with names and places mentioned to take to these as to old folk tunes we were so fond of.

To continue the tour of the house: we go up the stairs from the dining room. These are lighted by a small round window (*oeil de boeuf*).[5] There are four rooms on this floor: three bedrooms and the library. Where the stovepipe comes up from the heater in the office, there is an extra large jacket around it which constitutes a sort of secondary source of heat (*poêle sourd*).[6]

I slept at one time in the little northwest room, from which I have only faint memories but for two exceptions. One is the bed, which was homemade and had a straw mattress (*paillasse*). It was usually stuffed with hay which is finer than straw, and one year Mother used corn husks — the soft, inner shell of corn ears.[7] These were not as dusty as the hay. Making this corn silk bed was really a chore compared to shaking the feather beds of Grandmother's time.

The other memory is probably the most lively nightmare of my life. Snakes of the most spectacular sizes and colours were crawling thickly all over the floor and up the walls. I had been poring deeply and long over the magnificent engravings in Buffon's *Histoire Naturelle*. The colours in them were so vivid and the serpents so lifelike that they seemed about to uncoil and slither out of the book. My wails of terror awakened Mother, and I was gratefully shaken back to wakefulness and reality.

5 Bull's eye (window).

6 Muted, or muffled, stove. I can't find any English equivalent. (Lorraine)

7 That was the year we had such an abundant corn harvest that we had a regular husking bee, with a number of the neighbours taking part. When corn was thus plentiful, Mother kept some of it on the cobs, hung in bunches by the braided husks, to make hominy during the winter.

The southwest room was occupied by Christian and Serge, and I had the one in the southeast corner for most of the time I can remember. The furniture here was, I believe, a dresser chiffonnier and wash stand of oak, very common in those days, and a metal bedstead. One object of interest was a shelf in the corner above my bed on which stood a statuette of Joan of Arc. It was given to me because she was my patron saint, and I was very fond of this figurine. She was some ten inches tall, ivory in colour, and very delicately moulded and finished. Joan was clad in armour and with her gloved hand she held aloft the banner of the French king. She had a very beautiful face. I occasionally brought flowers to adorn that shelf. My feeling for her was hero-worship rather than piety. She was among the patriots I so much admired.

Though I was not long on piety, I might occasionally give some saint a chance to show his stuff. I once lost a little ring: a souvenir of my first trip to Sainte Anne de Beaupré. It was just a little circle of twisted metal with a tiny heart suspended from it. Not at all a valuable thing, but it was precious to me. I prayed: "*Good Saint Antoine, help me find my ring and I promise to make a novena in your honour.*" But Saint Antoine did not respond. The ring remained lost, having doubtless fallen through a crack in the platform between the house and the woodshed. Ever after that I refused in the litanies to respond the required '*Pray for us*' to the name of Saint Anthony. I was sulking.

We were allowed to read for a little while after going to bed, and we grew quite clever at lowering the lamp wick so that no light was noticeable from downstairs after the last call for 'lights out.' This caused the lamp to smoke and as a result many a sooty globe did Damienne and I have to clean on Saturdays.

The central room or library had two prominent features: the large bookcase with doors that locked, and a hexagonal display case on a base made of tree roots, polished and stained a pinky colour. The various compartments of this case were velvet lined and held a collection of coins and medals.[8] The library was a room with many attractions indeed. We did not have access to the locked shelves, and there were additional attractions out of reach on the very top. I managed, though, to decipher names sometimes, and made tentative enquiries. A large folio displayed the flamboyant title in heavy lettering: *ROCAMBOLE*. Mother said that this was not for young people.[9] Another time, I managed to get down another soft paper-bound volume of similar format, with a deep yellow cover on which was a gorgeous picture of a he-goat on a throne of sorts and surrounded with (presumably) worshippers. The title: *Le Diable au XIXe Siècle*.[10] This was too exciting not to warrant a look first before requesting permission to read. I saw enough to gather that certain ancient practices were being revived and that

8 Serge says that, when they were older and bolder, he and Christian removed some of the silver coins in Father's collection and spent them at Morin's store for cigarettes ('*petit bleu*' cigarettes and cigarette papers). They cached their booty under a stone at the Baie des Atocas (Cranberry Bay). (This note was added by Mother as an afterthought, and I have included it here, since she does not tell me where it goes — Lorraine)

9 Damienne was more resourceful; she appropriated a manual of human anatomy and managed to read it undetected.

10 *The Devil in the Nineteenth Century.*

Freemasons were involved in Black Mass and other execrable and unnatural exercises. It sounded much like science fiction or magic to me. Mother promptly put the book back in its place. Some years later, she told me that it had been sent to Father by the bishop for his opinion because this publication had caused a certain amount of alarm among some of the country clergy. Father's dictum had been that it was largely a 'pack of nonsense' with, conceivably, a bid for mischievous publicity.[11]

This bookcase contained, among others — when they were not scattered among the neighbours — what we called *les gros livres* — the 'big books': the choicest lot of assorted long and short stories, verse, serial features, fairy and folk tales, items of information of all sorts I have ever come across. They were bound volumes of a French publication entitled *Le Magazin d'Éducation et de Récréation*[12] and it was just that: a storehouse of learning and entertainment. These were a powerful factor in our early cultural development. The material ranged from the elementary level to about Junior High School, as well as I can judge. Included were, besides such works as the novels of Jules Verne, the *Swiss Family Robinson* and *Robinson Crusoe*, other tales of adventure, notably *Deux Ans de Vacances* — all about a group of young people shipwrecked and



11 I recently came across a mention of this work in *Man, Myth and Magic*, page 2429.

12 This magazine, founded in 1864, counted Jules Verne among its regular contributors. The first number, in March 20th of that year, contains the first portion of Verne's *Les Aventures du Capitaine Hatteras* before its publication in book form. The magazine was a resounding success and did much to add to the fame of this talented and many-sided author.

stranded for two years on some faraway island — such serial features as *The Memoirs of a Donkey* (comparable to *Black Beauty*), the amusing *Aventures et Mésaventures de Pataud et de son chien Fricot* and the life and times of a pet marmot: *La Marmotte en Vie.* There was also such excellent material as the fables of Aesop and Lafontaine — wit and wisdom admirably combined. There were other imposing tomes, among them Thier's *History of the French Revolution*, Bretagne and Dunois's *Great Captains of the Middle Ages*, Rollins' *Ancient History*, some Canadian history, the novels of Sir Walter Scott in French, some of Dickens, Chateaubriand's translation of *Paradise Lost.* Buffon's *Natural History* was a bit above us, but, oh — the illustrations! There was a medley of smaller books in a uniform edition called *Bibliothèque Paroissiale*, which included biographies as well as volumes of a devotional nature. I recall a paperbound copy of the medieval epic of *Reynard the Fox and Isengrin the Wolf*, those famed partners in crime, and a small copy of *Aladdin and his Magic Lamp*. This, of course, is to mention only what we were allowed to read, and leaving out what was strictly adults' fare.

In my earliest reading, an occasional idiom little used in conversation would leave me somewhat puzzled. One of these was "*fondre en larmes*" — literally, to 'melt into tears.' The picture I had in my mind was of a person dissolving away to a mere puddle like the wicked witch in *The Wizard of Oz.* I was always surprised to find the same personage continuing to live through further adventures.

It was almost an article of faith with us that Father could answer any question, but I stumped him once. I had been reading the New Testament, and I came across an unfamiliar word. "*Father,*"

I asked. "*What is adultery?*" He paused and his face took on a solemn expression. "*It is such a terrible thing, my child, that one does not speak of it.*"

It is not easy to say which of our books were most influential in our private world. Fiction? Adventure? History? Moral tales? We took them all in with avidity, entertained and stimulated by turns, strongly moved by the fortunes and misfortunes of the characters who thronged the printed pages: delighting in the frolicking humour of Jules Verne — fiercely partisan in our reading of history. All these, of course, informed, inspired and structured our play and superimposed on a naturally rich and varied environment an exciting atmosphere of unlimited possibilities. Not that we could not or did not draw the line between fact and imagination: there was a time and place for both.

Lest our lives appear to have been a perpetual holiday, let me hasten to state that all the foregoing was in the nature of extracurricular reading and nothing else. There were, first and foremost — and five days a week (except for school holidays) — lessons. Lessons were, unless our teacher (Mother) was (a) absent or (b) incapacitated, regularly assigned, studied, and recited.

Ours was a comparatively new parish, and there were as yet few children in the neighbourhood. Moreover, the concept of compulsory school attendance was still just that: a concept. Therefore we had no school, and Mother set about to remedy the situation. She had already done her bit by teaching several young people near us to read and write. We, however, got the full programme as outlined by the Powers that Were plus a few extras that occurred to Mother or Father. The texts I recall for these elementary grades were readers, spelling books, grammar, Catechism, history of Canada, history of France, history of England, history of the United States, biblical history (*histoire sainte*) arithmetic and copybooks for writing exercises with a model line in fine Spencerian script. In addition, Mother included a volume of general European history and history of the Church. Also, to develop skill in deciphering handwriting, a manuscript text which had been used by one of my great-uncles. Last but not least, there was a manual for learning English by the Ollendorf method. We learned, rather than were taught, but help was always available if we ran into difficulties.

Considering the burden of sheer work and responsibility that rested on her shoulders, Mother managed to do what everyone else frankly judged impossible. There are debts that can never be justly estimated any more than they can be repaid. For one thing, the benefits are too intangible to be clearly and fully grasped and too great to be measured. Literacy, though it enjoyed a general consensus of esteem, was by no means universal at the time.

I remember very well the daily *dictée*, the drill in verb conjugations, the recitation of the English lesson, over which Mother's head would sometimes nod, and we would quietly withdraw while sleep stole over her weary mind. *La plume de ma tante* or her *parapluie rouge*[13] were no more engrossing in those days than they are now.

Slate and slate pencils were common in the early days. We were happy to exchange them for scribblers and lead pencils. It was gratifying to hands and ears alike.

13 Or, presumably, the English equivalent thereof. (Lorraine)

To enforce rules, including that of study, there were sanctions, none more dreaded than deprivation of stories read aloud by me for myself and the others after supper. In extreme cases, free Saturday afternoons might be cancelled. Simon Legree could devise nothing more painful nor more effective.

Study did not require all of our time. Much of it was taken up by chores. Some of these were daily routine, some seasonal, some dull and some mildly interesting; some, like berry-picking excursions, we enjoyed so much that we thought of them more as picnics than as mere tasks. There was a thrill of accomplishment in gathering a bountiful crop of raspberries or wild strawberries and we were (glory be!) miles from home and thus out of earshot, safe from being forever interrupted for small errands — besides, one never knew what might happen in the forest on the other side of the lake, or, with luck, turn up along the way.



Among daily tasks that come to mind are such things as hauling water from the creek for drinking, cooking, and sometimes for washing, carrying two buckets on a yoke like those of Chinese coolies, which apparatus Father fashioned for me. Rain water was collected in a barrel, and in warm summer weather it was fun to watch the antics of mosquito wrigglers on its surface.



There was wood to split and carry into the house, ashes to be removed from the stove and disposed of, kindling prepared for the morning fire. There were cows to be fetched from the pasture, though they preferred to tarry in some cool, shady place, and then milking to do. There were pigs to be fed; calves also, and in winter horses and cows as well; and there was gathering eggs and feeding chickens.

There were potatoes and corn to hoe, other crops to weed, butter to churn. In the fall, there were potatoes to pick, and other vegetables and corn. The first taste of roasted ears was a delight. As for the potatoes, an additional task might face us: the war against the Colorado beetles who seemed determined to harvest the plants before the tubers got well on their way. Paris Green could, of course, help in this, but the use of poison was not favoured so close to the house. Our preferred method was to go along the rows with a bucket in one hand and a slender stick in the other, smartly shaking the plants to dislodge the adult beetles. Young, soft-bodied beetles clung firmly and were hard to remove. We collected the eggs by removing leaves adorned by the clusters of shiny orange-yellow oval structures.

Picking hops was a sticky job, but the smell of the soft dryish tassels was pleasant.

We grew tobacco on a small scale, but one year there was a considerable amount of it, and Christian and I had the task of stringing the fragrant leaves on wires extending from one wall of the woodshed to the opposite for drying.

Work that involved being outdoors at least part of the time was the least boring. Even sweeping the porch and steps and the firmly packed soil of the yard between the house and the 'hangar' or storage shed was preferable to sweeping the kitchen floor.

Indoors, there was weekly floor-scrubbing and polishing furniture with coal oil and then later with O'Cedar oil. Also, we had to fill the lamps with petrol, trim their wicks and polish their globes. There were tall, straight lamps for close work in the rooms downstairs, smaller ones for bedside lights in the bedrooms. There were bracket lamps on the wall here and there with reflectors to enhance illumination. A tall brass lamp with a large decorated globe stood in the parlour, and the dining room boasted a hanging lamp with a row of crystal prisms around the shade. When the early sun shone through the window, rainbow segments appeared upon the wall. There were lanterns which were used in the shed and in the stable. When they were all cleaned and polished and lined up in a row, they did make a pretty sight.

Then there was butter making. The churn I remember best is the first one, soon followed by later, improved models. This first one was a tall, earthenware crock with a hole in the cover to accommodate the handle of the paddle which was moved rapidly up and down to beat the thick cream until it would finally separate into butter and buttermilk. These churns can now be seen in most of our historical museums. One of the later types was a barrel on a stand with moveable parts. The barrel was rocked back and forth until the process was complete. The task became more interesting when one could be entrusted with the 'working' of the butter: that is, when the whole pale golden mass was placed in a large wooden bowl. Now, with a wooden paddle, one pressed the buttermilk out of the lump, a small portion at a time, until it was deep yellow and free of liquid.

There was the preparation of vegetables which might involve paring potatoes, picking and trimming wax beans, or picking and shelling peas. It often meant filling a bucket well packed with leaf lettuce and going to the creek to wash it, over and over, until every speck of dust or sand was sluiced away. Served with salt, pepper, a little vinegar, and gobs of thick sweet-sour cream, this was a salad fit for any king.

Daily cleaning and tidying included attention to sanitary facilities. Periodically, the outdoor toilet was scrubbed with a broom and a blend of water and lye. In the early days, hardwood ashes soaked overnight yielded the lye solution. Used on bare wood with a business-like scrub brush, it made tables and floors glow like soft gold. The beautiful pine floors of the pioneer houses were protected by strips of woven matting, for scrubbing those floors was very hard on the housewife's hands.

The most — perhaps the only truly harassing kinds of chores — were minor errands. There always seemed to be countless things to be fetched or put back; nothing ever was where it was needed. Since we had no refrigeration,[14] at least three times a day food had to be brought from the cool cellar and then returned to it. I hated those trips up and down the narrow steps. It was dark in that clammy cavern. Unhealthy ghostly plants huddled as if frightened near the crack which admitted a sliver of light at the outer door.

But enough of chores! Needless to say, these were distributed among all four of us according to our age and capacities, and the heaviest burden still rested on Mother, for Father's work kept him away from home for much of the time.

We did have hired help sometimes, and it is unfair to other men we employed periodically that the one I most clearly remember

14 In later years, an ice house was built across the mill road to store dairy products and such things.

was a gormless creature. (Mother said, not without justification, that he was a moron.) One evening, he was sent to fetch the cows for milking, and the wily beasts, who no doubt had his measure by this time, evaded him by simply crossing the creek. We (Christian and I), found him there, on the bank, standing on one foot and dangling the other, gazing helplessly at the stream. Mother said that Father had chosen this halfwit so that no one could conceivably start any gossip. There were others, at various times, whom I vaguely associate with construction rather than with farm work. There were several of these men, and they were engaged in working on the covered bridge in the village, which was built in 1908. Sometimes in the evening, Mother would read for all of us, either a story or a passage from the Bible. Thus it was that I became aware of the duplicity of Jacob in his dealings with his uncle Laban (*Genesis* 30: 38–40).





One day, Christian and I learned why it is that folks talk of 'cursing like a waggoner.' We were on our way home when we heard a wagon rolling at a great speed and a voice calling out loud injunctions to the horses. We hid in a ditch full of tall grasses and were treated, as the equipage galloped by, to such a display of picturesque and exotic curses as we had never before heard and as our imaginations could never conjure up.

The farm was not large and only part of the area was fit for cultivation. There were such crops as hay, wheat, oats, buckwheat,[15] barley, and rye: not all grown necessarily in the same year, and

15 Buckwheat is a very leafy plant; it was said to be an excellent crop to grow for ploughing under as a fertilizer for poor soil.

none in very large amounts. I doubt that we grew all we needed for the farm animals. A popular crop on neighbouring farms was a mixture of oats and field peas. More than once, torn aprons and shirts betrayed us when we yielded to the lure of the tender green pods in a nearby field belonging to Dolores Paquette.

One clear memory dates from some time after Father had purchased the acres from the Ruet place to the East. The grain was being threshed in the middle part of the barn, evidently so built for this purpose. Christian and I had been allowed to sit and watch, well out of the way. The sheaves had been stored on one side of the lane, open at both ends, in which was a treadmill as well as a rather small-scale threshing machine. Watching the heavy horse who, Sisyphus-like, patiently kept moving, dogged steps going nowhere, gave me a rather queer feeling that I never quite forgot. I would be curious now to see the machine itself; at the time, I only had eyes for the horse.

The hay was chiefly a mixture of millet, timothy, and red clover, and we loved to ride on the fragrant load. One time, having been particularly insistent, we were allowed to spend the night in the hayloft and were given blankets to spread over the new-mown hay. I cannot speak for the others, but I found the experience disappointing. For one thing, the hay was more lumpy than I expected, and then, the smell of the clover was not nearly as powerful as the effluvium that rose on the still night air from the horses' stalls below.

Of the farm animals, some stand out more clearly in my memory than the rest: for instance, "Vic" (Victoria), a handsome Percheron mare, with trim ankles and a glossy black satin coat. She was a real lady of a horse; so well-behaved, in fact, that Father set me on her back to see if I would care to ride. I do not know how old I was, but I felt as though I were on the back of an elephant, and I wanted only one thing: to get off and to find myself on *terra firma* once more. Another of these merits special mention. Barney was a horse of calm, staid temperament, and hence 'safe' for us children. If he was not in the mood to start out on a trip, he would limp quite noticeably so that once or twice we actually turned back in sympathy for our dumb friend. However, in cases of necessity, we had to keep going, and we soon observed that, coming back, Barney would, every time, trot contentedly all the way home. In the end, his symptoms found us rather sceptical.

Other horses were just animals whom Christian early learned to harness and who pulled either cutter or buggy, as the case might be. I had learned to keep my distance from the strange heavy Clydesdales who drew heavy loads of lumber away from the mill. On one occasion, I was reaching up to pat one of the noble beasts on the shoulder when he suddenly turned with a snort and bit me on the cheek — an unexpected mark of affection long remembered.

We had a cow by the name of 'Bossy' — much too common a cognomen for the outstanding specimen that she was. This was really a beautiful animal, large and well-proportioned, the undisputed leader of the little herd. Red with a white face, horned, intelligent, serene rather than placid, willing rather than docile, she was a top-grade milker for quantity as well as for butter production. One other cow there had to be dehorned on account of her uncertain temper. She lacked the contented mien of Bossy, and we remember her chiefly because one of the neighbours' boys remarked one day that she resembled his uncle Joe.[16]



One denizen of the barnyard could and did, during his fortunately not too long life, make things uncomfortable for us. That was a large black rooster with great, cruel spurs. He obviously enjoyed seeing us flee as he came after us in full chase, and, when we had been pursued far enough, he would retire behind the barn to the very top of the manure pile and crow his victory to the hens and all else within hearing. That bird could have written the book about the territorial imperative. Once he went too far: I was coming up the slope toward the house with Damienne, just a baby and not able to outrun the feathered menace. With my heart in my mouth, I seized the first stick I saw and laid him flat in the road. I was feeling pretty proud of myself when I told Mother about it, but what she said was: "*Did you have to hit him so hard? You might have killed him.*"

There were some seasonal activities or events in which we played little part except as interested onlookers. In the spring the carp would swim up the creek to spawn, and the men would gather in the water just below the first dam, fishing spears in hand, and make great havoc among the poor things. Actually, it was done mostly for the sport since this is a species not highly esteemed as

16 Resemblances between species had not escaped us. There was a girl whom Christian called 'Poulette' Sarazin. She had the timid, nervous manner of a pullet and something of the profile: receding chin, long sharp nose and all.

food.[17] The men would remain there, standing among the threshing mass, until they were tired or twilight prevented them from seeing the fish any longer. Some filled potato sacks with carp and then wondered what to do with them. When we had more than enough for a meal, the pigs enjoyed the rest. We were given a sackful once, and Mother commented wryly on the generosity of the neighbour who until then had not shown any sign of remembering our occasional presents of game or fresh-killed pork.

And every spring there was the *drive*. McLaren's had a timber cut past the woods where we used to pick berries, and some timber was cut for the mill as well. The company's logs were floated over the dam and by the mill. The crew had a male cook who did them proud. We were told how, one time when he was cooking a batch of beans on hot stones in the ground, one of the men brought him a partridge; he simply added the titbit to the lot! The story goes that there were never such beans before or since.





In the fall there would be hog butchering, and we were keen observers of the whole process except (speaking for myself) the actual killing. The carcass was scalded and scraped clean, then hung high from a rack. The entrails were removed, edible parts brought into the house, and the first of Mother's tasks was to make the blood into blood sausage before it became coagulated. For this

17 Though the carp were not much prized in themselves, they did provide a welcome treat: in the spawning season, they were filled with golden roe, which Mother fried in butter.

process, the blood had to be kept at a certain appropriate temperature while other ingredients were prepared: that is, onions, ground fat, pork, and spices to add to the liquid. The intestines were quickly stripped to provide the casing. Mother always used the outside membrane only. What a rush! What exciting sights and smells! Several roasts were cut up, some pork steaks also. Some of the best meat was ground to make a number of tourtières to be eaten, come Christmas. Traditionally, this was the main dish served for *réveillon*[18] after midnight mass.

A few choice pieces of meat were always given, as a neighbourly gesture, to people who lived nearby. Some would perhaps come to help out with the job as this was not easy for one man alone, especially if the animal were of medium or large size. The snow-white mass of fat (*panne*) was later rendered for lard, the crisp golden brown residue or cracklings (*cretons*) was kept, for it made a tasty spread for snacks.

Mother also made head cheese. All of the pig's head, including the brain, went into this. The present-day commercial product can only give a ghost of an idea of the rich, yet delicate, flavour of this dish. It should be mentioned that every particle of fat associated with the entrails was saved for the making of soap. The fatter portions of the carcass were usually salted for summer use and for pork and beans.

18 A snack shared with friends and neighbours in the early hours of Christmas morning, after the church service.

Sometimes the bladder of the pig was made into a tobacco pouch by first distending, then rubbing it, until it reached the consistency of soft leather. Father used the pouch and found it quite satisfactory.

# 3

# here, there and round-about

As we grew up, we were allowed to range farther from the house in our play, and to the neighbours' on occasional errands.

Onésime Prescott's house was the nearest. He was a gaunt, tall man with a straggly grey beard whose appearance was forbidding. Like many in those days, he was illiterate, but he had either been taught or had himself made up the rule about not sparing the rod. On his two boys, he used a horse whip. They often escaped to the trees to avoid (perhaps well-earned) chastisement. He enjoyed a measure of importance in the parish. He was the beadle and rejoiced in the imposing title of *connétable*,[1] which, to our amusement, he pronounced as "*connectable*." At every service on Sundays,

1 See Note 1, *Connétable*.

*Home and surrounding district.*

he sat at the southwest corner of the church wearing a bandolier and holding a staff topped by a gilt ball as badges of his dignity, watching for any dog that might stray in, any young whippersnapper whose giggles might reach his ear, or mayhap some woman who might feel faint from the long fast and be in need of assistance. In those days, no food or drink was allowed from midnight to the time of communion, and the high mass was late in the morning so it was no strange thing to see ladies, especially young ones, turn pale with the strain of fast and fatigue during the long service.

Sometimes, our hens chose to take a rest. One expected this to happen periodically before the days of special diet and extended daylight hours in the poultry pens. When this happened we were sent to Mr. Prescott's, across the creek, to fetch eggs. The main room of Prescott's house had one feature which we found fascinating: it was entirely papered with the Saturday comics from *La Presse*. I do not know who read the news, or if anyone did, but the Chinese do say that a picture is worth a thousand words and Mrs. Prescott was heard more than once to say that "*there certainly are a lot of funny people in Montreal,*" and who could say her nay? I remember walking home with a crick in my neck from trying to read the words, for the pages were pasted without regard for normal orientation.

In the other direction, past 'the corner,' lived the Davids. There were only adults there, grown daughters and their parents. Mr. David (Jean-Baptiste) would sometimes come and pass the time of day with Father. One fine afternoon, Father, who had just returned from some long trip and was having a look around the garden, made him a present of the season's very first cucumber. Needless to say, Mother was not enchanted with this neighbourly gesture. Their house still looked very much the same when I saw it again[2] complete with elaborate gingerbread trimming along the roof and front porch, but the outdoor oven was gone. Mrs. David used to bake bread in it every week, and we watched with keen interest a succession of fragrant loaves being taken out of the cavernous interior.

A son-in-law, Isidore LaRocque,[3] worked with Father for McLaren's. He was a good friend and later continued to correspond with Father after we left Val-des-Bois.

Along the road which goes towards Lac Pelletier lived the Dubucs, Lacasses, and later on the Frappiers. The Dubucs were old acquaintances of Mother's. While I was still but a small baby, she would go with Mrs. Dubuc to pick raspberries while Berthe and I, being of an age, would sleep in one basket: not, however, always in perfect harmony. Mother used to say that she bit me in the back, once. (It was her basket.) Their farm was somewhat beyond the point where White Deer Lodge is now situated and was the farthest we were allowed to go visiting, though we did walk on to the Portelance farm beyond.

2 A German farmer owns it now, so I was told by Mrs. Thom, the former Emérence David, one of the daughters of Jean-Baptiste.

3 The author of the history of Val-des-Bois, 1908–1983, is Marc-Claude LaRocque. I am sure he must be of this family. I refer copiously to his history in my Epilogue. (Lorraine)

The elder of the Dubuc boys was married and lived also along that road. George Dubuc, Sr., was a carpenter and a pleasant, easy-going man. The elder daughter was pretty Solange, whom Mother taught to read. Solange married the best-looking young man in the parish: tall, handsome, dark, curly-haired Edouard Plante. Solange's husband was the man who eventually bought the property from Father when we left Val-des-Bois. As of this date, they are both alive and well, surrounded by many children and grandchildren. The younger daughter, Berthe, the one girl my own age I occasionally saw, was a serious child, fond of cattle and horses. It was said that she was in love with a Portelance boy who married someone else. She has remained single until now.

Both Mr. Dubuc and his son-in-law were for years working in the mill and in the carpenter shop. That shop was very interesting, and we loved to linger there and watch the operation of the various tools. There was a lathe, a vise, and an assortment of apparatus of which I learned the names, if not the skill to use them.

Speaking of the carpenter shop brings back a related memory. Sometimes, birds might get caught in traps intended for other game. One was a large, grey owl which the men kept in the shop until his injuries healed. He stood there, outwardly impassive, while work went on and we came as close as we dared, to admire him. Towards spring on a day when we were present, he was released. He flew away up over the yard and promptly swooped on silent wings on a cat who, all unsuspecting, was sauntering across. The poor cat was killed, eviscerated and devoured in little more time than it takes to tell about it. I don't think I had a chance to scream before it was all over. It had been a long, and possibly a meatless, winter, except perhaps for the odd mouse.

Another interesting guest was a blue heron whose leg had to be put in a splint until it became strong enough to stand on. This, too, was a well-behaved and patient guest. One that could not be trusted to behave in the same way was a magnificent bald eagle, which gave the men who got him out of the trap no little trouble. He was brought to our place and put into a crate made into a sort of cage with stout bars. He had a broken leg, which was duly splinted and bandaged. How he hated the bandage, the splint, the cage — the whole humiliating business of being prisoned in the midst of the poultry yard! We often came to look at him. His proud gaze never faltered. What a king he looked! Frustration must have all but destroyed his spirit as the hens unconcernedly cackled all the day close to his cage. On a couple of occasions, too close: in a flash, the razor-sharp powerful beak had slain the witless fowl and pulled the bloody mangled flesh through the bars. From the house, Mother kept an eye out much of the time. He never made a move while she was watching. At last, he too was allowed to fly away, back to his wild freedom. The picture that remains fixed in my memory is that of his eyes — deeply set yellow orbs, unblinking in the brightest sunlight on the snow — windows into an unconquerable soul. Thus must have been the eyes of those heroes of legend whom harshest fate could not destroy and who mastered their destiny by accepting it. I have often thought that for any group of humans to claim this bird as an emblem (as many groups have done) is sheer presumption.

After Christian became proficient at steering the small flat-bottomed boat (*chaloupe*) with a paddle, we were allowed to do a bit of fishing. Catfish and eel were speared from a raft which was anchored in the lake. We rowed to it in the *chaloupe*, and the boys had a lamp strapped to their forehead so that they could see the fish. Serge recalls that once they had gone there in company of some friends and brought along the gramophone. When they rowed back to the shore, they found about twenty people assembled by the road in the moonlight. The music had attracted the attention of passers-by who waited to discover whence the music came.

There were fine pike in Lac Pelletier, catfish (*barbote*) and lots of carp. These seem to have been the chief food of the voracious pike. 'Eat and be eaten' seems the way of nature. I once opened a large pike and was highly intrigued to find four fish inside him, in the fashion of those fascinating Russian dolls or Chinese carved ornaments. There was talk of an eel once, which, having been mistaken by the fisherman for a black water snake, was hastily thrown back into the water.

I was never much of an angler, hating the touch of the wriggling worms that we used for bait. Trolling was rather more to my taste. Chris always removed the hook from the fish after a firm blow on the head had stilled its squirming.

The lake was large enough for a sudden wind to raise waves. On such occasions, Christian was calm and competent, skilfully guiding the boat into the current and safely to shore. His cool reliability served as balance to my imagination and initiative. I suppose I shall never know how much of the timidity I felt when faced with the unexpected was due to the fact that I was extremely myopic, a condition which was not corrected until I was in school in Montreal and past fourteen years old. It is difficult to feel confident when difficulties or obstacles are only dimly perceived. Certainly I have never experienced such difficulty in driving a car as I felt in trying to steer a course in a boat.

One of the places we were allowed to go and play — ("*you may go and look but don't make a nuisance of yourselves!*") was the saw mill. "*Look, but don't touch!*" was an oft-repeated injunction when machines were going, especially when the circular saw — its outer edge visible only as a streak of light — would scream as it cut through green logs drawn up relentlessly on the carriage until a board would drop and the ponderous contraption would go back: a hand would adjust the log's position and the process would be repeated all over again. We gazed with great respect at the great disc, gleaming and sharp. We were told about a dear little old lady who could not believe that the saw was going because she could not see it move, so she went to make sure by touching it with her little old finger — with the result easily anticipated by everyone but herself. We did not need to have this moral underlined.

Indeed, Serge contributes this: there used to be visitors at the mill occasionally. Families: wife, husband, and children would be led through the building to watch the operation of the various machines. The saw for cutting shingles was twenty inches in diameter. Because of the tough fibres of cedar, the saw had very fine teeth. It was placed horizontally on the machine and could be canted to produce an uneven thickness — one end thin, the other thick. On one of these occasions, the operator's wife was looking at the saw and carelessly put her hand a little too close. The tip of the finger was neatly sliced off and, drawn by centripetal force, it travelled to the centre of the saw, leaving a bloody trail. The saw was stopped, she snatched the finger tip and stuck it back on. Mother bandaged it carefully, and it grew on again!

On the lower level, there was the grinding machine (I always thought it looked like a giant coffee grinder) which served to make a coarse meal (*moulée*) from various grains: corn, oats, mixed oats, and field peas, etc., for hog or cattle feed.[4] Further back, overlooking the place where the flume carried the water from the dam to the giant water wheel, we would stand with the cool spray on our rapt faces watching the making and bundling of shingles, mostly cedar in those days of bounteous forest wealth. There was a very pretty shrub which grew at the edge of the water, among the rocks. It had small flowers in profusion, yellow and amber in colour, shaped like snapdragons. We often had to invent names for the flowers we found, having no manual to consult. We were better off with trees, since Father taught Christian a good deal of forest lore. He used to be able to identify all the timber that was processed at the mill, even without the bark! I thought this a most admirable achievement.

I used to turn the handle of the grindstone for Christian or father when they sharpened axes. Christian and I sometimes sawed wood with that huge contraption a cross-cut saw (*godendard*). The

4 In addition to this, the grinder also produced flour for making bread and buckwheat flour for pancakes. The fee for this work was usually paid in kind.

*The mill, circa 1900. W. D. Richer in foreground.*

most ear-splitting sound I ever heard was the filing of the teeth of those saws to sharpen them.

Out in the mill yard were piles of lumber, neatly arranged for seasoning. The smell of fresh-sawn wood was a delight quite unforgettable. All the spices of the Far East would not have tempted me away from the clean scent of pine, fir, hemlock, or cedar, as the sap slowly dried in the warm sun. The people who rented the mill from Father were very forbearing, I should think. My memories of the place are of quite unmixed interest and enjoyment.

For a while, a couple lived in the house near the mill. The wife was reputed to be the dirtiest housekeeper in the parish. I was sent there once on an errand, and I remember the husband particularly. He was a very tall, thin man with a quiet, deliberate manner. While I was there, he came into the kitchen to get a drink, took down his cup, which was hanging on the wall, drank, and put it up again on the hook, out of reach of anyone but himself. I was struck by this gesture, which seemed to set him aloof from the rest of the household.

The walk along the water between the first and second dams was pleasant, if rather moist underfoot. There were some bright red flowers there, which I have since learned are Cardinal flowers. The second dam provided an adequate crossing to the other side. Christian would proceed with splendid assurance; I, in trembling dread. I have a persisting phobia of heights. We rarely explored this part of the land. I can see a fine red fox on the rocky promontory (excuse the word, if it is too grand for that jutting rock, but I invariably thought of it in that way) — a fine red fox with his fine sharp nose in the air, his handsome bushy tail like a banner behind him. My! How beautiful I thought him! I am so thankful that Father was not inclined to hunting.

Another picture is that of a deer in early spring, peacefully browsing on the mountain slopes facing our house. He was so clearly visible that we could imagine gazing straight into his limpid, innocent eyes. Mother excitedly called Father to get his gun. Fresh venison was not to be sneezed at when the main item of meat was salt pork. Father took the weapon and, with a reluctant sigh, went out in the garden. He aimed, stood for a moment, lowered the gun, shook his head and said: "*It is no use; I cannot do it.*" I could have hugged him. It is understandable that Mother did not share my sentimental feelings. Her reaction was probably just — resignation.

I had no objection to snaring wild rabbits. Christian and I would sometimes set copper wire snares under the tall cedars near the road. Mother was willing to cook any game which came our way. We had beaver, rabbit, even muskrat once. Once she cooked some frog legs which we found delicious: more delicate in both texture and flavour than chicken. This was the bullfrog, the *ouaouaron* who provided the bass notes in the spring symphony to which we would go and listen when not only young man's fancy but that of practically every living creature would turn to thoughts of courting. The theatre was the portion of the stream swollen by the dam, a most satisfactory habitat for animals of amphibian habits such as frogs, toads, lizards, water snakes, and turtles. The sheer variety of sound appears almost unbelievable now, it is so long since, and I have never again heard anything to compare with it. From the shrill pipe of the tiniest one to the deep, solemn croak of the largest one of all, no note was absent. The volume of this chorus would swell, recede, and swell again until we were carried away on a wave of ecstasy with Nature in the throes of its rite of spring. We would sit there enthralled until it was practically dark, and walk home with our heads filled with the music gradually fading in the distance.

I have mentioned turtles. One day, the boys found a turtle with a hole drilled near the edge of its shell and a piece of wire attached to it. We had read about how strong these animals are, and, to test the reports, Christian and Serge stood on the turtle's back and lo! It walked off with both of them! There is a fairly large species in that part of the country, and Christian and I once found a nest in the sandy shore of Lac Pelletier near the bridge. Full of Swiss Family Robinson lore, he was all for making an omelette, and we accordingly raided the nest. The omelette was beaten and cooked, but proved disappointing. We concluded this time, as on other occasions, that hunger and paucity of choice must have lent charm to some of those highly praised feasts of which travellers tell. There were numerous clams in the creek, but Mother was not interested in cooking them.

Once I saw a lizard in low water at the edge of the artificial lake (Lac de la Carpe). It must have been no more than seven or eight inches long, but it was so exactly like a miniature crocodile, and it moved so smartly over the stones that I ran all the way home without reflecting that this was, after all, a harmless cousin of the monster I was seeing in my head. Probably, some might say, I had been reading too many books. I saw a yellow and green garter snake, too, one day that I was coming back from the creek. It slithered across my path as I walked past the cow stable. Naturally, I told about it, but no one ever believed me. What a comfort it was, if somewhat belated, to find the description of this reptile in *Encyclopedia Canadiana*. Vindicated at last!

There were few maples of large size near home, but, some years, Christian tapped those that were within reach and brought home little lard-pails full of the sweet, tasty sap. A treat for us, and evidence that anything anyone else could do, we could do as well.

Some of the people who occasionally came our way should be mentioned. One who stands out in my inner vision is a tall, serious, patriarchal Scottish gentleman with a long white beard and a fine head of silver hair. Very handsome and dignified Mr. Bradley looked as he sat down to join us for breakfast one day. We listened more or less attentively as he discoursed on the virtues of "*oatmeal porrritch*" as a morning dish. We had no warning of the consequences of that fateful meeting, but Father had been uncommonly impressed. The next lot of groceries contained a bag of the unfamiliar stuff. Like Dr. Johnson, we had been used to associating oats with horses, not human beings. The ensuing period was a trying one for Mother, who, like many another, might find herself between the devil and the deep blue sea, or, more specifically, between Father's commands (or wishes) and the resistance of the offspring to the same. A compromise was finally arrived at: we would eat a not-too-generous helping of the mess if it were smothered in grated maple sugar and thick cream. Eventually, we came to accept brown sugar as a substitute for maple, as this was never plentiful enough to be anything but a luxury.

One of the familiar features of country life at that time in our part of Canada was an occasional visit from itinerant salesman or peddlers. They would generally be recent immigrants, and, until profits had yielded sufficient capital for the purchase of a horse and buggy, these men would actually trudge the weary miles between farm houses with — some one, some two — suitcases of goods and samples.

Camille Assad, a pleasant, good-looking, curly-haired Syrian, was the first. With him, as with almost all who came to our door, there would be a place at the table if the time was suitable. Camille had a remarkable stock in his cases: small items like buttons, hooks and eyes, shoe laces, etc., could be purchased then and there. For yard goods, orders were taken and the goods delivered on the following trip. There was one case which contained a wide assortment of jewellery and related articles, arranged in trays for ready display. This was a hard, square, box-like affair, and how he could stand to carry it on his back was more than I could understand. We were almost as pleased as he when he made it to the next stage and turned up with a smart little horse and buggy. Fairly soon after that, he opened a store in the nearest town, Buckingham. There is a fairly large establishment there today that bears his name. His brother took over the route when Camille went and presumably followed in his footsteps on the road to success. He had a son around our age. One day, the youngster came to have a tooth extracted. He never even whimpered. His cool, self-possessed manner commanded our sincere admiration. I even invited him to join our play in the role of 'Father,' which part usually fell to Christian. That was a genuine compliment.

Another travelling *colporteur* whom we found interesting was a Turk, a real, live Mussulman. Until then, our acquaintance with followers of the Prophet was chiefly through stories in which they captured luckless Christians who subsequently were given a choice between conversion and death ... or, at the very least, an arduous life of slavery. This man had a gentle enough manner, and when he repaired to our *montagnon* (little mountain) to say his prayers, he graciously consented to let us stand nearby and watch as he knelt and faced the East in the prescribed ritual. He explained rather apologetically that he was not a very good Muslim because he prayed only four times a day. I think we silently thanked our stars that we had not been born under the sign of the Crescent. Once a day was quite sufficient for us, especially when Father was home and we went through the complete programme. Creed and beads were not so bad, but when came the litanies....

Another memorable stranger was a Jew. A tall, blond, blue-eyed, handsome chap who could fit perfectly the description of Feuchtwanger's hero, Süss.[5]

There was a shoemaker who was also, some of the time, a travelling artisan. This was no ordinary shoemaker. Clément Capet claimed descent from that very Hugh Capet who founded the third

5 Feuchtwanger, Lion, German novelist and author, among other novels, of one entitled *Jew Süss* (1926).

dynasty of French kings in the tenth century. We were impressed with this, although the little man himself was not impressive, being of modest stature and swarthy of complexion. His wit, however, as well as his pride, were remarkable. Asked if he would like to return to his country (that is, France), he replied with scorn: "*Avec une telle famille?*"[6] Evidently he did not feel that, considering his illustrious bloodline, his Canadian relatives would be equal to the social presence expected of them in the Old Country.

Monsieur Capet was very good with puppets. Mother stretched a grey blanket across the door of the dining room, and we were the delighted spectators of our first Punch and Judy show.

Guests of many types — common farmers as well as strangers from faraway lands, the local priest who came regularly on his pastoral visits, lawyers from the city who called on Father on business or paid a courtesy call on their way — they all gave some colour to our quiet existence, as we watched and listened.

One of these gentlemen, a lawyer from Buckingham, was in the office with Father one day, chatting sociably while I listened from the parlour, beyond the open archway. Monsieur the man of Law was expounding to Father his method of making friends and influencing people, "*There is,*" he said, with an ineffable look of self-congratulation, "*no surer way to win the favourable disposition of parents than to praise their children.*" And, as if on cue, Christian at this moment walked in, holding a pipe-like toy he had himself fashioned, and wearing the distrustful look he reserved for

6 "*With such a family?*"

strangers. "*Monsieur Richer!*" exclaimed the visitor: "*What an intelligent-looking boy you have!*" Christian fixed the visitor with a baleful glance and declared in his most ferocious little-boy tone: "*Vous, monsieur, si vous vous fermez pas, avec mon tortillon-tortillette j'vas vous boucher!*"[7] and he strode out of the room, mortally insulted, still shaking the *tortillon-tortillette* like a weapon. This incident greatly amused Aunt Arthémise, whose favourite Christian was, and who relished the discomfiture of the slick city man of Law.

There was a slow-spoken individual from another parish who would sometimes bring us apples. These were packed in sawdust, in a tub or barrel. Some there were that would keep fairly well, and some were for immediate consumption like the snow apple, light with very red markings, sweet and so tender it would practically melt in your mouth. This visitor was an ingenuous creature. He had been told that there was money in bee-keeping, and he had purchased a hive which he had, he confided with a sly, secretive look, placed in the most remote corner of the orchard without telling his wife.

Father, ever helpful, fetched from the library shelves a treatise on apiculture and offered it to the good man. He hemmed and hawed a little, and then it transpired that he could not read … "*but*" he said ingratiatingly, "*could you maybe read me a little passage, Monsieur Richer?*" Mother, who was in the next room with

7 The name of the toy was Christian's own invention. *Tortiller* (infinitive) means 'to twist"; *boucher* (infinitive) means to stuff a plug into something — from *bouchon*, a cork. In other words, "*if you don't shut your face, I'll shut it for you!*"

tante Arthémise, missed none of this dialogue. When our guest had gone, she approached Father and slyly queried whether he had found a satisfactory passage for the would-be apiculturist. Father was a bit nettled but took it goodnaturedly enough. Later references to "a little passage" showed that the incident was by no means forgotten.

The Ruets were our neighbours to the east until the owner of the land died and we bought his small acreage. There was a story told of a child born to the family (or in the family) — a child who was born deaf, dumb, and blind and who moved about by hopping like a toad. Father went with the parents to the city to place the poor little creature in some sort of institution. The parents were first cousins — not that it is easy to understand what unusual combination of genes could produce such nefarious results.

There was a man who lived not far from us and who had several strapping sons. The Simards, father and three sons, were at our house one late afternoon talking over some business with Father. When dinnertime came, they were naturally bidden to join us for the meal. They demurred a little. Mother politely urged them, for it was getting late. The old man sat down but the sons held back: after a pause, long enough to be uncomfortable, the father turned to the boys and, with a jerk of the head, indicated the chairs set for them. Mutely, eyes on the floor, they slowly advanced and sat down. Gradually, the atmosphere cleared and talk was resumed.

A number of anecdotes were told of this old gentleman with the authoritarian manner. One winter, one of the boys went to work in the lumber camps, and, before coming home, invested some of his hard-earned money in a watch. The father, on being shown this treasure, examined it, and, after a moment's reflection, he said to his son: "*Give it to Médéric*" (who had remained at home to help his parents) "*he likes it better than you do.*" A Prodigal Son would hardly, in the Simard household, have been greeted with a fatted calf.

The Simards had the only maple grove of any importance in the neighbourhood, and they usually supplied the rest of the parish with sugar and syrup — at a price. One spring, Father's cousin, Ludger Frappier, was courting Virginie, a daughter of the house, Monsieur Simard invited everyone roundabout to a maple taffy party. Everyone knows that this is a very delectable sweet obtained by cooling some of the thickening syrup in the process of becoming sugar. When the right stage is reached, gobs of syrup are poured out on the snow to harden, and, presto, you have maple taffy. Of course, everybody came, including Ludger. After they had all been abundantly regaled, Simard Père stood up and said, "*I hope you have all enjoyed yourselves; that will be two bits apiece!*" General surprise. Also, consternation for those who had come with empty pockets, among whom our Ludger. Virginie, ever loyal, to save his face lent him the required fee.

This same Ludger was one of the best storytellers we knew. He was pleasant, good-natured with us young ones, and obliged with fairy tales without end, or at least as long as we were allowed to beg for more. He and his sister Mélina, wife of Napoléon Lacasse, were first cousins of Father and lived along the same road as the Dubucs. Relations with them were not as close as with relatives on Mother's side, but we were quite friendly, and, as children, we were allowed to visit once in a while. Mrs. Lacasse was a 'fun' person, and her little house one of the most cheerful I have ever seen anywhere. Everything in it was spotless, colours were bright, and I can only think of it as filled with cheer, warmth, and sunlight.

Serge recalls well our visits to Lacasse's house — the cheerful, pleasant living room and the delicious slices of fresh-baked bread spread with home-made butter and golden molasses. No one made bread like Mélanie Lacasse.

She had a keen — perhaps not always gentle — sense of humour. She came to stay with us on occasion when Mother had to be absent, and we found her very amusing. Once she said to a neighbour "*I don't know what Eliza feeds these children: they are always hungry.*" Naturally, this was repeated to Mother who never forgave her for it.

She was always gay and full of fun. She could tell a fib with a perfectly straight face. Once she was staying at our house in Mother's absence and was preparing a lunch for the hired man. As she looked for a clean cloth to wrap it in, she came upon some of Serge's baby garments which, having served their original purpose, were being pressed into another lifetime of use. "*I hope,*" she said blandly, looking the man straight in the eye, "*that you don't think I am wrapping your lunch in a diaper.*" And who could — seeing those big, brown, candid orbs — doubt her word? It was well that he did not turn back at the door to catch their mischievous sparkle.

Her last act was one of helpfulness. While caring for a sick neighbour, she contracted pneumonia and died after a few days' illness.

There was a son, Hilaire, a pleasant fellow, but too old for us to become much acquainted with.

Mlle Barre was an elderly maiden lady, sister of Mme Dubuc (Geo. Sr.), who lived with them and occasionally would help at the neighbours' when people were ill or in need of help for some other reason. She stayed with us a few times. She shared my bed, and I can recall lying next to the wall, very quiet, for she did not like to be disturbed, my feet slow to warm up since I could not curl up as usual. She was quite thin, and her sight was already failing because of cataracts. There was a chair in the kitchen which had varnish on it, and, thinking that it needed cleaning, she scrubbed it with lye until the wood was completely bare, to Mother's wry amusement. Mlle Barre died some years later of a fall from the attic where she slept. She had become quite blind, and there was no railing around the trap door opening. We children were surprised at this, used as we were to Mother's repeated cautions about ours. The use of such trap doors was common in houses which had no central heating.

One visit was commemorated by a photograph, taken by Mother. It occurred in the year that Halley's comet made its fourth appearance since being sighted by the astronomer who gave it his name. There was much talk about this impending phenomenon, as always when something strange or ill-understood is expected. Some predicted the end of the world. We were much amused with these stories. The spectacle of the comet, streaming through space with its long trail of light fanning out towards the end was an exciting sight to witness. We were all out in the garden, waiting, when it appeared. The visitors were a Mrs. Bertin and Mrs.

Noëlla Pilon, both of Montreal. Mrs. Bertin's deceased husband had owned some property near the farm of George Dubuc, Sr., and Father was asked to attend to the sale of it on behalf of the widow to a man named Portelance. They stayed on while the matter was dealt with.

Mr. Bertin had been a 'real' Frenchman and a professed atheist: a character; he had treated his tall, rather masculine-looking wife like a servant, and she had absorbed something of his philosophic views. She spoke to me as I walked about with her in the garden and said that no one knew what God was, and it might as well be the sun as anything else, since it made life possible. That did not sound too bad to me, but I was a bit too young to take it to heart.

Mrs. Pilon was young and charming and a member of a smart social set. Her father was a canon of the Church. He was exceedingly proud of his beautiful and talented daughter and saw to it that she made an advantageous marriage. She was probably the most glamorous guest we had, at least, that I can remember.

The following Christmas, there was a marvellous box full of goodies for the children. I blush to admit that the only item I recollect is a dress for me, made of silk pongee and trimmed with ruching. That was a fashion wrinkle I promptly appropriated for use in embellishing dolls' clothes, feeling quite the little dressmaker.

# 4

# toys, games, pastimes, outdoor play

Now, I would like to say something about the 'fun' part of our lives.

A French writer said of life that it is like a door in which nails have been driven. These nails, said he, are the happy days. Seen from afar, they appear innumerable; pull them out, and there are barely a handful.[1]

Perfect days are few, and time spreads a kindly veil over many a doleful childish memory. But by the same token, the feelings and pictures that endure were surely those that produced the sharpest and deepest impressions at the time. Looking back, I do recall a great many enjoyable experiences. Granted, these are spread over a

1 I searched high and low for the source of this quote, but I can't find it anywhere: I recognize neither the writer in question, nor the passage. (Lorraine)

number of years, and there were dull days — days when nothing worthy of note seemed to happen — days filled chiefly with chores (and, of course, homework) — rainy days. In every life there are those. The tedium of such days was usually redeemed by the story hour, unless — irritated by boredom or fatigue or being simply out of sorts — we had misbehaved and forfeited the privilege.

We were not short of toys or other aids to amusement. We had a swing made by Father. It stood on the east side of the house, near the vegetable garden. There were toboggans and wagons in season. We used the toboggan on the slope of the *montagnon* — the little hill where wild plum trees grew, on the way to the mill, and also on the hill beside the house. There were sets of tools for the boys, toy soldiers, and various dolls and such for Damienne and me. Jacks-in-the-box were fun but were soon worn out because the springs were not equal to the demands made upon them. The boys were very skilled at making whistles from the stems of sumac; the soft, corky texture of the heartwood makes it relatively easy to remove in order to obtain a hollow cylinder. Police whistles suspended from a cord around one's neck were much prized and party noise-makers would find their way sometimes into Christmas stockings.

Christian had a bicycle which I attempted once, with dubious success, to ride. My excursion ended in a ditch filled with sharp-edged stones.

The first doll I remember was made of wood carved by Father with his jack-knife. Lili had a wig when she was new, but I can only visualize her now with a bald pate. Her limbs were articulated with straps of leather at shoulder, elbow, thigh, and knee. There were others later, mostly composition dolls whose nose and ears diminished quickly once the paint was cracked. There were dolls with eyes that opened and closed, whose waxen eyelids, alas, would, after a while, lift to reveal empty sockets. I must have been rather hard on my toys. Damienne was far more careful of hers. Her Eaton's Beauty doll lived to a ripe old age, as did a little cabinet made for her by Father and painted red, and a set of blue enamel play dishes.

There was a *Polichinelle* (Punchinello) of which I was very fond. This personage featured in story and song. There were puppets on strings. These were, I fear, short-lived, but, while they lasted, what amusing antics Christian could make them perform! Christmas stockings might contain, besides oranges and candies and nuts, a variety of things — crayons, little Chinese dolls: gay reminders of the children in that faraway land. We had toy dishes. There was a gem of a little toy stove that was Damienne's. It could hold a real fire, and there were a frying pan and a kettle to match! A doll carriage was also Damienne's.

Such toys there were as rubber balls, skipping ropes, brilliantly coloured musical tops, and a number of mechanical toys. The one that comes most readily to mind is an enormous beetle three inches long with red wings spotted black. The wooden floors provided an excellent surface for the feet of these tin creatures. There were toy soldiers. There were also guns and cap pistols. Christian whittled guns and swords out of wood, made bows and arrows, and, inevitably, catapaults or slingshots. Here I use the plural advisedly because they, even more than other toys, were liable to confiscation when injudiciously employed. Confiscation of tools or toys, as well as suspension of privileges were the sanctions chiefly relied upon by Mother to maintain order and discipline. Once, when very young, I was deprived of playing cards for a whole week because, having lost a game to Arthur Paquette who good-naturedly had consented to amuse a (no doubt insistent) small girl, I had, in a fit of temper, scattered the deck over table and floor. The sentence caused me to shed bitter tears, but it was very effective.

Corporal punishment was limited to the use of a switch (*hart*) which we were usually sent for (adding insult to injury) because they somehow tended to disappear around the house. One day, Christian and I were on that unwelcome errand, and he spied some tall specimens of the last year's goldenrods. It was a clever idea, but it did not work. We had to go out again to cut a willow sapling of suitable length and size.

We really experienced harshness only for a short period, and not at the hands of our own parents but rather at those of one Marie Sarazin, who was left to care for us while Mother was in St. Luke's hospital in Ottawa. Mademoiselle Sarazin was possibly in her late thirties, tall, angular, of forbidding aspect. Perhaps she had resolved in advance not to stand for any nonsense, and certainly no nonsense was offered by us. I truly feared the creature. Serge says he recalls Marie Sarazin, and he was afraid of her. He thinks that was the time when he started to call me *Mama Jeanne*. Perhaps he felt he needed protection. After Mother returned and it was decided that she was finally able to do without the services of

Marie, I could hardly believe the good news. It was as though a dark, lowering cloud had been lifted to let the sun shine on the world. Poor Marie, perhaps she had done her duty as she saw it. If she had been unkind to the little ones, it is doubtful that it would have escaped us so she was probably not as much of a Gorgon as she appeared to me.

Penances for lack of docility might be: kissing the floor, remaining on one's knees facing the corner of the room, or being deprived of some desirable activity: even being confined in the darkroom, which had served, at one time, for developing photographs. Father left the burden of our disciplining to Mother and contented himself with fearfully earnest adjurations on his departure for long trips, embellished with those impressive quotations in which the Old Testament is so rich.

We were not unduly repressed. We were actually supposed to leave the conversation to the adults at table, but Christian often managed to evade that rule by making amusing remarks which would elicit a smile and even a little laugh from Father. Obedience was insisted upon — as indeed it should be — and we were from time to time reminded of our duties in that respect.

We had various games to while away winter evenings: dominoes, checkers, cards. I never learned to play games with marbles, but I was very fond of the beautiful striated alleys. I had a larger marble of clear glass with a tiny polar bear inside.

In the summer, we liked to remain outside as long and as late as possible. We played croquet in front of the house on the lawn, and we would skip rope, play ball, run around the house with cap guns snapping madly until the adults rebelled or the twilight would bring the whippoorwill and the bats out of their daytime sleep. Twilight was a noticeable period because of the long shadows cast by the surrounding mountains. How the birds would swoop on soft wings with their enormous bills wide open to gobble up the mosquitoes and other evening insects! Bats too, but they were less pleasant to watch as they would occasionally get entangled in our hair (ugh) their poor eyesight and membranous wings making for a flight less swift and sure than that of the birds. *Whip-poor-Will! Whip-poor-Will!* The sound is engraved on my memory and the mere thought of it conjures up the whole scene in soft, grey tones and muted colours.

There were other evening sounds: the song sparrow (*rossignol*), the cuckoo, the mocking bird, and many of which I never learned the names. There were the bittern and other water-loving birds, owls, and, in season, the toads and frogs. I suppose it is because all is still at that time that these voices assume greater resonance than that of birds who pour out their hymn to life in the warmth of the noon-day sun. Or maybe it is the mountains, enduring witnesses that were old when life began and may well see the end of all we know.

Once indoors in the evening, only stories could keep us awake. There were pastimes for rainy days: whittling, board and card games, building houses of cards, while large wet drops ran down the window panes in lively little rivulets. We had a stereoscope with a lovely collection of scenes. The three-dimensional effect was so convincing that I remember thinking that I could actually detect the swirl of the garments of the whirling dervishes.

Sometimes we made candy, or prepared our own snacks. Our favourite home-made candy was pulled molasses taffy. It was fun to pull it until it was light gold in colour, then to cut it into handy bite-sizes; then we would set it on tin plates to harden outside. With molasses in a frying pan, we made molasses toast by putting in a slice of bread and letting the molasses cook to the consistency of taffy. This was a favourite snack. In winter, Mother used to make doughnuts in large quantity and freeze them. She would fill a crock of three-gallon size, and, though that looked a lot, especially when they were being fried, they would soon be gone. We were also fond of 'dough boys,' fried strips of white bread dough.

For us girls, there was dressing up and making dolls' clothes. Also, paper, scissors, mucilage, and wax crayons provided materials for countless hours of activity. Business letters that came to the house were used for writing on the blank side, envelopes were unglued, turned inside out, glued again, addressed and stamped with facsimile stamps made with pencil and crayons. Every scrap of wrapping paper was made into stationery or cut out in rows of paper dolls or in lace patterns. We had no colouring books, but we drew, and then coloured, pictures without end!

We relished keenly the comics in *La Presse*. There was a French version of the Katzenjammer Kids in which Hans and Fritz (*Toinon and Polyte*) were partners in mischief and Mrs. Katzenjammer was translated into *Aglae*, an older sister. The Captain was an uncle. Any imitation of the boys' antics was obviously out of the question. We had to content ourselves with quiet cheers when they successfully turned the tables on the adults, especially as harsh treatment would at times lend justice to their cause.

One of the series of comics we most enjoyed was entitled *À l'Hôtel du Père Noé* (At Father Noah's Hostel) a take-off on the legend of Noah's Ark. The animals chosen to play very human roles were amusing either in appearance — ponderous hippos and elephants — or, in behaviour — like the playful and mischievous monkeys. As I remember this strip, the humour was not hostile or malicious, but it constituted, rather, a satire on human pretensions: a picture of social, rather than of family life. The drawings were on a generous scale, fulsome in line and colour and delightfully droll. I spent hour upon hour filling scribblers with free-hand copies of these pictures, each figure painstakingly outlined in black to make every line, every rich curve, stand out distinct and eloquent. Our supply of pencils and wax crayons must have been well-nigh inexhaustible.[2]

Before leaving *La Presse*, I must mention another feature which contributed to our fun and, incidentally, to our education. This was the weekly column written by a Montreal lawyer and called LADÉBAUCHE. There was a pun in the name itself, since *débauche* means corruption. In homespun conversation with his

2 Creator of this comic strip was Montreal native Raoul Barré (1874–1932), a North American pioneer in the field and in film cartoons. My thanks to Estelle Dansereau, University of Calgary, for this information (I.A.)

wife Catherine, Baptiste would discuss a variety of topics, chiefly political, but extending also to popular ignorance, stupidity or superstition, with the insight of a seasoned campaigner who has 'been around the block' and who is not easily deceived. The whole was expressed phonetically in the idiom more recently dubbed *joual.*

We relished this all the more that we were often admonished to avoid such older French provincialisms as *toé*, *moé*, and so on, and we had nothing of that nature in our reading material. Huckleberry Finn, Tom Sawyer, Uncle Remus, Hillbilly songs, and comics — even Westerns — were still to come to us. Only in quotation could one roll with impunity on one's tongue such delectable bits of elocution as "*les pétaques pourrites pusent!*"[3] The column was rich in picturesque choice of words. For example: speaking of someone who had not done credit to his illustrious ancestor: "*Y'a pas descendu! Y'a dégringolé en scie ronde!*"[4] An expression we liked: "*Ça t'en bouche un coin!*"[5] I heard recently in a contemporary movie made in France.

Christian often quoted one of Ladébauche's wise sayings: "*Il faut réfléchir avant de faire une bêtise*"[6]

3 *Rotten potatoes stink.* This isn't even Joual; it's just slang, and maybe funny. (Lorraine)

4 *He didn't descend: he tumbled (like a circular saw?).* I guess you had to be there. (Lorraine)

5 *It plugs a corner for you.* Mother seems to have taken it for granted that her readers were bilingual. (Lorraine)

6 "Think carefully before committing a blunder."

That particular vernacular known as '*Joual*' which has made the delight of more than one of our philologists is well preserved in the incomparable verse of *Jean Narrache* (a pseudonym). It would be nice if some day some of the best of these examples might be resurrected for the pleasure of the curious in matters of language, politics, or perhaps sociology.[7]

Storytelling time sometimes came with visitors: cousin Laurence, the aunts and Ludger Frappier and his sister Mrs. Lacasse all had a fund of fairy and folk tales. Some of these — notably a story about a little green horse — have never turned up in any of our numerous collections. When Grandmother (mémère Côté) was with us, the stories might take on a more thrilling form: ghost stories, accounts of marvellous happenings such as spectacular punishment for sins:[8] for example, a man who had his tongue destroyed by a canker because he had been guilty of gossiping about the local *curé*; a rain of sulphur had caused widespread conflagrations as punishment for the hardened, unregenerate behaviour of the population of a certain parish. One woman had mysteriously given birth to a little imp, complete with tail and all.... Exploits of werewolves were related in hushed tones ... we would

7 I am surprised at this comment; Mother had in her library, and I have, part of a set of books containing just such material. It's entitled *Les Vieux m'ont conté*, by the Reverend Father Germain Lemieux, S.J. and it's an attempt to document Franco-Ontarian folklore. I found it difficult to read, although I'm pretty well acquainted with the argot. I don't think the print medium is the best vehicle for this stuff. Did you ever try to read Uncle Remus? I'd rather hear it than read it: but what do I know. (Lorraine)

8 The most famous of these, the story of Rose Latulipe, we had read in the *Almanach du Peuple*, a yearly publication full of fascinating data of all kinds. (I don't know this one, either, and I have yet to look it up. [Lorraine])

listen, spellbound, letting delicious shivers runs up and down our spines, while the tales lasted. I do not recall that any of us every lost any sleep over fear of the supernatural. Our religious education had made us, strangely enough, rather trusting in that regard. Perhaps we identified (sublime confidence!) with men of good will for whom peace on earth was intended.

I have mentioned before that we liked to sing: not only the songs learned from Mother and relatives, but we learned many on our own. We learned the English songs that I've mentioned and others, including the songs of Botrel. We relished his folksy humour, and sympathized with the lonely belles of Paimpol whose lovers were long absent with fishing boats on the cold waters of Iceland or on the coast of Newfoundland.

Besides the piano, we had a gramophone. Father had won it in a raffle for a fifty-cent ticket, with a number of tubular records. Only one of these do I recall: the touching aria from *Madama Butterfly* where Cio Cio San sings her trust in the constancy of her lover. We were allowed to take the gramophone along on evening excursions on the lake. We thought the sound of music on the water should be interesting. We also had a music box or euphonium with records in the form of large metal disks with notes produced by indentations in the metal. Favourite pieces: *Le Carnaval de Venise* and *Les Cloches de Corneville.* Some of those music boxes are still extant, mostly in museums. I have seen one at the home of a retired Edmonton photographer (Gladys Reeves): as good as new, the tinkling melodies charmingly nostalgic.

Outdoor play, which, at most times we greatly preferred, varied with the seasons. Snow, which creates troublesome problems for adults in the pursuit of their daily occasions, was for us a source of endless diversion. With sleigh or with toboggan, on snow shoes or walking precariously on the crust of ice which followed a thaw or simply rolling ecstatically in enormous banks of fresh fallen snow, every day which was not really cold found us outside as long as we were permitted to stay.

Oh! to be out on those mild days when moist air brushes your cheeks like a feather while large, perfect snowflakes fall so gently that you have time to admire their fairy-like beauty on your mitt or on the sleeve of your jacket before they dissolve into tiny droplets of moisture. Sometimes there's snow that clings together to make firm snowballs, snowmen of imposing stature or snow forts that, with luck, might last several days. As it says in *Alice, "There's glory for you!"* Once the wind had piled up a very large snow bank in a corner of the fence, just left of the gate to the stables: piled it so firmly that we used spades to tunnel a space inside of it large enough to stand up, and for us all to sit in it. We discovered to our happy surprise that we did not feel the cold at all; so we decided that living in igloos made very good sense after all.

In winter, the frost on the windows would sometimes get very thick and assume the most wonderful forms: fern fronds and a profusion of leaf-like structures which brought to mind the jungle paintings of Rousseau (*le douanier*).[9] They occasionally

9 Henri Rousseau (1844–1910); a 'naïve' painter; unschooled. He became a customs inspector on goods brought into Paris, and that is why he is nicknamed 'le douanier' (the customs officer). See the *New International Illustrated Encyclopedia of Art*, Vol. 18. (Lorraine)

caused me to lapse into day-dreaming when I ought to have been studying my lessons.

We were always glad to see the bare ground in the spring because, by the time the snow was all but gone, we had had enough of the slush and icy water. The first bit of green was likely to show in some young aspen growing on the little rocky hill near the house. I would nibble some of the silky, paper-thin leaves, enjoying the clean, slightly bitter flavour. This would also be the first spot to be dry. Since the area was within call and observation, we were generally pretty free to go there in spare moments. Once, when I was very, very young, I had wandered to the top of the rise and managed to turn over a flat stone, revealing a crawling mass of newly born snakes. This was a small garter snake, sand-coloured above and coral below, less than a foot in length adult size. I must have called out something which alerted Mother for she gave such a shout that I was thoroughly shaken and headed for the house without delay.

Summer was the best time of all because there were more things to see, and we were allowed more freedom to play. And, of course, summer days are longest. Random walks along the road or through the fields would generally turn up something of interest. Grass stems were tasty bits, the soft, juicy part just above the node. Gum could be carved out of the bark of venerable spruce trees; thimbleberries were more or less everywhere; blackberries lined the ditches along the road in some places; dewberries favoured shady spots, strawberries the sunny places, though the best and largest were among tall grasses. Pincherries were fairly common along the road to the lake; the *amélanchiers*[10] had few fruit, but were tasty. If we were out early, we might come across spider webs still unmarred by the wriggling of some unwary prey, the morning sun making each bedewed thread of these incredible structures a row of scintillating crystal beads. We would crouch to admire them, our feet in the cool wet grass: for we discarded our shoes as soon as we were permitted.

The first flowers of the season were the object of an eager search: the wake robin (red trillium), dogtooth violet, a blue violet and a yellow violet, and clumps of wintergreen whose leaves are not deciduous and make quite delightful chewing. This plant is a little parsimonious as to blossoms and, to find fruit in any quantity, we had to climb the nearest mountain — an exciting, if arduous, undertaking. There were rarer sorts, like the graceful yellow and red columbine which were mostly found in woodsy places.

In June, ox-eyed daisies and yellow buttercups were all over the fields and roadsides. We sat in the sun in the fragrant meadow making endless flower chains of buttercups, daisies, or dandelions until we were tired or were called in for a snack or a meal.

Of course, even in summer, the sun did not always shine down on our play. There were sudden warm showers that were rather enjoyable unless they caught us far from home or at some inopportune time. Clouds would come down until they would hide

10 The English equivalent of this word which Mother uses in French is 'serviceberry,' or 'shadblow' or also 'Saskatoon berry.' I got this from Mademoiselle Annie Bourret who wrote *Pour l'amour du français*, an admirable book which I added to my library in 1999. (Lorraine)

quite the top of the near mountain. Then they would burst, perhaps with a lively accompaniment of thunder and lightning, pouring a torrent of enormous raindrops like a benison on plants and beasts.

We often took a snack along to eat in some favourite spot. Such a spot was a large stone jutting out from the montagnon at the turn in the road to the mill. It used to be shaded by a tall tree: a liard. This is a poplar which resembles the balsam but has a smoother trunk, larger and glossier leaves. Buds have the same spicy, resinous smell when they open. On the nether side of the stone was a cluster of sumac. We liked to crush the red fruit for the pleasantly acid taste which gives this plant the pseudonym *vinaigrier*, or vinegar-bush. We sat there contentedly in the cool shade, looking down on the stables and the hog pen and at the woods beyond the stream. The pen was fairly large. How or when Jerusalem artichokes were introduced there we did not know, but occasionally we would bring a spade and help ourselves to some *topinambours*. The tubers are the size of small potatoes and grow so deep in the soil that no amount of rooting by the porkers had succeeded in eradicating them. We ate them raw, having found that the delicate texture and flavour diminish in boiling. It seemed a shame to rob the pigs, but at least we dug our own, unlike French farmers who, they say, allow their pigs to hunt out those savory fungi they call truffles and then snatch from them their hard-won prize.

Just across the road from the *montagnon*, not far from the tall cedars under which Christian and I set snares for unwary bunnies, he decided one day to play pioneer and clear a small patch of land.

He did so, turning the sod over with a spade, and sowed a little wheat. We thought it quite wonderful that the wheat germinated, and grew, and produced grain ... it was a page of *Swiss Family Robinson* come to life, or maybe Jules Verne's *Ile Mystérieuse*.

Attempts to build viable shelters were seldom successful. One of our best ones was erected on a grassy flat not far from a clump of alders bordering the creek, at some distance from the stables. That had a frame that supported walls and roof of woven branches, these made more opaque by the addition of fir boughs. We were very pleased with this, but a young bull took exception to it and butted it down. No one tried to argue with him. It was the memory of this brief success which prompted my statement often quoted by the others with derisive glee: "*Give me four posts and four good nails (spikes) and I'll build you a house!*" I felt that the rest was within my competence, but no one ever took me up on the offer.

On some sunny Saturday afternoons, we would start out on what we called voyages of discovery. This called for flags to plant on, or near, heretofore unknown topographical features of land or water, somewhat in the fashion of the professor in Jules Verne's *Five Weeks in a Balloon*, recently revived (the portly professor played by the well-known Cedric Hardwicke). It is quite remarkable how many things like bays, straits, promontories, dangerous reefs, mountains, and valleys one may discover if one scales down one's requirements. One might say that the more demands on the imagination, the greater the thrill of achievement. Anyone can recognize a port large enough to accommodate a fleet, but how many truly appreciate an inlet just big enough to allow a small boat to rest in comparatively quiet water out of the wind?

We had flags of two persuasions: the Union Jack and the *Tricolore*. Quebec's beautiful *Fleur de lys* came later. Being a girl, and the eldest — though which one carried most weight is not too clear — I carried the French flag. Christian carried the Union Jack. There was only one party and only one boat, so the rivalry could not have been too keen. I cannot recall any occasion when there was any serious clash of political interests, except one time when we had built a very creditable snow fort on the *montagnon* near the house.

It was in late winter, and we were anxious to make the most of this structure before the sun could bring it down. I was to man the fort with one of the younger ones, Christian to storm it with the other. The siege was to begin on the morrow, and we laid in a good stock of ammunition, both inside the citadel and in the enemy camp. The *Tricolore* flew proudly from the highest point of the walls. To the surprise and discomfiture of the garrison, we realized that the impact of the enemy's guns was proving fatally effective. Christian had had the foresight, the night before, to even the odds by soaking his snow balls in water. We rationalized this clever piece of strategy by saying that since he was flying the Union Jack he was not bound by the protocol which regulates gentlemanly war practices. There was, however, a lack of conviction in this expressed view. We had read too much history not to have a healthy respect for the victors of Crécy and Agincourt.

A good deal of our play was inspired by our reading. There were no close neighbours with youngsters of our age, and, as Christian sometimes complained, there were not enough of us to make even one team, let alone two. We would imitate some of the things we saw in the newspaper — Christian and I would go through the motions of what we thought was wrestling — the loser being the one whose shoulders were held to the floor for the count. We would also sit at the table with wrists locked, straining as if much depended on it. In any contest of strength, he was a match for me in spite of the age difference between us. He was more agile and wiry. In spite of all the horseplay in which we indulged, we did not really hurt one another that I can remember. Our squabbling was mostly verbal. We were well equipped for that.

I do not remember Damienne well as a small baby. At five, I was too young to be entrusted with her care. As far back as I can recall, she was a dainty, quiet little thing, pretty as a picture. Everybody said she looked like a doll, and she certainly did, with big, dark eyes and lovely curls which Mother took pleasure in coaxing around her finger.

Young Serge is the one we remember best, not only from, but in the cradle. When very small, he often had earaches which caused Mother anxiety and wakeful nights. Dr. Matte called and gave useful directions, predicting that he would grow out of it. Dr. Matte was a tall, fair man with a blond beard and gentle manners. He said more than once that a mother is a child's best nurse as she knows more about him than any physician can. He called once when I had scarlet fever, spoke soothingly and left a bottle of a medicine: a pretty green in colour and bitter as gall. We rocked little Serge and sang him to sleep as Mother had done for the rest of us. When earaches made him fretful, she walked the floor with him — or Father did, if he was at home.

Serge lived to see the earaches diminish, and they finally went away. His yellow curly hair grew down to his shoulders before Mother could bring herself to cut it, yielding to his protests against the combing out of tangles morning and night.

Serge was especially amenable to suggestion, ever ready and willing to lend his toys. He used the word *donner*, which means to give, and, when the time came that he had given all of his toys and wanted them back, he would cheerfully say: "*À c't'heure, je t'l' dédonne.*"[11] We accepted very readily his version of property rights in view of his general co-operativeness.

The younger ones went along fairly well with our games of pretending — Damienne often under protest; she had more domestic tastes. There was little scope for them under our direction until they became old enough to plan games of their own, which, indeed, they eventually did. One project of theirs which provided amusement for many a pleasant hour was the little store which was erected on the *montagnon*, more or less on the same principle as our other buildings for shelter purposes, only, of course, with shelves, in imitation of the general store where we went occasionally on errands and to fetch the mail. Little boxes of all kinds and small bottles containing liquids of mixed provenance stood upon the shelves. My contribution was one containing stale rainwater and labelled *Aqua foetida* — a notion picked up goodness knows where. The little store was a lasting source of varied activity. Here,

11 "Now, I *ungive* it you!" (*À cette heure, je te le dédonne*).

Damienne might in safety make a fire in her lovely little stove and heat things on it in the pot and frying pan that were part of the kitchen equipment that came with it.

Christian's humour tended to be mocking. He loved to relate some elaborate tale of adventure or mischief and when Mother expressed concern or disapproval he would shout in glee: "*You believed me! You believed me!*" She never knew for sure whether he was lying or telling the truth. He could tell outrageous stories with a completely straight face and then rejoice at the gullibility of his audience. Sometimes she would shake her head in despair and mutter: '*Gibier de potence!*'[12]

Christian was fascinated by the Latin prayers and liturgical chant. When very small, he made up a song of his own, which went like this:

*Atte sepprietté a sanqueto sanquetola*
*Spiritus ré gloriae in excelsis doé Dodoé Déo*[13]

We all sang it with gusto.

Christian and I had a great fondness for teasing, but Christian had greater ingenuity, which was sometimes expressed in practical jokes. One day, he conceived the notion of hanging Damienne's lovely Eaton's Beauty doll. Damienne walked into the kitchen to behold her darling swinging from the end of a rope fastened to the

12 Gallows bird; but in English it isn't funny, whereas in French it's not even very severe. (Lorraine)

13 For those of you who might be misled, it means nothing. (Lorraine)

top step of the attic stairs. She was so outraged she could not speak, but her screams brought Mother running. Mother took down the doll, but Damienne was hysterical. Words of comfort had no effect and Mother, fearful of convulsion, seized a dipper of cold water and threw it in Damienne's face. Damienne subsided, finally, but she never forgot nor forgave that dipper of water. It was an insult. Christian was considerably taken aback at the result of his caper. I do not remember what punishment was meted out to him, but, to my knowledge, nothing of this nature ever occurred again. Damienne herself recalls that she was of a rather prickly disposition. The squabbles that went on between Christian and me were in a manner of speaking part of our play, like the mock fighting of pups and kittens. We were evenly matched. Damienne would not join in any horseplay, and indeed she wanted no part of any games of ours. She resented our bothersome coaxing. "*Laissez-donc votre petite soeur tranquille!*" Mother would remind us, in a tired voice; "*Elle n'entend pas à rire.*"[14]

As Mother said, Damienne (like most children, for that matter) was lacking in humour, especially when she felt herself belittled. One day, she and I were playing on the platform between the kitchen and woodshed. Father was engaged in repairing the steps on the north side. Damienne had disregarded some caution given, and Father, in a mock serious tone, said: "*Écoute, ma petite fille, encore une fois*"[15] — and with twinkling eyes and his mouth a tight



14 "Leave your little sister alone; she has no sense of humour."

15 "Listen, my little girl: one more time —"

line to repress a smile, he picked up a two by four and made as if to apply it to her little bottom. She turned and ran, crying with vexation. But this had been too amusing to forget in a hurry, and, on subsequent occasions, when she proved unco-operative, we would say warningly: "*Damienne, la planche.*"[16]

Damienne and Serge used occasionally to fantasize that they were not our parents' real children; some day, they said, it would be revealed that they were orphans or members of some other family. Christian said he wished he were an orphan because then there would be no one to tell him what to do.

Children's property rights were not necessarily respected. Mother justified giving away Damienne's doll without consulting her. She said: "*You are too old to play with dolls.*" That memory made Damienne fanatically careful, where her own children were concerned, to avoid such an error.

The creek was a never-failing source of interest along the whole of its course near us. Starting at the bridge which marked its issue from Lac Pelletier, the stream was almost filled with water weeds.[17] Christian would guide the boat along the narrow clear channel. In places, there were yellow water lilies — golden cups floating among the round green pads on the surface of the water. There were blue flags (a species of wild iris) along the bank. Early in my young life, I had been reaching for one of these, leaning perilously over the stream, when Aunt Arthémise snatched me from a watery



16 "Damienne — the stick." (the *board*, actually).

17 *Elodea.*

grave. That, at any rate, was her story. I had been left in her care, and she had suddenly realized that her charge had disappeared. I find it pleasant to think that there was a time when I seem to have known no fear of physical danger — even though that happy state was of short duration.

The swollen part of the creek came to an end at the upper dam, at least when it was closed. It was below this, I think, that there were crayfish. Christian used to tease them out from behind stones, and we would watch them with amusement as they scuttled backwards into hiding. The channel was fairly deep in some places, but at others we could wade across easily. The crossing we used for fetching cows from the pasture was below the mill. Just a few yards further down was a tall walnut tree: the nut meats were bitter — not really edible.





We longed passionately for islands. Christian and I would work for hours tirelessly heaping sand and gravel in a shallow stretch. If the mill were idle for a day or two we might even thrust a few branches down as token trees; but that was only make-believe, for we knew full well that the first moment of high water would wash away all traces of our labour. When the water was low, it was fun to watch the minnows and a variety of aquatic insects, either walking with confident step on the surface, or diving deep.

In the bank just below the stables, we noticed one day a vein of blue clay. That looked interesting. We tasted it tentatively — I don't know why. It had a pleasing flavour. We spoke about it at the house and were enjoined not to repeat the experiment. Since then, it has come to my knowledge that the people of a certain part of the Eastern United States make a regular practice of eating this type of clay.

Some little way further down the creek, alders grew on the bank. These looked particularly interesting because of the cone-like structures which remain on the tree long after the seeds are scattered. When leafless, the branches rattle as the wind blows through them. It was from one of these that a blue-grey cat of ours, having reached a crotchety and infirm old age, was hanged by uncle Charles during one of his visits. She was over nine years old and obviously had lost all zest for life, but none of us had the heart to put her out of her misery. Whether putting her head into a slip knot was less repulsive than a blow on the head or whether this macabre procedure appealed to Uncle Charles' sense of humour, I don't know, but at any rate there she was for many a month afterwards: a forlorn little skeleton swinging from a tall leafy gibbet, and when the fall winds came, she added another rattle to the rest.

The next part of the creek with which we were familiar ran along a flat grassy area which must, at some remote period, have been under water. We thought of this spot as the cherry orchard. There were several kinds of chokecherries: one clump near the water had fruit that were very nearly black and grew tightly pressed together, like grapes; another sort occurred in a clone[18] about the middle of the area. These trees were taller than the others, the cherries larger, more loosely arranged along the stem and with a rich, mellow flavour. Also worth noting was a large tree: this was the

18 A group of trees formed by proliferation of the roots of one single individual.

black cherry, whose wood is used in making furniture. It had late-ripening fruit, and we found it difficult to get at it because the trunk was so tall. Further still was another clump of cherries unlike any we have seen since: the fruit a clear, light red, very small-stoned and juicy. The flesh or pulp was of the consistency of the Nanking when quite ripe.

Below the stables, a curve in the course of the stream caused a strong eddy current and that place was too deep for our usual play. Father sometimes swam there, and so did Christian, after a fashion. There were water wings of inflated rubber for the rest of us. I was urged to swim, but Father, unfortunately, was inspired to duck me. I came up spluttering and gasping for air, and I did not care to pretend any more that I was a frog.

Near the bridge which led to the Prescott farm stood an enormous spruce tree. We liked to sit under it and talk, playing the while with the cones which littered the pleasant, dry spot. Before leaving, we generally checked the ancient trunk for a bit of spruce gum, a good stimulant for the appetite — not that ours needed much sharpening, especially after our walks in the fresh, sweet country air. We were not allowed to go very much further along the creek, but one place, just below the site of the Ruets' old house, we found particularly fascinating. The bank was almost perpendicular and fairly high, and it was riddled with round holes which we discovered to be the nests of bank swallows. There were several kinds of swallows: barn swallows, chimney swallows (who would at times accidentally find themselves prisoners in the house), and others. We found the bank swallows particularly interesting. The creek is deep there, and a mountain rises from the opposite bank. We were told that there was a mica mine somewhere near the top, but it was no longer being worked.

There were many mica mines in the country roundabout. Window panes for chicken coops were made of it, of various thicknesses according to the amount of light desired. It was used in stove doors, and insulators are still made of mica. There were flat surfaces where the mica was exposed on the side of the east mountain, and they would reflect the rays of the sun at sunset. We found asbestos, too; the mill was built on asbestos rock, a greenish stone. Chris and Serge used to scratch the rock and fluff off some fibres.

After we reached an age when we could be depended upon not to get lost or too easily carried away by distractions, our excursions might often have a definite goal or purpose. One of our favourite places was the wooded area across the creek where the cows were pastured. Another was the wilderness on the other side of Lac Pelletier. The first was criss-crossed by cow paths which made it easy to explore. If we were sent to bring back some item of wild harvest for the table — wild garlic or cress — we made a point of going and returning by the most circuitous path possible. There were so many interesting things growing all through these woods. Sweet-smelling pink clover and fine grass abounded under the sparse growth of willows and poplars. In certain spots, one could pick long streamers of running club moss, so convenient for making decorative garlands with the addition of tissue-paper flowers. Other club mosses were the ones called 'ground pine' and 'ground cedar' because of their resemblance, on a minute scale, to those trees.

On a stone about forty inches in height and approximately the same in diameter — (and goodness knows how it had landed so far from the nearest large, rocky mass!) grew the only patch of polypody fern I have ever seen. One had to revisit these special places every season to make sure those fascinating plants were still there. The wild garlic grew considerably further in a small area surrounding an enormous oak tree. That spot was sufficiently unusual to attract us for its own sake: a cool, shady glade with lovely plants such as maidenhair and other ferns. A spring flowed near the oak tree, and in the water-soaked leaf mould of its banks we dug with our hands for wild cress. This cress has a knobbly underground creeping stem with many roots growing out of it. It is this stem that is edible, having a flavour which partakes of mustard (it belongs to this family) and horseradish. Like the mild-tasting wild garlic, it was a pleasing addition to a meal.



One time our quest was soon completed, and, having time to spare, we took the notion to push further into less familiar terrain. In a clearing, we spied a novel spectacle: bright green grass grew on a level expanse broken by little else than rushes, small shrubs, and a marvellous plant which we had never seen. This was the pitcher plant, as I learned later. Great excitement. I must have a complete specimen to take home to study and draw. We went to fetch it, and, reaching for a clump of the coveted plants where they bloomed in the sun, we suddenly realized that the turf underfoot was resilient as a bed spring. Gleefully we jumped up and down — especially little Serge, until Christian became suspicious. He bethought him to inquire as to just what lay underneath. He took a willow stem about the size of his wrist, stripped it of its branches and pushed it down until there was only the part he held above the surface — a portion somewhere between five or six feet being submerged. As he pulled out the stick, he found it coated with the blackest thin mud one can imagine. With fast-beating hearts, we urged the younger ones off the treacherous bog. We had much to relate when we got home, and it was no surprise to us that the mysterious area was declared by Mother to be out of bounds. We recognized that danger existed outside of adventure stories.

When Grandmother was visiting, we might be sent for medicinal plants. Like the good Hercule Poirot, Grandmother placed a serene confidence in the efficacy of certain tisanes. One was made of the flowers of the blue-fruited elder or *Sureau blanc*. Incidentally, there is only one other part of Canada which is said to have this shrub as a native plant, and that is the southwestern tip of British Columbia. Another errand for her sent us to dig — (I say "us," but I recall that it was Christian who held the spade) — in wet ditches for the large white roots of cattails. On one occasion that she and Mother were dyeing wool for socks, we were directed to fetch alder bark. This yielded a brown dye of a rich sepia hue. I have never since then beheld any dye of that colour.

In June and July, gathering fruit was the most important of our activities. Wild strawberries we found almost everywhere. For amounts worth preserving, however, it was necessary to find patches of wild grass — preferably with partial shade. That was where large spreading clusters of luscious red fruit could be found. What a thrill it was to part the soft green mat to reveal the

*Covered bridge over Lièvre River between Val-des-Bois and Poltimore, circa 1910.*

heavily laden stems! The best place we knew was a meadow which belonged to a man called Ferdinand Villeneuve. He lived along the road to Notre-Dame-de-Pontmain, just past the junction of our road with that one. Finally, probably to protect his hay crop or simply because he was displeased with our trespassing or even because he may have wanted the strawberries for himself, he invited us to stay out of his field. That was that! or, as we liked to sing: *un point, c'est tout.*

One place rich in associations was the forest across the lake. There were timber trails through there. Father had a cutting permit in that area, and Jas. McLaren's had a considerable timber lease. In the winter men would cut the commercially valuable trees, haul them on sleighs, and pile them on the ice until spring, when drivers[19] would guide the floating logs to the dam and over it, down the creek to the Lièvre where it joined other lots on the way to the great mills. As far as we ever ventured there was no land under cultivation; in that enchanted wood the world belonged to the birds, the squirrels and other animals, and to us.

Occasionally, we would find trees from which the bark had been scraped by mighty claws, but the bears did not dispute us our harvest of raspberries. Sometimes we heard a wolf howl in the distance, but we never had any close calls or genuine frights.

19 The local expression in French for 'driver' was 'draveur' and the 'drive' is 'la drave.' This word, as noun as a verb, occurs in *Bélisle's Dictionnaire Général de la Langue Française au Canada*, but is nowhere to be found in Larousse. It does appear in the Robert & Collins. (Lorraine)

Raspberries grew in abundance all through that expanse of hardwoods. Mother would send us early after breakfast, with an ample provision of slices of home-baked bread and home-made butter with cucumbers or other filling for some sandwiches, the rest to be filled with fruit at the scene of our lunch. We chose, of course, the fattest and juiciest raspberries we could find. We had vessels of suitable size in which to pick these, but if some other goodies such as thimbleberries, red or black currants, should turn up — acceptable treats but not abundant enough to preserve — we would make holders for them out of the large round leaves of basswood and relish them at leisure. Once we found a patch of black raspberries (*catherinettes*). These were not common, and Mother mixed some with a portion of the red fruit to give it a beautiful purple colour. This was a trip repeated at intervals until the season was over, and, although it was tiring, the way long and the weather often hot, it would be difficult to recall more pleasant occasions.

The immediate rewards for this labour were happy freedom and tasty fresh berries. There were also raspberry pies, and a dish called *cipaille* or *cipâte*.[20] To make it Mother lined a cast-iron pot with pastry and filled the space with thick layers of raspberries separated by layers of pastry. The fruit thus cooked had a very special flavour.

20 You may know that the origin of the word '*cipaille*' is the English '*sea-pie,*' a word that Quebeckers learned from English-speaking sailors who frequented the coast.

Fruit was cooked, in those days, by the open kettle method and stored in bottles with the help of a funnel and a wooden stick. It was later removed — somewhat like catsup. Canning jars came later. One year we counted two hundred bottles on the shelves.

We found gooseberries wild but only in small quantities. Mother combined the ones we picked in the fields with the ones from the garden, where we had only a couple of bushes. Picked ripe, they were made into jam without cooking. The pulp was pressed through a collander to eliminate the skins, sugar in equal amount was added, and the whole well blended. Jars were filled and sealed and placed in the window in full sunlight for several hours. The result was a preserve of an exquisite flavour and a delicate pink colour.

September brought other delights. There were hazelnuts and beechnuts to gather. In the fall the hardwood forests are ablaze with glorious colour. The balmy air — the clear carrying quality of sound through partly leafless trees — the thick cushion of freshly fallen leaves underfoot — the shrill protests of squirrels as we searched for nuts under the beeches — it all made for a mood of such exhilaration as I associate with no other time. We would shout and jump up and down on the springy yellow-brown carpet — scream back at the indignant squirrels — until we were nearly exhausted. The harvest of nuts was not as constant as that of fruit. Beechnuts were dinky little things to shell. However, we mostly managed to do pretty well with hazelnuts. The crop might sometimes even fill a potato sack. The fruit were left for the outer envelope to dry or rot, thus becoming easier to remove, and the nuts stored.

Mother would sometimes add these nut meats to a soft fudge that she made with maple sugar: the famous *sucre à la crème*. Recently, I heard Monique Leyrac say that when she gets homesick for her native Québec (she lives in France), she makes *sucre à la crème* or *tourtières*.

Re-reading these pages, they seem so idyllic that I must remind myself that all of our paths were not forever smooth. Bare feet are vulnerable to small sharp pebbles, to dry, prickly thistles; burrs get stubbornly entangled in clothing; there are stinging nettles in the richest berry patches; there are wasp nests among fallen logs in the most exciting forest thickets, and, occasionally, we did experience insect invasions that cast a shadow over otherwise unclouded summers.



The Colorado beetle was not alone to create difficulties for the farmers. To be sure, we could not boast of anything so spectacular as the plagues of Egypt, but tent caterpillars and grasshoppers are distressing enough in their way. Either of these can make of a pleasant outdoor retreat a place of shuddering revulsion. The caterpillars are the worst. They are so silent and so insidious, and so unstoppable! One year, they invaded in their billions our happy preserves. They defoliated trees, travelled — a moving, breathing carpet — along roads and across meadows; they covered fence posts, crawled up walls in enormous dark, writhing patches —

entered buildings at every crack, dropped on unwary shoulders from tree branches, curiously peered at us from the brim of our hats, or, if we were hatless, stuck in our hair or crawled down our necks. For the duration of their larval existence there was no pleasure in anything we did outside the house.

The grasshoppers were different but not much better. They were noisy and destructive. Where green, healthy crops had been, a devastation of chopped-up straw was left. Especially on a hot day, they would jump endlessly in all directions, hitting everything in their way with the speed of hailstones driven by a hurricane wind, leaving at the point of impact a brown spot which Christian likened to tobacco juice. Those were not our happiest days.

There have long been variously effective ways used for dealing with such cases of Nature's excesses, but she still springs the odd surprise: for instance, the plague of army worms in the sugar beet fields of Alberta last season. There's always something.

Still, those were not frequent trials, and in fact they were seldom remembered afterwards. The pleasant moods, the misty enchantment of the climate and the country — that is what remains.

The few pets whose company we enjoyed should not be forgotten. The blue-grey cat whose hanging has been mentioned was, in her heyday, a businesslike mouser and never did put up with too much nonsense from us. My favourite cat was a tortoise-shell I had when I was very small. This was a handsome, gentle cat who submitted with incredible patience to being picked up, rocked, dressed up like a doll and laid in a crib where she would even pretend to sleep. Minette was a loyal friend, and I assert this in spite of what is commonly believed of her tribe. Once I was ill and too feverish to pay her the usual attention. She practically pined, and Mother found her asleep one morning, head and front paws on the covers between the bars of my crib while her hind feet rested on the floor. How the dear animal could have rested was a mystery.

Christian had a nice little retriever spaniel called Trim who followed us everywhere. He liked to swim after the boat when we rowed on the lake. One day, the trip was too long for his strength, and he drowned. Later on we had, for a while, a Great Dane given us by uncle Charles Lemieux.

There was a crow which we rescued when we found it with a broken leg. Aunt Arthémise spliced the injured limb, and, after it was healed, the bird, christened Diane, remained a long time about the place. When we came back from a jaunt, Diane greeted our return home with loud caws of welcome.



Damienne once had a young marmot, which became very tame. The boys captured him, a mere baby, as he emerged from the home burrow near the old Ruet house. Mother fed the little fellow with a medicine dropper until he could take in food by himself, and when he grew larger he lost every vestige of shyness. He would follow Mother or Damienne to the garden where he nibbled the pansies, holding them daintily in his little paws. At the table, he would run up Mother's long skirts into her lap where he would eat with relish bread with jam, molasses, or apple sauce, sitting up in squirrel fashion and gazing interestedly at the company. Fall came, and, in his marmot wisdom, the little fellow dug a burrow near the house, preparing for the long winter's sleep. But now an unkind fate took a hand: two mornings in succession, two hens were found dead in the coop, their throats slashed. The marmot was suspected, simply because no other animal had been seen about. Damienne was sent away on some errand, and when she returned her pet was gone. The next morning, Mother was early at the chicken coop, and the culprit was caught *in flagrante delicto*, having just perpetrated his fell deed. It was a weasel.

# 5

# relatives, household crafts

Those of our relatives whom we got to know in the early days did not live at great distances from us: Grandmother Côté and the two elder married daughters, Alice, wife of Uncle Marcel Charbonneau, and Rose-Anna, wife of Charles Lemieux, lived close to one another on farms in Poltimore, and Uncle Omer Richer was a blacksmith at Notre-Dame-de-la-Salette. This village, like Poltimore, was about fifteen miles away, though in a different direction.

Uncle Joseph Côté had a house and blacksmith shop in Val-des-Bois, approximately two and a half miles from our place. Uncle Joseph's wife was Alexina Lauzon. She had a pretty face and a genteel manner. I do not remember seeing her otherwise than pregnant. They produced ten children. Mother and she had attended school together but were not fond of one another.

*Visitors from Notre-Dame-de-la-Salette with W. D. Richer family on front porch, 1914. L. to R.: Madame Omer Richer (Alphonsine), Madame W. D. Richer, Jeanne, Damienne, Alzire, W. D. Richer, Christian (at front), Serge and Omer Richer.*

Uncle Joseph had a portrait of Mother which he had made from a photograph when she was about seventeen. I saw it on more than one occasion in their parlour. It was framed in an oval moulding in the fashion of those days. Alexina would sometimes turn it face to the wall or, if so moved, turn it back to make derogatory remarks about the subject. Mother begged Joseph to give it to her, but Alexina was adamant in her refusal. There was bitter feeling between the two, and Father did not mend matters by occasionally praising the good manners and behaviour of our cousins, Alexina's children.

This aunt had a fine talent for embarrassing people she did not like. I can see her at our table one Easter Sunday. She had the great good fortune to find a hair in her soup. Not much of a hair, 'tis true, but, by dint of lifting it very slowly with her spoon and holding it up to study it as if it were a rare specimen, she managed to get the attention of everyone present. Never looking to right or left and maintaining an expression of bland indifference as she placed the offending filament upon the edge of her dining plate, every pore of her face exuded satisfaction. If she had been a cat, she would have purred. We found her only moderately cordial when we went there on Sundays before Mass as we might do if we were early. (Also, we had observed her surreptitiously pinching the girls' arms to secure instant obedience.) Nevertheless, they came to visit, along with the others.

On one occasion, there were several of us sleeping on the floor in the library, all beds having been pre-empted by the older generation. Jeanne, the eldest of Uncle Joseph's children, was with me. She attempted to confide to me some things she had overheard from behind the door when neighbouring women called on her mother. I refused to listen. Truth to tell, I was not interested. I did not know the people, and I had only the vaguest notion of what she was talking about. She must have thought me socially hopeless, and she was probably right.

Whatever might be said about Aunt Alexina, she was a good dressmaker, and she was more aware of fashion trends than was Mother. Jeanne and I, being of an age, made our first communion and received confirmation in the same year and our respective mothers made our dresses.[1] At our age (eleven) and for such an occasion, the importance of apparel was just about equal to that of a wedding gown. The current fashion was what is called 'princess,' and the material used was all-over embroidered cotton of more or less fine quality. I suppose that the religious significance of the day should have blotted out of my mind all frivolous considerations: for a year, off and on, Father had been pointing this out. But I confess that the contrast between my cousin's dress and mine caused me keen, if not enduring, grief. Hers was of a finer fabric, and there was more embroidery on it. Moreover, unlike mine, her dress was unlined and showed (most discreetly, of course) fine lacy underthings. My mother's skill was by no means negligible but her performance was inspired — or perhaps inhibited — by her modesty. Mother produced a garment so thickly opaque that it might

1 This was the last year before Pius X decided that the 'age of reason' comes as early as seven. When confirmed, one was expected to ratify personally the vows that had been made on one's behalf at baptism.

have been worn with anything underneath it — or even nothing at all. Ah! how I envied Jeanne's slim smartness that year!

Uncle Joseph was an excellent blacksmith. He had, in his youth, taken full apprenticeship training with paid tuition. His blacksmith shop was a popular place. Even I got to watch him occasionally, his face ruddy from the heat of the fire fanned by the action of the bellows, until the piece of iron that he held with pincers was white hot. Then I marvelled at the loud sizzle as it was plunged into cold water for tempering. Shoeing horses seemed to me a wonderfully brave and clever thing to do. It still does, because the feet of horses are submitted to so much strain and sheer wear, and the blacksmith requires some adroitness in handling the animals.

Uncle was the darling of his family. Also, being of a jolly disposition, he was popular. Aunt Alexina was a teetotaler, but he was not. In those days as in these, friendliness often suggested a 'wee drappie' from a flask which at the appropriate moment would emerge from the back pocket of almost any man who had business with him. There were no cars or tractors then, and any service for transportation or farm work involved the local blacksmith. He was generally, in practice, a wheelwright as well. Everyone was his client, and to be a client of Uncle Joseph was also to be his friend. It is therefore not surprising that (as we heard discreetly whispered)[2] on one occasion — having celebrated the New Year





2 Mother's text reads *à travers les branches*, but for the non-initiated I have changed the wording. (Lorraine)

not wisely but too well (or, at any rate, too late), poor Uncle found the door of his house locked against him and spent the night in the shop. His mother and his sisters were profoundly shocked at Aunt Alexina's high-handedness. At any rate, the shop was a cosy place to be and may, on this occasion, have held more comfort than he might have expected at home at the hands of his wife.

Uncle Joseph was a school trustee, and it was he who contributed many of the texts which were to fill so many hours of our lives. He had a very fine voice and was *Maître chantre*[3] at the village church. His singing of *Minuit, Chrétiens* (in English, *O Holy Night*) was always the high point of midnight mass and made it a solemn and deeply moving experience.

One evening, I recall sitting on the back steps while Mother played the piano and Uncle Joseph sang the *messe du second ton* (a mass for feasts of second degree). That was a beautiful composition, and, listening there in the twilight, God seemed somehow closer than He did in the little church.

I never really knew Aunt Alexina very well. I would like to add, though, that, much later, I came across a card written to Uncle Charles' wife, Aunt Rose-Alba (the thing was given to me because of the photograph on the other side), and I found her style as well as her writing to be of considerable elegance and delicacy. She had more of what I might term "social consciousness" than did Mother. Mother had been indoctrinated, not only by her father, but also by her husband. It is true that 'what you are is what matters; — not

3 Lead singer.

what the neighbours think,' but that rule does not always contain the Alpha and the Omega of all wisdom.

Uncle Charles was my godfather. At the time I have in mind, he was still unmarried and what they called a *voyageur*. That is to say, like most young men of his day who had been raised in rural districts, he travelled about in search of employment according to the season. Farms were for the most part too small to require the labour of several growing sons, and there was much migration to other places where industries were being developed, in Canada or even in the United States. This was even true, sometimes, of girls. Aunt Eugénie had gone to the city to live and work. Aunt Arthémise and her youngest sister Émilienne were still with Grandmother.

Aunt Émilienne was the youngest of Mother's sisters. She did not visit us very often that I can remember, but she was with us one Christmas. She received as a gift a pair of pretty boxes for gloves and handkerchiefs. I was smitten with the satin lining and the gorgeous painted pansies on the covers, and I was sorely puzzled when she barely glanced at them: with a frown, she tossed them indifferently into a dresser drawer. She seemed often dissatisfied, a stormy sort of character. Grandmother was said to have 'spoiled her.' She was the 'baby' and may have been indulged more than the others.

Our relatives came to see us periodically. We enjoyed their visits very much, and these occasions passed most pleasantly for everyone. The Lemieux, Charles and Rose-Anna, had a boy my age, Edmond, and another called Emmanuel, as well as two older daughters, Laurence and Rose. Laurence and Rose visited us now and then by themselves. We met other members of the family in later years.

Father was a genial host, and Mother, of course, put herself out for family gatherings. I can see the table set, open to full size for dinner on Easter Sunday. There was an enormous omelette near the centre (we had been saving fresh eggs for this for a couple of weeks), and here and there thin, crisp, light brown slices of pork dotting the golden surface. That was one of the times we had *sucre à la crème* for dessert. I can see it now — dropping slow and rich from the spoon as Mother served it.

Father was well liked, I think, by Mother's people, and his pleasure in their visits was genuine. He would even permit slight familiarities upon occasion. Once an argument arose about the difficulty of lifting a dead body, and Father lay down to prove his point. There were several adults there, and at least three of them were men, but, try as they might, they could not budge him. (It makes one wonder at the ease with which fictional murderers tote their defunct victims about, even before rigor mortis has set in.)

We were not spoiled with lavish praise. It was, perhaps, to cover up a touch of embarrassment at the kind remarks of our guests that Father broke into a gay little ditty, improvised on the spot, to reply to a compliment addressed to one of his children:

*C'est mon oncle, 'pi ma tante*
*Qui nous font des compliments.*
*Les compliments font 'flic,' font 'flac'*
*Les compliments font 'flac' partout.*

*La queue du chat fortille, fortille —*
*La queue du chat fortillera.*
*La queue du chat a tant fortillé*
*Que la queue du chat s'en est cassée —*
*Les compliments font 'flic,' font 'flac'*
*Les compliments font 'flac' partout.*[4]

My memories of the adults' conversations are rather vague for the good reason that, as the oldest of the children, my duty was to see that the younger fry were kept entertained.

Arthur Charbonneau, son of Marcel, a quiet child and thoughtful, found Damienne a congenial playmate. Mother and the aunts were amused to see them walking about pushing the doll carriage, as sedately as any grown couple, with never a word.

Pictures and stories were the chief fare after it was too late to play outside. Mother would play the piano sometimes for the rest to sing. Mother could chord accompaniments to anything. This was fortunate because most of our song books had only the melody and some of them only the words. We had a rich repertory not only of folk and children's songs but of ballads and other songs, mostly





4 If it was improvised on the spot, it remained, so to speak, in the répertoire, along with its tune. In English (more or less)
"*Uncle and Auntie pay us compliments;*
*The cat's tale wags — so much that it breaks off.*"
(Compliments are foolish and not to be taken seriously.)
[Very loose translation] I can even sing this song; I learned it as a child. (Lorraine)

from France: a trifle sentimental, perhaps, but with often very beautiful lyrics. What a collection of 'old-time' records they would make if they were played and sung. Memories of these may be the reason why popular tunes of later years always seem so mediocre, somewhat lacking in delicacy of sentiment and elegance of speech.

Uncle Charles Côté, when urged, might contribute a solo. Aunt Eugénie avers that his voice surpassed in tone and richness even that of Joseph. When he sang *Dernier amour de ma vieillesse* or *L'Autre côté du ciel*,[5] he had everyone in tears.

As he was my godfather (*parrain*), it was to him that I appealed one day to get parental permission for me to visit in Poltimore. I felt quite old enough and, Uncle helping, permission was granted. I was the most delighted and excited child imaginable as I rode in a crowded two-seater on that day. I stayed at Grandmother's house, and some of the time I was allowed to go and play with my cousins who lived not far away. At Uncle Marcel's house, Margot was about my age, but I did not find her particularly companionable. My favourite playmates were Edmond and Manuel, who, moreover, enjoyed more freedom of action than their sister (that old double standard). Emmanuel and I, one afternoon, filled a potato sack with acorns we picked under the oaks near the mountains. These were destined for the pigs.

I did not see much of Aunt Rose-Anna. One picture of her lingers, standing at the kitchen window, swatting flies with a folded newspaper. At that time the only flypaper came in large sheets

5 *Last Love of My Old Age* or *The Other Side of Heaven.*

which were laid on tables, with occasional vexing results. We had not yet graduated to the handier coiled strips, which at least hung from the ceiling out of the way.

Uncle Charles Lemieux, with his two brothers Nazaire and Phidime, had migrated from the Gaspé some years before. They had grown up in a fishing settlement on the coast and were unfamiliar with many features of inland life. Phidime loved to tell about their first day in Montreal, exploring this world of things new and wonderful. In one display, they saw a heap of what looked like the reddest and most luscious apples they had ever seen. They bought a large bagful and bit eagerly into the tempting fruit. Ugh! The thing splattered all over their jacket fronts. "*This is no apple!*" shouted Charles, and with a curse he hurled the bag of ripe tomatoes all the way to the other side of the street.[6]



He liked to talk of the fishing along the Atlantic coast and would describe the many virtues of cod as a food: especially the delicate texture and flavour of the fleshy parts of the head, until everybody's mouth watered. Some time after they were married, he took his wife Rose-Anna to visit his native village. She was less impressed than he might have wished, and somehow, when she returned, she seemed to have lost her appetite for cod: perhaps a case of surfeit. She had seen acres of fish spread out on the beach to dry. Possibly they did not then use the racks that are a common sight today ... but she would not go into detail. She simply passed up the fish, even during Lent.



6 For another account of rural alienation in the city, see Note 2.

One thing I recall from Aunt Alice's house is her garden. She had lots of red and white currants, which her Margot and I picked for dessert. We did not have any of these at home, and I wished that they grew in the same profusion as our wild raspberries and thimbleberries in Val-des-Bois.

Grandmother Côté's little house was of squared logs, whitewashed every spring. Inside, it was full of warm, bright colours, not unlike Lacasse's house: pine floor almost white, mostly covered over with strips of *catalogne* (woven rag rugs).[7] There were ladder-back chairs painted red, with woven seats. On one shelf, there was a doll's house, probably belonging to Émilienne: on another, a statue of Mary, seated, suckling her child. This proceeding was discreetly covered with a veil.

We did have a touch of excitement while I was there. One night after we were all in bed, a sudden clamour woke us: loud bawling from the sheep pen, hysterical squawking from the henhouse. Uncle Charles was up in a jiffy and out of the house with his gun. It was pitch dark, but by the faint lamplight which barely relieved the gloom we caught, through the window, a fleeting glimpse of a sinister shape. It streaked past the steps where I stood, around the corner of the house and into the night. Its dire deed was done. A luckless ewe was found with her jugular neatly severed. Here, as

7 *Catalogne* is a fabric woven on a string warp of a weft of strips of miscellaneous rags. The word comes from the old French castalogne which means 'bed cover.' The French-Canadian dictionary gives the term with a 'fleur de lis' asterisk, and *Le Petit Larousse* does not contain the word, so I take it that it's a Canadianism. (Lorraine)

at home, the mountain was very close to the farm buildings, but the trees grew much more thickly, and visits from bears, as well as wolves, were not a rare occurrence.

Aunt Arthémise was a gay, amusing person. She was Mother's favourite sister and came fairly often to see us in Val-des-Bois. She had a never-failing fund of songs and stories: the stories were chiefly hilarious anecdotes about the people in the neighbourhood. After listening to her, we had reason to think that there were funny people indeed — and not only in Montreal.[8] The family must have known every soul in the district: for one thing, they had been going to the local school with the other children of the settlement, and, in her capacity of midwife and nurse extraordinary, Grandmother had helped bring many of that generation into the world. She had seen many out of it, too.

Aunt Eugénie came also, but more seldom, since she lived in the city and was free only during her holidays. She was fun, too, but in a slow, quiet way. Her humour was more gallic in flavour, less sharp than her sister's. Aunt Arthémise did not shrink from using ridicule to spice up her quick native wit. Even today, her contribution to any gathering is worthy of note. In her younger days, she could keep an audience in stitches as long as she cared to go on. Mother could enjoy this and preferred it to Aunt Eugénie's more

8 When I called on Henri Masson (a well-known painter from whom Mother bought a picture) in Ottawa, with my sister, Leila, some years ago, he was telling us about that country (the Gatineau Hills and beyond). He said it was very interesting and lovely to paint, and he added with a little grin: "*Do you know that there are people there who still believe in werewolves?*" These, too, are interesting. (Lorraine)

kindly but sometimes faintly risqué little stories. 'Eliza,' her family said, 'was a prude.'

If she was, she had learned it from no stranger: my Grandfather Côté, whom I never knew, was a dyed-in-the-wool Puritan. He died not long after Father and Mother married, and he played his part in the affair at the time.

Father did not mind Eugénie's salty wit. In fact, he rather seemed to enjoy it as he enjoyed her company. One time that he was in Hull on Mother's birthday he took Eugénie to a movie — as he wrote to Mother, 'to celebrate the occasion.' I doubt he ever understood women very well.

Once when we were still very young, Mother went to Ottawa to take a month's course in photography. She boarded at Rossignol's with Aunt Eugénie. She let herself be persuaded to take some dancing lessons. Mother did not reveal this to us until much, much later. Father never knew. The girls could, and did, keep their own counsel when it seemed advisable to do so. It was when Mother returned from this course that the small house or shed was fitted up as a studio with a darkroom for developing. She took a number of wedding photos and the like, and some for ourselves, but there simply was not enough custom in that sparsely populated district to make such a business profitable, and she gave it up.

I thought very highly of both our younger aunts, but Aunt Eugénie used, on the grounds that I was her *filleule* (goddaughter), to give me special attention. I would sit beside her at table, and she would unobtrusively help herself to the crust which I always detached from my slice of bread and always (but unsuccessfully), tried to avoid eating. Eugénie was ever one of those people who would, whenever possible, remove stones from the path of others. She possessed in rare degree the qualities of tolerance and kindliness. I considered her beautiful — a fine city lady, and the most pleasant person in the world.

One Christmas, she was with us when we set up and decorated the tree. Since Charles Morin's local emporium did not offer such fancy objects as commercial decorations for Christmas trees, we had to make some ourselves. Eugénie taught us how to make paper flowers from available materials. Some were like dahlias, others resembled large chrysanthemums as seen in Japanese paintings, giving us the glory of winter bouquets. All the equipment that was required was paper, scissors, wire for stems, nimble fingers and a stout hairpin: that last was for curling the chrysanthemum petals. There was something I could learn, and I did so with zest. What a lot of these paper blossoms served, on subsequent occasions, to adorn summer garlands made of running club mosses or, in winter, Christmas wreaths or streamers made of hemlock boughs! Small twigs of this lovely tree, bound with string, were almost as manageable as daisy chains.

Aunt Eugénie had a little game she played with Serge when he was still a baby. She would sit in the rocker and rock. The chair travelled slightly forward with every backward motion so she would say, "*Now, we are going to Hull,*" or "*to Ottawa,*" and describe a series of interesting sights along the way until the rocker got too close to the wall and had to be moved back again, whereupon she started on a new journey. Needless to say, the travelogue was for the benefit of the older children. I used to like that as I liked everything she did.

Encouraged by her playful manner, we would venture to tease her a little at times. Then, she would put on a disapproving look and say, in a stern voice: "*Miserable child! Respect my black hairs!*" — which would send us into gales of laughter. My godmother was popular, and not only with me. My brother Christian once tried to talk me into trading godmothers, for he was not partial to his own. He went so far as to offer his jack-knife to boot! I suppose he figured to get the knife back without too much difficulty; otherwise, what boy in his right mind would part with a tool so useful and almost a badge of masculinity?

Of the people who lived then in Poltimore, only Edmond and Emmanuel Lemieux remain there today. Uncle Marcel and Aunt Alice Charbonneau moved to the city with their family. They are both gone now, but a number of their children and grandchildren are still in Hull and Ottawa. Marcel, the eldest, went to live in Northern Ontario, where he is farming unless, of course, like the rest of us, he is retired. Margot married and came to visit us out West twice — once with Aunt Eugénie and Lucien, Uncle Charles' eldest son. Charles Lemieux remained on the farm. His daughter Laurence married a local farmer, now long dead, and she lived for many years in Sudbury, where I saw her later, when her three children were already grown up. Her father was visiting there at the time — a handsome, white-haired old man whose eyes twinkled with youthful mischief as he poured a drink for Damienne and me. He had been a hard worker all his life and had managed to survive both the perils of a fisherman on the Atlantic seacoast and then the hardships of farming on the scant soil of the Laurentian region.

Edmond took over the farm from his father. When I was there in 1959 with cousin Ivan and Aunt Eugénie, I found a pleasant and well-tended farmstead. The squared log structure of Grandmother's little house had been incorporated into the complex of farm buildings.

Emmanuel also was still in Poltimore. We saw him and his wife on the same trip. There were several magnificent pine trees in front of his house. I gazed at them with frank admiration and envy. They showed us a fine flock of white turkeys: the most profitable crop, they said, of that season.

Uncle Charles Côté came home one day from his travels and married pretty, fourteen-year-old Rose-Alba Charron, the daughter of a neighbour. They went to Hull to live and there raised a family of several children. Rose-Alba still lives with her son Lucien, who never married, and Jeanne d'Arc, her daughter. Uncle died many years ago.

Margot died a relatively young woman; so did Rose Lemieux. Aunt Arthémise married Nazaire Lemieux, Charles' brother, and they went to Ontario to live: first at Blind River and then at Sault Ste. Marie. Their children were the only eastern cousins whom my youngest daughter Leila got to meet as a girl when she accompanied Mother there for a visit. Lorraine met some of them as well as other relatives in Hull and Ottawa (also in Montreal), while she was at National Defence Headquarters during the war.

Émilienne married during the First World War and died a few years afterwards, leaving one child, Jeanne, whom Aunt Eugénie brought up. Aunt Eugénie had married late in life one Joseph Tremblay, and she had no children of her own. Later on, she more or less adopted Suzanne, Jeanne's eldest daughter, who is with her to this day.

Uncle Joseph moved to North Bay in Ontario.

Alexina, like her mother, tended to embonpoint, and she was much troubled with the consequent strain upon her legs. Eventually, she became very nearly a complete invalid.

One of the boys, Lorenzo, gratified his mother's dearest wish by entering the priesthood. He is now Mgr. Côté in Sudbury. Most of Uncle Joseph's other children are still in Ontario with the exception of Marie, who is in Montreal. Clémence also lived there some years and later in Toronto where in 1951 Chris[9] and I met her and her husband George Clark. After the death of George, she moved to Sudbury, where live several of the Lemieux. Her brother Fidèle lives some miles out of Sault Ste. Marie. Jeanne is in Windsor.

We knew more of Grandmother Côté than we ever knew of the others, except Aunts Eugénie and Arthémise. We not only saw her most often, but Mother often spoke of her and so did the aunts. Grandmother Côté, née Marie Tremblay, daughter of Adèle and Alexis, was a personality. When she reached the appropriate age, she was duly sent to school. On the very first day, the teacher noticed that little Marie was paying more attention to

9 My husband, Chris Olsen.

some (devotional) pictures she held in her hand than to the lesson and scolded her in front of the class. The following morning, the new scholar declared that she was never going back to school. She never did. Nevertheless, she learned how to read. She had a gift for finding a way through any difficulty. No language or other barrier ever stood in her way. It was said that she married Phidime Côté, son of Jules, at the urging of her family.

Phidime had been promised a farm in the Lac St. Jean country, where the Côtés and the Tremblays lived. This promise was not fulfilled, however, and along with a number of other couples they later moved away from the harsh pioneer conditions of the region and came to High Falls where a mica mine was being exploited and where there were other opportunities of employment. In time, they acquired land in Poltimore.

Marie was not only thrifty and imaginative; she was indefatigable. She was a born nurse, and doctors were so scarce, travel so slow and difficult, that they were only too glad to instruct, insofar as they could, persons of sense and competence in the proper care of patients. Nursing meant then chiefly ordinary sanitary and other precautions plus such helps and remedies as were available in almost every home. Grandmother knew them all, as well as useful Indian lore gathered goodness knows how or from whom. She would trudge through miles and miles of dusty roads or winter snow; no one ever appealed to her in vain. More than once, she nursed back to health patients whom their doctor had given up for lost. She could learn from any situation and from anyone she met. She spoke no German, but from some of the new immigrants

*Phidime Côté and Marie Côté (née Tremblay), with their eldest son, Joseph.*

got fascinating pickle recipes; she spoke no English, but she had no trouble in getting to Saskatchewan when the fancy took her to come and visit Mother in Ditton Park. We never actually knew how much she did or did not know, only that when she wanted to do a thing she found a way to do it.

On Father's side, Uncle Omer was the only one who lived near by. He was a quiet, kindly man with the bluest eyes I have ever seen. Father's eyes were blue, too, and they could flash like a steel blade in the sun when his face was stern. Uncle Omer's eyes were different: they were deep and serene like the Mediterranean on a still summer's day. There were three daughters: Alzire, who died fairly young, Yvonne, and Alice, now living in Mont Laurier (Madame Dominique St.-Louis). The boys we knew were Antonio and Nilphas. Another brother, Oscar, later came to settle down in La Salette. He married a local woman, and there were three children: Irene, a sister of Providence and Ph.D. in Education, and Rita, a school-teacher before her marriage and who still teaches occasionally, and one brother, Eusèbe.

Some time after we left Val-des-Bois, Alice married Dominique St.-Louis, and Omer moved to Notre-Dame-du-Laus, where he bought a blacksmith shop. Cars had come into fairly common use by then, and the blacksmith shop gave way to a filling station. Nilphas took over the business after Omer's death, but he was not inclined to commercial undertakings. When I saw him many years later, he had moved with his family and his mother, Alphonsine, to Pointe Gatineau. Here he acquired an acreage of several lots. When the municipality wanted to put in a paved street and offered to buy the necessary land from him, he gave it on condition that the street would bear his name. His own house, on *rue Richer*, is set on a large lot planted with a number of trees, some of them very large and beautiful willows. He furnished the property like a children's park with all manner of play equipment made by himself. He loved children (he had ten) and enjoyed making things.

At first, he had worked for a while in an axe factory, but the last letter I had stated that he was on the maintenance staff of mechanics caring for the huge heating system of the building complex on Parliament Hill. His last act was to go out and water his dear willow trees — there had been a long, dry spell. He came into the house, sat down and complained of chest pains, asking his wife for something to aid digestion. Within twenty minutes, he was gone. He must have cherished his childhood memories. He still had a letter that I wrote to him in my teens, decorated with a pink cabbage rose in watercolour.

Antonio continued for many years to travel from place to place. He was a diamond-drill operator: spent a number of years in Australia and once, some years ago, wrote me from Manitoba to ask for the address of Christian and Serge. I sent them to him, but he left the province without visiting them, later explaining that the distance was more than he could conveniently cover in the time he had. This Christmas, I heard from cousin Rita that he is back in Quebec, in Rouyn.

While in school in Montreal, I met father's sister Amélia, Sister Antoine-Marie of the Sisters of Providence, who was then business administrator at a convent of the Order in Mascouche. She invited me to spend the Christmas holiday with her, and we subsequently kept in touch, more or less, on a yearly basis. Damienne knew her better, as she spent a year as a student in Mascouche. In later years we both made a point of calling on her whenever we were in Montreal. By then, she had retired and had been assigned lighter duties. I had more than one afternoon with her at St. Vincent de Paul. She obligingly let me photograph the interior of her bedroom, and I thought her rather a dear in her own slightly prim, serious way. She had not a noticeably keen sense of humour.

It was through her that I became acquainted with still another cousin, also a member of the same Order: Françoise Richer — Sister Marie-Médard, daughter of Médard, an older brother of Father's who had remained in St. André-Avellin. Françoise, at the time, had charge of an orphanage for boys on the rue St.-Denis. She remembered Father and had had some correspondence with him.

I last saw Aunt Amélia at the new Providence Centre near Montreal.[10] She was truly retired by then, having reached a rather fragile 85 years. Her last admonition: as I was the eldest of the family, I had a duty to see that the rest did not stray from the path of righteousness, and also she repeated an earnest injunction from Grandfather to his children not to forget that we belong to the Louveteau branch of the family and to keep on using the name. Lorraine and her husband Joffre called upon her on the way to Quebec City in 1964. She died not long afterwards (1966), the last of her generation.

10 My nephew Kenneth Adam (Damienne's second child) drove me there once, and we ran into a blizzard on the way back.

Mother did not speak often of Father's people and, except for Uncles Omer and Oscar, only Aunt Amélia had visited at our house. The rest lived mainly in St. André-Avellin or had removed to distant parts. Father did not frequently discuss his old home or his family, but his correspondence with Omer and Oscar indicates a lively interest and affection on both sides.

In 1913, he received from Aunt Amélia news of his mother's last illness. She urged him to come home, but he did not respond. When the black-bordered envelope came, it remained so long unopened in a pigeon-hole of his desk as to pique my curiosity. I asked Mother about it, but she just shook her head. I think he had known better than to subject himself to the pressure of death-bed requests, a favourite ploy of those who have not succeeded by ordinary means in getting their way.[11]

I have already spoken of Grandmother Côté, but her visits are associated in my memory with certain activities, and her name comes up inevitably as I describe these now. Though she was a fairly frequent visitor, her stays always elicited on our part a pleasurable excitement. I remember more than once running up to her on arrival with the eager question: "*How long can you stay, Grandma?*" She was not a particularly demonstrative person and did not spoil us with attention, but she would sing for us, tell us stories, and

11 As I read through this text, it occurs to me that Mother herself was the recipient of a 'deathbed request.' As I shall mention in the Epilogue, Grandfather on his deathbed left the care of Grandmother to his daughter, Jeanne, our mother and the author of this memoir. I wonder if it is very wrong of me to read into this sentence a small sigh. (Lorraine)

occasionally deliver herself of choice bits of wisdom of a stern moralistic nature. She averred that, at the Last Judgment, we would all be expected to give an account of everything we had possessed (wealth was but a trust). We heard these words without alarm; it sounded a bit strict, but fair. However, when she added that we would also have to account for every word ever spoken, I had an uncomfortable feeling that she had particular reference to me and that I might well have an unpleasant quarter of an hour with the recording angel.

If I had one habit which must surely have proven tiresome to our elders, it was my constant chatter. How many times Father, especially, reminded me of it by touching his finger to the tip of his tongue. This was probably why he occasionally dubbed me 'bird brain'[12] and, I fear, only half in jest.

Father once said of our maternal grandmother that he had the greatest regard for her sound common sense. Probably this was, coming from him and concerning a woman, high praise.

There was usually a good deal of household activity when she came. Such things as rug making, quilting, spinning, knitting, etc., are in my memory associated with her visits, especially during the winter months. Mother not only knitted our socks and stockings, but she got the wool straight from the sheep. The fleece had of course to be washed, pulled, carded, spun, made into skeins, and dyed. Sometimes the dyeing was done before the plies were put together, two colours being used for a mixed or 'heather' effect.

12 This comes out less harshly in French; we say '*tête de linotte*' (head of a linnet). It need not be as pejorative as 'bird brain' must be. (Lorraine)

We helped with such tasks. The pulling was tedious but well within the capacity of little fingers. I found the dyeing fascinating. Diamond dyes were used then, and Mother combined the various colours to make new and wonderful shades of blues and reds, oranges and browns. It was to dye yarn for socks that we were sent to fetch alder bark, and no commercial product ever equalled that particular rich sepia brown. We could turn the handle of the reel on which the yarn was stretched to make skeins as the twisted strands were brought together. We could also wind the yarn into balls for knitting.

Mother, for years, made our everyday stockings out of this homespun yarn. I suffered (not in silence) from nagging discomfort from wearing the rough itchy stuff. My long black Sunday hose were made of silky Merino wool from Australia, knitted in an elegant lacy pattern. I was very proud of those. The boys had long, double-knit socks for the winter. Father's were especially attractive in colour and pattern, with tassels to decorate them where the contrasting cuff was turned over the top of the boot.

Rugs were home-made: some hooked, some braided, and some woven. Grandmother would sew the strips of rags end to end, and I, sitting on the floor at her knee, would thread her needles not to waste time (which no doubt, like all else, would have to be accounted for). Some of the strips would be used for hooking, and some woven into widths of *catalogne*. One year, Mother had dyed some burlap bags for making fringes for some fur rugs. But what to do with the threads that had been pulled out to make the fringe? Besides, the stuff was already dyed, and, surely, speculated

Grandmother, something could be done with it. Mother rose to the occasion. More burlap bags were dyed, unravelled, and then rewoven. The material was of a variety of bright colours and the widths were gay. They were then sewn together to make bed covers. One of these was used on Christian's bed. Horizontal stripes contributed greatly to making the fabric appear smoother and more neatly finished than one might expect of such crude material. This was the best fun yet! No one, as far as we knew, had ever thought of it.

Mother made a number of patchwork quilts — not anything so elementary as crazy patchwork, but patches assorted carefully into lights and darks and in colour groups to produce well-balanced effects. She had quite a lot of fine woollen fabrics at one time: a long baby cape of fine white wool cashmere, among other things. From these, after dyeing the cloth in eye-filling hues, some of which were never seen on land or sea, she made an unforgettable log-cabin quilt.

Grandmother had uses for pieces that were too small for any regular design. If woollen, scraps were cut into tongues which were sewn onto a burlap backing in an overlapping pattern. Then she decided that even bits of cotton some one by two inches could be attached to a firm foundation by one end to make a shaggy, deep-piled bedside mat. I thought for sure that thrift could no further extend. Grandmother's books were ever ready for the final audit. There was another sort of mat which we made, a quick job, more to my taste. This was made of the usual strips of old materials, making sure that the strands on and near the surface were of the desired colours, and when the number of strands added up to a sufficient thickness, they were tied firmly with string or yarn where they met. This produced a mat of small squares: less smooth underfoot than some, but rather neat in appearance. The last one of these Mother made was for Christian's firstborn, Rodolphe.[13]

At various times, fads made their appearance. One of these was ball fringe used to decorate piano covers, what-not shelves, and so on. So we learned to make little woollen pom-poms. When it came to finding tasks for idle hands to do, Old Nick had nothing on Grandmother. This, too, was something that could be fun, when one considered the patterns that could be produced by using several colours. The knick-knack shelf in the parlour, a small one in the dining room upon which a clock rested, and probably others donned this Victorian garb than which nothing is more redolent of the fussy taste of the days of our good Queen.

Another thing was bead *portières* (door curtains). Ever since the time that the whole house had been papered all at once, a store of left-over parts of paper rolls remained. These leftovers must have been 'burning a hole' in somebody's consciousness. We took to making beads from wedges of wall paper rolled tightly on a pencil, with the end of the wedge firmly glued down. I seem to recall that round wooden beads were strung between these long paper ones. The last time I saw such *portières* was in 1954 in a small town in Southern France. I guess they do not lightly discard things there, either!

13 I can't figure this out; I swear this is how she wrote it, but I can't picture this rug. (Lorraine)

It was during days and evenings devoted to such pursuits that we might hear talk of the past, principally from Grandmother. She told of her life as a young bride when she and Phidime lived with his parents, Jules and Eulalie, at St. Joseph d'Alma. Eulalie had been a weaver of unusual skill, ornamenting her woollen blankets with original border designs. She was also a tailoress: she made not only suits for men but overcoats, and that, it should be remembered, in the days before sewing machines.

There were also wry tales of the young wife being expected to do chores for the whole family, including doing the washing at the stream on spring or autumn days too cold for comfort. Marie was not a girl to submit without protest to treatment she deemed harsh or unfair. Doubtless her influence hardened Phidime's resolve to move away from Lac St.-Jean to find a home of their own.





Grandmother told of other interesting people: a cousin, whom everyone called Aunt Anna, caught my fancy. She was one of those people who can cope handily with any practical problem: she built her own house in Hull, where it still stands!

Our clothes were largely made at home. Christian belongs, I am sure, to the last generation of boys who wore dresses instead of rompers as a prelude to short pants. I can remember him in a little suit of black velveteen with shirt collar and cuffs trimmed with a ruffle of embroidery edging in a Little Lord Fauntleroy style. Of my own clothes I recall (not with affection) the plain, long-sleeved coveralls we wore every day over our dresses. My view was that, with such an ugly and all-concealing garment, a pretty dress was wasted. On Sundays, of course, we had white aprons trimmed with ruffles and embroidered edgings which revealed the sleeves and the neckline of the dress underneath.

For whatever reason, there are exactly four dresses that I can remember from babyhood to my eighteenth year. One I have already mentioned.[14] The next one I am wearing in a picture Mother took. It was of blue cashmere with lace around the yoke. I did not like it. The first time I wore it to church, I managed to tear the lace in some brambles. Had Mother been at that time acquainted with the theories of Freudian psychology, she would assuredly have suspected me of doing it, as they say, 'accidentally on purpose.' She was, with good reason, not amused. She must have repaired the dress, but the next thing I remember about it is that it turned up in that gorgeous log-cabin quilt I spoke of: so it had a long and useful life, after all.

The other two dresses I will speak of later in this account.

Mother made some of our shoes for daily wear in winter.[15] These were cowhide leather moccasin-style foot gear to be worn with thick woollen stockings. For such shoes as these, the fitting presented no problem. She had, however, a set of lasts, a small hammer and fine tacks, awls, and leather needles and heavy linen thread. With such equipment, she managed to repair 'store shoes.' Descendants of French royalty were not always available for such tasks! For going out, mainly to church, winter dress boots were of felt with fine kid trimming, laced half-way up the leg. In summer,

14 My first communion dress; see pp. 102–03.

15 We called these *souliers de boeuf* (ox-hide shoes).

the very best girls' boots were buttoned, with velvet uppers. More ordinary ones were of laced calf leather. The feelings aroused in our young breasts by such finery were very like what our own daughters felt about high-heeled as against low-heeled (baby) shoes.

Once, Grandmother taught us to braid wheat straw for making hats. It took patience: soaking the straw to make it flexible, then keeping the braid moist while it was being sewn and shaped to the head. But such hats were readily available, and Christian found the commercial ones somewhat more comfortable. As for the girls, we wore sunbonnets — at least, we wore them when Mother was looking. I felt about them as most youngsters feel about rubbers, and only frequent warnings of impending sunstroke made me keep the stifling things on in the warm, still summer afternoons.

I learned to sew, after a fashion. What I remember best is putting patches on the knees of Chris's cotton fleece underwear and the elbows of his shirts. I even got to like it as my work became, with practice, a little neater. The shirts were easygoing, but after a number of washings the cotton fleece acquired the consistency of shoe-leather. It presented a challenge. I also learned something of what we called English embroidery,[16] padded scallops and raised solid patterns. That was rather satisfying, as was crochet. I never took to knitting.

As the years went by, we, like everyone else, became more dependent on commercially manufactured products, but the memory of pioneer lore remained vivid as well as its incidental lessons.

16 I believe that the correct English-language term for this is *broderie anglaise*. I met it in a novel by Margery Sharp (*Cluny Brown*). (Lorraine)

Most of our shopping was done by mail order. We were among the regular customers of Eaton's.[17] Mother was as provident with sewing supplies as she was in matters of food: pins, needles, safety pins, sewing cotton, shoe laces, hooks and eyes (and later on, snap fasteners), buttons of all sizes, various trimmings for dresses, ribbons, all of these along with sundry combs, pencils, crayons were stored up and available in what we called her 'little store.' Its bounty may have, in a way, contributed to our comfort and security.

After Aunt Eugénie had been in the city a while and had become an employee at an emporium called *Chez Pharand*, the largest ready-to-wear establishment in Hull, she inspired in us a certain interest in fashion. She was an excellent seamstress — a perfectionist, they said, if rather a slow worker. She made a crimson velvet blouse for Mother, which I very much admired. Once, Mother made for herself one of those excruciatingly elaborate petticoats that were so popular at the time — quite full, of fine white lawn. It had a ruffle about twelve inches made of widths of fine tucks separated by strips of insertion and finished with lace. This served admirably, after it had run its course in its original capacity, for making underwear for dolls. To think of all the hours that went into the making of such garments!

Sewing in those days was far from simple. Patterns were not locally available, and Mother, who did most, if not all, of our

17 As children, we acquired a practical acquaintance with Eaton's catalogue because Mother thought to let us, come Christmas time, spend a whole dollar on merchandise chosen out of this cornucopia of delights. No money was ever laid out with more careful consideration.

clothes, had to fit the garments on the only forms that there were: ours. How I hated the cold scissors slithering around neck, shoulders, and armholes! Poor Mother — with me squirming — literally unable to stand still — it is a wonder that she did not give up in despair. In spite of or perhaps because of the difficulties under which she worked, she developed considerable skill. I never knew her to be faced with a task of this sort which she was unwilling to tackle, and usually she tackled it successfully.

Home nursing was another feature of our lives. We were a reasonably healthy lot. We had few visits from the doctor, and Grandmother Côté possessed a store of nursing lore which she passed on to Mother, an eminently apt pupil. Treatment for colds or chest congestion included, according to the severity of the attack, rest, warmth, hot drinks with brandy and/or ginger, hot foot baths with mustard added, mustard plasters applied to chest and back. Inhaling camphorated alcohol helped to relieve sinusitis. For deep-seated inflammations such as serious bronchitis or abscessed teeth, croton oil was applied, and later on capsolin, which has croton oil as the active principle. To relieve surface inflammation, emollient poultices were made of bread or onion. To draw stubborn slivers or thorns beyond the reach of Mother's needle, a plaster made of mixed yellow soap and brown sugar was applied to the affected part.

Grandmother favoured a course of sulphur and molasses as a spring tune-up for us children. We protested as a matter of principle that we were not sick. Mother herself did not insist, and when the need of a purgative or laxative arose, Epsom salts were generally used. A cough syrup was made of a patent preparation added to syrup. Dr. Matte's prescription for anaemia, general fatigue, and debility was *Peptonate de fer Robin*, an iron tonic which put new life in several generations of women, young and old, before disappearing from the market. One of Grandmother's favourites in cases of arthritis or rheumatism was Meynard's liniment. Mother also had a manual of home medicine which she used to very good advantage. In later years she was to show remarkable talent in the care of the sick as her mother had done before her. Doctors were few and far away, and nursing skill was much esteemed.

Altogether we grew up in an atmosphere of competence, confident that help would be available where and when needed. Transportation was somewhat slow, but medical assistance was not lacking even when contagious diseases required special measures. More important than anything else, our little illnesses or injuries were never treated lightly but got all of the attention and the concern that they deserved.

# 6

# the city — school days

I must have been nine or ten years old when Mother took me on a trip. We went on a pilgrimage to Saint Anne de Beaupré, and on the way we stopped in Hull.

This was my first experience of the city, and in many ways it was extremely interesting, but we had read so much about the great cities of the world and had seen so many pictures that I felt little surprise. We stopped at Rossignol's where Aunt Eugénie was staying, and the boys there were rather taken aback when, in answer to their questions, I replied that Hull was very much what I had expected. This was no way for a "country cousin" to react. However, if the city was no cause for astonishment, it offered much that was new to observe for a child fresh from a remote parish of the wild Laurentians.

I could not sleep in the ultra-feminine room where I spent the night with Aunt Eugénie. Such an attractive room! I had never seen such ornate (and, I thought, supremely tasteful) decorations: frills of pink, starched crocheted lace on everything! Unfamiliar noises — cabs rolling by — locomotive bells, factory whistles, the heavy *clip-clop, clip-clop* of massive Belgians and Clydesdales on the macadam as they drew loaded delivery wagons — all these things were exciting. The lamp lighter came along and gas lights did their dim best to relieve the gloom of the night, street sounds abated somewhat, but I never closed an eye until early morning.

The next day we went to some of the shops. Woolworth's stands out among the rest like a beacon in a fog of misty memories. Never before (and, thank goodness, never again) did I see so many things at one time that aroused in me a craving to possess them. Countless colourful and novel things had my head all in a whirl. I remember specially a large and varied collection of trinket boxes decorated with numerous small sea shells. These must have been very common at the time because the boxes were liberally covered with them, and they were not expensive. Since then, I have seen some in Vancouver at many times the price. My heart's desire fastened on these. Mother either did not realize how I felt or had become inured, by now, to foolish requests. She was adamant. My very soul writhed in bitter frustration as we walked along the counters laden with bright temptations. I learned that life is rife with disappointments.

The National Museum was better. Many new and strange things were there but none that I would want to take home or even play with. The Dinosaur was impressive, still sleeping the sleep of Ages in his prehistoric rock bed. What did command my attention, though, was the Albatross in one of the display rooms, stretching his bony arms in a vast span to form a macabre frieze at the junction of wall and ceiling. Both were still there the last time I looked.

We went to visit the Houses of Parliament. The guard at the door was magnificent in his neat blue trousers and red jacket, from his well-polished shoes to the very top of his bear-skin Busby — his gold chain gleaming under his manly chin. So tall, so soldierly, so utterly gorgeous! I gazed at him in reverent awe. I had heard the night before that Lord Roberts (General Commander of British troops in South Africa) was expected shortly to visit Ottawa. Surely this splendid creature could only be someone of importance. I whispered softly to Mother: "*Is this Lord Roberts?*" I hope he heard me; that question together with the look of unbounded admiration on my face must surely have made his day.





The trip on the train to Ste. Anne was a novelty too. Montmorency Falls made such a lasting impression that they actually looked familiar when after some forty years I saw them again. We reached Ste. Anne. The Basilica was an imposing building indeed, its lofty pillars laden with crutches showing more or less evidence of wear. Ex-votos of various sorts were everywhere displayed. There was a huge crowd, and, as we came out of the church, a number of beggars circulated among the pilgrims in front of the door. Having rashly given all the pennies I had to the first one, I was upset because I had nothing left for the others. It seemed terrible to pass by a poor man who implored in pitiful tones: "*Charity, for the love of God!*" and to have no way of responding to his appeal. But Mother again turned a deaf ear. That would, *höffentlich, larn* me to manage better.

Another thing I remember is the Cyclorama of Jerusalem: one of the world's largest panoramic paintings. It measures 360 feet in length and forty-five feet in height and depicts the city of Jerusalem, Calvary and the surrounding countryside as at the day of the crucifixion. That was very impressive. The perspective gives a marvellous feeling of distance.[1]

There is little more that I recall from this trip, but at least I had seen a real live city and heard its city sounds.

Some time after this, Mother having decided that my elementary education was complete, I was sent to a convent in Hull to continue my studies. This was the Convent of the Sisters of the Good Shepherd, a cloistered Order whose members engaged in teaching as well as in other good works. I never knew such a dismal place as that convent. The nuns who taught us and looked after our needs were dressed in white, and we had to address them as "Mother" and kneel to speak to them (at least to the one who supervised us in the general assembly hall). There were five flights of stairs between classes and sleeping quarters and going up and down those was the only form of exercise we had. I ran up and down like the wind, on tip-toe.

1 It was conceived by the German painter Bruno Pighein, under whose direction seven painters laboured for four years in Munich to complete the masterpiece in 1882.

The recreation hall was depressing — we were silent so much of the time. The food was depressing. The black grill that stood between us and visitors was depressing. The chapel services were depressing because we could hardly see the priest at the altar through that ubiquitous black grillwork. We had to queue up to use the sanitary facilities, and, as the queue was frequently long and the facilities few, there were always some who could not wait — and *that* was depressing. I don't think I ever saw the sun shine while I was there. I was homesick. I wept buckets of tears.

In class, I could not distinguish anything on the blackboard. My only bright moment occurred when I was asked to recite the conjugations of verbs. I did all four without a pause and without a flaw. That did not suffice, however, to lift my drooping spirits. I went home at Christmas and was not sent back. Mother's heart was not, after all, really made of stone.

I felt like a prisoner released from jail.

Mother now faced Father with the problem: "*I have taught her all that I can,*" she said one day. "*Now, you can take it from here.*" So I was given a grammar assignment (syntax by now) to prepare and the time came to recite the lesson. Mother was sitting by the table with some knitting or sewing, and I, inwardly quaking, stood nearby when Father came out of his study to hear my recitation. He took the book and asked the first question. Instead of answering, I burst into tears.

It was not that I was afraid of Father, but he had always seemed to me a little more than an ordinary mortal. I am sure he did not mean to appear particularly imposing: but to me (and not to me alone) he was like a judge clothed in the majesty of the Law (the Law both of God and Man). His enormous dignity when he spoke seriously seemed to set him apart from lesser beings.

It was not a wall that stood between us but rather a kind of *distance.* He was a very private individual, and few, I think, ever really traversed the zone of aloofness that surrounded him. My reaction disconcerted him. Father comforted and reassured me, looking very much at a loss the while. I finally stopped my blubbering and Mother sighed deeply. The problem had been tossed back once more into her lap, and so once more she set about to find a solution.

Now I went back to boarding school, this time in Montreal. Here I found a much more congenial atmosphere than that of the cloister from which I had been delivered. Perhaps, also, by that time I was ready for a change of scene.

My new school was a small academy conducted by the Grey Nuns of Montreal. The building, a modest stone structure situated on Richmond Square, had served originally as an orphanage, and hence was called *The Bethlehem Home.* The name, soon afterwards, was changed to *Bethlehem Convent.* It was pleasant and homelike. This was no cloister. The Order had been founded with the object of ministering directly to the people, helping the poor and the sick, sheltering the homeless, spreading the blessings of education as well as of religious instruction. Conditions had changed materially since the beginnings of the country and with them the work of the good Sisters. The purpose of the House was now almost exclusively teaching, though a couple of elderly nuns devoted some time to charitable activities. We were surrounded by a human, open atmosphere.

I arrived in September 1913. There were about one hundred students in residence in our convent, ranging in age from eleven or twelve to sixteen or seventeen years. There were also a number of day students from the city. One of them in my class, a pretty and slender girl with some pretension to elegance and sophistication, was heard to express delicate sneers at those country girls who "*did not even wear corsets!*" Most of us were from the country, however, and, as taunts and jibes were frowned upon by the nuns, we suffered little teasing during our period of adjustment.

We lived a busy life. Usually awakened about five A.M. by the clanging of locomotives arriving in Bonaventure railroad station, any remaining shreds of sleep were dispelled half an hour later by the insistent tinkle of Sister's morning carillon. Shaking her little bell with the energy of a brand new day, she would intone the "*Let us bless the Lord,*" to which we would respond "*Thanks be to God.*"[2] We would then begin to dress. We must have looked like so many little white ghosts as we stood by our beds putting on, in the correct order, as best we could under cover of our long nighties, the garments arranged the night before on the back of a chair. Then we would troop to the spacious bathroom to wash, each one in her appointed unit of space, sometimes helping one another with tying a hair ribbon or combing long curls.



2 To those of my readers who may find the translation irritating (which I do), I append the Latin which I so well remember from my own convent days: "*Benedicamus Domino*" — "*Deo gratias.*" (Lorraine)

On Saturdays, there was great activity on this floor as we had our weekly bath in turn. A curtain was drawn around each tub, but modesty was further secured by the rule that required us to wear our chemises throughout the process.[3] I suppose these garments still exist and may be worn in some places and under some circumstances as protection against winter cold; but as there are many windproof fabrics nowadays, maybe even there the undershirt is becoming obsolete.

Now we made our beds. If visitors were expected, we carefully spread starched and pleated pillow shams over our pillows. We were required, too, to tidy our lockers. Each student had a deep shelf or unit in which all her possessions were kept. Every month without fail, during the first two weeks, I lost my marks for order and neatness; then, without fail, by the grace of dear Sister Saint Hilaire and by dint of heroic effort on my part, I won them back in the last fortnight. Tidiness on a daily sustained basis did not come easily to me.

I took to school here as a duck to water. During my first year, we had Sister Rose-Anna Dion as a classroom teacher. Sister Dion was a fine woman and a highly skilled teacher; she was wise, passionately devoted to the education and training of youth, and she was blessed with wide and deep insight. By her understanding and

3 In my convent, we had hospital gowns to wear in our bath, to avoid shocking our guardian angel. My guardian angel just looked the other way as I slyly dunked my gown into the water to make believe that I had complied with the rule. (Lorraine)

her tolerance, she promoted our adjustment to this new style of life. She had been brought up on the farm and had a great store of homely common sense. Her sense of humour was slightly earthy, never coarse. Should some child from a remote country parish appear to harbour undesirable fauna in her hair she would chuckle, remark that it was evidence of a healthy scalp, and send the patient to the infirmary for appropriate treatment. She would make jokes about the puréed pumpkin served for dessert, about the sempiternal veal stew, about the porridge which came with molasses or with milk and white sugar on alternate days.... The food, she pointed out once, could not be too bad because one cook had become so fat on it that, when she died, they had to widen the kitchen door to carry her through it. When we found the regimen a little hard, she would tease us back into good humour; she praised us generously when we deserved praise and freely gave encouragement to those whose performance fell short.

She discovered within the first week that I was very short-sighted and needed glasses. I realized now why I saw flying birds only as a blur of colour; why I must hold my book so close to my face; why distant scenes were always so soft in outline and even in colour. I was jubilant! This was a new world. We had a small yard at the back of the convent where we spent recess. After vainly coaxing me to join the others in playing ball or other games, Sister gave up, and I sat under a huge ancient willow tree on a bench with a book or with a pencil and my ever-present little sketch pad, as blissful and serene as Ferdinand the Bull under his favourite cork tree, smelling the flowers.

Sister Dion was not too rigid in the matter of discipline as long as we got our work done. I had a habit of scribbling in the margins of my exercise books (even of some texts). One day, she came up behind me and caught me putting the finishing touches on a cartoon of Sir Robert Borden. His hair and moustaches were a delight to draw. Having first made sure that my assignment was completed, she deigned to smile at my art work. I wondered later if she would have been amused had the subject been — say — Sir Wilfrid Laurier.

I provided some light moments for the good Sisters. I had brought with me from home my treasured scribblers full of drawings copied from the comic section of *La Presse*. Sister Dion borrowed them, and the guests of *L'Hôtel du Père Noé*[4] were a huge success as they were circulated among the nuns. (Incidentally, I never saw the scribblers again.)

Once, during the Bible study lesson, I was asked to tell about the arrangement whereby Jacob was allowed to build up a flock for himself during the seven years that he worked for Laban in order to win Rachel (which turned out to be fourteen years after all). I gave full details, including the willow branches partly peeled and placed in the pool where the sheep went to drink — with the result that many of the lambs were born spotted white and black. It was obvious that the bit about pregnant ewes and prenatal influence had escaped me and thus the real point of Jacob's clever little

4 The animal cartoons hereinbefore referred to; see page 70.

trick was way over my head. It seems that great was the general merriment as Sister Dion related this to the sisters at their recreation that evening. All this, of course, was relayed to Mother by the sisters themselves. Channels of communication between parents and school functioned admirably.

Apart from our studies and routine household duties such as dusting and sweeping, we were allowed, on a volunteer basis, to help in the laundry. If we proved sufficiently able and trustworthy, we might graduate to ironing the accordion-pleated pillow shams which, on special occasions, adorned our beds. Our very best work went to the starched linen and lace vestments from St. Joseph's parish church. It was with great pride that I hung up the handsome chasubles and surplices ready to be sent back to the rectory.

We were expected to do some sewing. My first undertaking was turning and cutting down a navy blue serge dress for one of the younger girls. I do hope it held together when subjected to the strain of play. As a project in fancy work I chose a lace of darned net about twenty inches wide and yards and yards in length: well anyway, several yards. This was destined for an altar cloth. It took me two years to complete it.

We sometimes attended services in venues other than our pretty little chapel. In the beautiful Notre Dame church we heard a famous preacher on the conversion of St. Paul. We were much impressed with his oratory. On a few occasions we went to St. Joseph's in an older district of Montreal. A couple of little children would sometimes wander in during the service; barefoot, with tangled blond hair and stained little faces — angelic little faces such as Michelangelo loved to paint.

On sunny days we often went out for walks, two by two in a demure little procession. Our special outings were usually to museums, schools or churches. Once we visited an orphanage. This place made an unforgettable impression on me: rows of little white cribs, a drab and colourless play room with rows of tables and chairs and, above all, the feeble, doleful wail of infants — this was very sad. The babies were picked up only to have only their most basic physical needs attended to, for the place was very short-handed. The older children were listless and pale, with lacklustre eyes: all but one who looked alive, her gaze quick and bright. We soon learned why. A young nun came into the room. The child ran to her and she was taken up and hugged while the others looked on, forlornly as souls might gaze upon the blessed from the joyless depths of limbo. We walked away depressed.

The end of our first year was as exciting as its beginning. Exams were for me such a novelty that they were almost like a game: a competitive sport. Thanks to Mother's more than adequate preparation and Sister Dion's teaching and encouragement, the little country girl came through with flying colours. In those days it was the custom to give prizes for first, second, even at times third standing. The prizes were usually books donated for the purpose by friends of the convent, individual or corporate, and sometimes provided by the school itself. Large volumes in brightly-coloured bindings, piled up, one on top of another, they made an impressive showing.[5]

It was glorious to drive home from Ottawa with Mother and Serge in the buggy drawn by that same handsome Percheron mare, Victoria, whom I had long ago declined to ride. It was lovely, too, to get back to the little farm; to see again all the familiar scenes, but now there was a difference which became more apparent as the holidays wore on. We all were a little older.

Some of the David boys came sometimes to play with Chris and Serge. Since I was not allowed to play with boys, I remember little about them except that when I was just back from first year in convent one of them, because I was barefooted, teased me. He muttered, with a snicker, something about 'big feet.' By now, my dresses were ankle-length, and some were made with hobble skirts in the fashion of the day. I suddenly felt awkward. I couldn't straddle a drainage ditch or run across a field. Much as I did not like to, after that I kept my shoes on. This David boy may well be

5 Mother modestly refrains from pointing out that she brought home several of these books. I have some of them today: gorgeous volumes: *La Gerbe d'Or*, a collection of essays, inscribed '*Jeanne Richer, 1st prize for music, 1915.*' Then Georges Pradel, *Jeanne d'Arc*, 1st prize for excellence, 1915; *Travailleurs et Hommes Utiles* with fifty illustrations, '*Jeanne Richer, 1st prize for excellence, 1916*'; *L'oeil-de-Tigre, 'Jeanne Richer, 1st prize for literature, 1916.'* Of course. they are all in French. There are also a couple that belong to Auntie Damienne — one for catechism!! and a couple that were won by me, *moi qui vous parle.* (Lorraine)

the same who opined, after I had spent a couple of years away at school, that "*Jeanne est si instruite à- ct'heure, ch'cré ben qu'elle est ben proche folle.*" [Jeanne is so well educated now that I guess she's pretty near crazy!] I did not escape occasional use of this quotation by my ever-loving brothers. In fact, the sentiment was somewhat shared by my Aunt Alice.[6] Any kind of difference has to be paid for, I suppose. Being grown up had its disadvantages.

We now became aware of new and different matters. In August of 1914, war had been declared, and the long and fearful conflict began which we were to call the Great War, or later, the First World War. To my generation, war was something out of books: something exciting, something heroic. My response to the headlines was to jump up and down shouting: "*Oh, good! Now France can recover Alsace-Lorraine and get even for 1870!*" Later, I wondered how I could have been so unrealistic, and I learned to my surprise and dismay that I was but one of many in my thoughtless reaction. While the bloody struggle spread over Europe and eventually to the New World, country after country became embroiled willy-nilly, and nations discovered that their resources and the lives of their citizens had been committed by secret treaties.[7] While the fields of the Old Country were cut up by deep trenches where

6 Indeed, Aunt Alice made that same remark to me about my mother, when I was in Hull, just before the war; she did not think much, either, a bit later, of my enlistment in the C.W.A.C. The Catholic clergy were much opposed to our participation in the war — especially that of the women. (Lorraine)

7 An aspect of diplomatic relations which Woodrow Wilson was later to condemn and proscribe in his Fourteen Points.

men combatted mud, vermin, and claustrophobia between bouts of fighting strangers, no more aware than they of the issues at stake, I found myself back in the convent for yet another year: in a snug little world, in some ways more homelike than home itself.

We did not hear very much about the events which filled the pages of the newspapers day by day, but we were aware of general hardships. Most of us were from families of modest income, and the good Sisters did not let us forget the sacrifices our parents had to make in order to send us to boarding school. The fees were sixteen dollars a month, and such things as music, art lessons, laundry, and so on were extra. This does not seem a large sum, but on a percentage basis it represented a considerable portion of Father's salary. When a general appeal came for clothing and other useful articles, I was in a quandary. At home, owing chiefly no doubt to Mother's skill and prudent management, there was always enough to share with victims of fire, long illness, and the like. The present drastic need seemed to call for exceptional generosity on the part of those like us who were safe, fed and sheltered, lacking for nothing.

During the holidays, Mother had made me two dresses of a summer material then popular, a Japanese cotton crepe. The fabric was not expensive, but one of them pleased me particularly because of the style and the colour. It was a soft rose trimmed with blue. Like that of Abel, I thought, my sacrifice must be of that which I most valued. Almost tearfully I packed my rose-coloured dress in mint condition and sent it to the Belgian refugees with my true (if a trifle strained) sympathy. When later I had to account to Mother for this, she did not say a word but looked at me with something of despair in her eyes. What was to be done with a child like that? Had the question been voiced, I might quite truthfully have replied: "*T'was the parents Thou gavest me.*"[8]

My music teacher during my first year and part of the second was Léonie Ferland de Beaugrand, a sister of Albert, dubbed "the country poet" ("*le poète du terroir*") by contemporary litterateurs. The family was among the few landed aristocrats who remained in Canada after the conquest. Léonie was beautiful, intelligent, charming, with a slightly reserved manner. She had early signified her intention of entering the Order, but her health was delicate, which factor delayed her admission to the novitiate. I adored her. A touch of fragility added the fragrance of martyrdom to the halo I could already visualize above her head. She was kind and gave me a book for my birthday, *The Beatitudes*. Responding to my obvious interest in things literary and historical (and who knows? perhaps touched by my no less obvious devotion), early in my second year, she invited me to spend a Sunday with her family. At the very prospect I was transported at once into the seventh heaven. However, by this time, another teacher (of whom more later) had been assigned to my class, and somehow she managed to find some niggling pretext for denying me the privilege of the visit. This Sister held the view that this life is a vale of tears and the sooner we get used to it, the better.

8 This quote is one that Mother used often: in a different guise. The original is "The woman whom thou gavest *to be* with me," and it's from *Genesis* 3:12, where Adam puts the blame on Eve. (Lorraine)

The nun who replaced Sister Ferland as music teacher used to talk interestingly of the composers she admired. I can never forget her enraptured tribute to Beethoven whom she held to be the king of them all. Naturally, I responded to her enthusiasm in kind.

She told me, once: "*take care, it would be easy for you to forget God in your love of music.*" On another occasion, she asked me if I planned to get married, and I said that I probably would. She looked at me and laughed. "*I can see you, now,*" she teased: "*half a dozen little ones around you in various degrees of déshabillé; dishes on the table and in the sink, — 'Come, children, come out and look how bright the stars are tonight!'*" It was not difficult to perceive that in me she was seeing her own self.

Times have changed in the convents as well as out of them. For some time now, young nuns have been encouraged to develop their natural talents. It was not so then. Obedience to the rule, mortification of the flesh, and rigid disciplining of emotions by frustration — this was held to be suitable preparation for eternal bliss in heaven. Sister "—"[9] was a very talented musician. Upon entering the Order, she was deprived of all use of her piano for two years and put to work in the pharmacy. Irrepressible, she healed her bruised soul by learning chemistry to such good purpose that she invented a new preparation (I was not told what this was) which proved of permanent value. Finally, she was allowed to play again and to teach music.

I was told (not by her) that a very warm attachment had developed between her and a certain young priest. (The grill of the

9 I can't find her name and I suppose it is irrelevant, anyhow. (Lorraine)

confessional does not a prison make.) This highly sublimated affection produced beautiful mystic poems for which she wrote no less beautiful music.

I never became much of a pianist, but I played on various occasions when we at the convent entertained visitors with music and song (mostly of a religious nature). When I was not playing, I sometimes led the choir and won praise by my "modest demeanour" — an echo of home. And speaking of praise, it is, I think, fair to say that we were not spoiled by an excess of it. When I wrote home to tell that I had completed a painting and asked if I might purchase a frame for it, Father replied "*certainly, and a nice one so the folks will have something pretty to look at in case the painting does not amount to much.*" Even when we got compliments, they might turn out to be somewhat left-handed.

In my last year of school, I had learned to paint on velvet, mostly cushions. There were accordingly a number of these at our house, which Mother would on occasion display to visitors. One of these guests after examining long and admiringly my handiwork turned to me and cast upon me a thoughtful gaze: "*to look at you, one would never know you had done it.*" How the family enjoyed that one (even I).

We had Art lessons, too. The Art studio was at the Mother House, a few blocks away, and I went there once a week.[10] The

10 The Old Building is still standing, not materially changed. We had been there on visits and had wandered through the huge crypt under the Convent where lie buried the remains of members of the Order and certain grisly souvenirs are displayed, such as glass urns containing hearts that once beat with devotion to the interest and welfare of the Order.

hours spent there were hours of happiness unalloyed. The teacher was a pleasant, friendly person, and as we worked we chatted of many things. I much admired the painting she was doing, including a number of illuminated addresses[11] on celluloid sheets intended for various VIPs in the Order. I am certain that these rivalled in delicacy and wealth of detail and colouring many a famous decorated manuscript of an earlier age. One picture intrigued me: it was a religious subject, painted on glass from the under side. The work had to be done while the first coat was still soft and other colours could be worked in and show through. This technique produced painting of a peculiar translucent quality. Amid all these beauties, I was entranced. The outcome of that year's work was the charcoal drawing which is in Lorraine's possession[12] and the panel in oils dubbed by a friend of Leila's '*the Green Horror.*' It is true that it is very green. Plants standing in or near the water are apt to be more verdant than those with dry feet. I was amused. I do tend to favour green in many things.

'*Les Grandes*' (second-year boarders) were allowed more latitude in the matter of circulating through the various parts of the Convent. We might help in the kindergarten in the early morning, washing little hands and faces. The teachers were sometimes nuns who had been sent back from distant missions for a refreshing contact with civilization, and they had much to relate about the Far





11 These were called *Bouquets spirituels* (spiritual bouquets) and consisted of a list of prayers offered for the recipient or in support of his or her wishes or requests from the Deity.

12 I'm ashamed to say I've lost it. (Lorraine)

North. In those days, that meant Fort Smith and Fort Providence. One of them told us that sometimes supplies were delayed in coming and an infusion of hay had to substitute for tea. She spoke of her charges, too, of whom she seemed quite fond. She smiled as she talked of "little blond Eskimos."

Our second year was marred by the loss of our teacher, Sister Dion. She was, I suppose, too good to waste on a classroom of Sixth Form students; she was made Superior. The day she came to announce the news, she was anything but happy. Her face wore a drained look as she gave us the fateful tidings. The whole class broke at once into uncontrollable sobbing. This was real, spontaneous grief such as I have never witnessed before or since. Many years later, she told me that her 'promotion' had very nearly cost her her life. She functioned as Superior for some time, but her heart was broken. Before too long, she was rapidly fading away in a T.B. sanatorium. Desperate, she appealed to the Superior-General to allow her to go back to teaching. Education was her vocation: children, the love of her life. They did not send her back to the classroom, but she was placed in charge of educational activities for her Order, and in this post she brought about several important reforms. She had a long and active life and died past her ninetieth year.

I have already mentioned the Sister who took her place. She was of a different calibre. My friend Beatrice Bourget tried to be kind when describing her, explaining that she had never been attractive or lovable and that in her youth she had lost fingers from one hand. This added to her general grievance against fate and further soured her acid disposition. Beatrice contended that allowances should be made for people who are not happy. They might hurt others 'unintentionally,' Beatrice thought.

I had serious doubts about the 'unintentionally' part because of the unerring skill with which Sister would find and exploit the most sensitive spot in the feelings of others. I once read that Socrates, asked why he had taken two wives, replied that, patience being a virtue, he wished to have ample opportunity to practice it. Here was someone perhaps placed among us by a beneficent Providence that we might become proficient in the practice of Christian forbearance.

We did not always suffer in silence her punishing manner. I made up verses, and one day she caught us in class (our voices, though somewhat muted, had drowned the sound of her step) singing to a lively hymn tune, with me beating the measure, the refrain of my latest song in which I had likened her to Attila the Hun.





Some years later, when I attended a summer term of normal school in Prince Albert and boarded with several other teachers with the Sisters of Zion, the food and restrictive discipline gave rise to new songs which were no better received by these nuns. The favourite one was performed, with great gusto, by all the girls in the dormitory to the tune of *Sur la Route de Louvier.*

Refrain:

*Ah ! Que la vie est belle belle*
*Chez les Soeurs de Sion.*

*Prenez garde aux échos de la maison zon zon zon zon;*
*Car en bas ainsi qu'en haut*
*Il y a des soupiraux.*[13]

It was here too that I learned from a comrade a particularly irritating tune for an old ditty: "*Un elephant se balançait ait ait ait ait, Dans une assiette de faïen en en en ce..etc*"[14] I heard it said before we left that they intended never again to take in teachers as boarders.

To return to the convent in Montreal: I suppose that to be asked to accompany the nuns on their charitable visits was to be considered a privilege. These were not happy-making occasions, at least for me. The few scenes I recall were not of a nature to make me optimistic about illness and old age, though, in all fairness, the best one can do about these is really to accept them as part of the reality of existence. I went along to deliver food to a family in unbelievably depressing surroundings. A sick mother little more than a skeleton lay in a very poorly furnished bed; thin, pale children stood near her. Everything was grey and drab around the room. More disheartening than anything else was her pathetic mumbling of 'thanks.'

Sometimes we visited the sick: some of them with open sores. Oh, my queasy stomach!

13 "Oh, but life is beautiful, beautiful
With the sisters of Sion.
Be careful of the echoes of the house — ouse — ouse
For downstairs as well as up
There are small windows with bars."

14 "One elephant (and then two, and then three) were swinging on an earthenware plate."

We stopped at a hostel for the aged. Most of them just sat, staring at nothing, or rocked, faces dull and indifferent to our approach. The room existed in a stale and silent atmosphere. I hated it. I felt — not fear, or even compassion, but rather disgust and horror at the inevitable dissolution of all flesh.

The second year saw several of us graduate with a certificate which entitled us to teach in the intermediate schools of Quebec. We had had a course in Pedagogy which dealt with the general principles of education. One of the books we read for this course began with these words: "*Education is a work of authority.*" We were very far indeed from the democratic concepts of today. The minds of children were still wax tablets upon which the wise educator could write: a triumph of theory over experience.

I had had two happy years in spite of the fact that learning with our new teacher was not the pleasant and inspiring activity that it had been under Sister Dion. Music and the Art lessons had made up for that to some extent. My music teacher was an artist in her own right, a dynamic personality such as I have seldom met: a very intelligent woman. Toward the end of the year, she said to me: "*Now you have to learn more English and you must go to school in Ontario. Ontario has a school curriculum fit for a man.*" So my next year was spent in Ottawa, with the Ottawa Grey Nuns, a branch of the Order which had seceded from the rest to devote themselves exclusively to nursing and teaching.

I must go back a little — a matter of three or four years, to pick up the threads of a story of which we children, and especially I, at Convent, was not aware.

During the summer of 1911, something had happened that was to bring about the total disruption of the even tenor of our lives. Mother gave birth to her last child. Mother was four days in labour. The baby's head was engaged in the pelvis, and a doctor was called in from Buckingham. This was a person very different from the gentle, kindly Dr. Matte. He decided to use instruments to expedite delivery. A craniotomy was performed: the skull of the baby was crushed. Father baptised the child, as anyone may do in Catholic theory in an emergency (*ondoyer*), stipulating 'if there is life,' etc. Little Oscar was a beautiful boy. We had been sent out of the way during the process, but we came back after it was over. All that day, Father wept without ceasing, the tears running down his face as he went about doing what was necessary. There were women there, but I cannot tell who they were though Grandmother was sure to have been present. Mother was very ill and after some time was taken to St. Luke's hospital in Ottawa.

While she was there, a certain Father Côté came to visit her, someone having suggested that he might be a relative of hers. As he said to her, they undoubtedly were in some degree related, since there was only one original settler of that name.[15] They chatted, and Mother finally confided to him the burden that had lain so heavily upon her heart for so many years. Father Côté promised that he would give the matter some thought and make inquiries. No more was heard from him for some time, but his words had kindled a small flame of hope and expectation.

15 Jean Côté, who came to Canada from Perche in 1635. See Drouin, Volume III.

Mother recovered and came home. Years went by. I had my time in Montreal, and, after I had obtained my intermediate certificate, I went to school in Ottawa. Here I found myself under the tutelage of the same nun who had taught Mother when she was sixteen, in 1894–95. This was Sister Ste. Herminie, a martinet of a teacher, or so it seemed on the surface. She had been born into a military family (the Jacksons), and she was proud of that fact. She was a marvel of efficiency in everything she did. I admired her very much and was by no means misled, intimidated, or deceived by her gruff manner. She would scold us mercilessly, assuring my best chum (another Beatrice) "*You're going to fail ... blue as a grape*"[16] unless, of course, she put more effort into her studies.

My knowledge of English was still very sketchy. I found myself faced with a situation wherein French might be used at least in part in the course of teaching, but every text was in English. My Geography book was a revelation: it was a thick, well-illustrated manual, with many photographs but relatively few maps. Unlike the ones I had been used to, it dealt less with boundaries and extent of states and provinces, number and length in miles of rivers, location of cities, lakes, mountains, etc., and more with natural resources, industries, and such things, and the effect of these factors on human populations. Now, this was something meaty with which to work. I was elated.

16 I just can't translate this one; in French it comes out '*tu vas faillir, bleue comme un raisin,*' and in English it just makes no sense at all. Maybe it makes no sense in French, either, but it's a 'saying.' This might give you some little notion of how difficult this translation business can be. (Lorraine)

The first lesson in English grammar was 'Greek' to me. No part of it had any meaning. I complained in some distress to Sister Ste. Herminie but she answered, quite airily: "*You know your French grammar; this will present no problem. Just ask Beatrice to explain the terms to you.*" One session with my pal Beatrice and all was clear. I plunged into the analysis of English paragraphs and parsing of words with such zest that this became one of my favourite subjects. Nothing was dull.

Sister Ste. Herminie dispelled the faintest shadow of uncertainty from the most involved math problems. I had been used to thinking of this as my weakest area. Once, I had asked Sister Beauregard why one multiplied the diameter of a circle by 22/7 to get the circumference. She replied that "*it had always been done that way.*" In frustration, I had written to Father and asked him. The answer should have been obvious without my asking.

There were no such difficulties here: when our teacher had finished the exposition of a principle or a formula, there was no need for questions. I took physics and revelled in the precise definitions of familiar phenomena. I made a hundred per cent in (Euclidean) Geometry. This was the life! With my English–French dictionary at my elbow, I felt equal to anything Egerton Ryerson[17] might have

17 Ryerson, Adolphus Egerton (1803–82): Canadian clergyman, educationalist, and political figure. A Methodist minister and editor. In 1844, he became superintendent of education for Canada West (later Ontario) and created the province's educational system. From 1830 to 1845, he was active in politics to combat Church of England privileges, but he opposed the Reformers of the period on other questions. (*The Book of Knowledge*, Copyright 1958 by the Grolier Society of Canada). (Lorraine)

plotted for or against us. The Ontario course of studies was living up to my highest expectations. This was 1916, the year of the great controversy over the use of French in the schools of Ontario. Regulation 17 effectively abolished the use of French as a language of instruction in the province as had been already done in Manitoba. There was great outcry. Crowds paraded in the streets in protest; classes were idle until the question had been settled and routine could be restored.

Sister Ste. Herminie did not regard with favour this waste of time. We would have exams to write at the end of the year, regardless of what transpired in Toronto. Since she had been instructed not to do any teaching for the time being, she sat at the back of the room and observed while I led the class through its paces. I was thrilled, yet torn between pride in her confidence in me and anxiety to justify it. Beatrice, who was talented at drawing, assisted at the blackboard in Art class. I dealt with the Crusades, adding to the material in the text some details from my own remembered reading. We managed to keep up to the schedule. Our examination results attested to that fact!

There was little difference between the regimen of this convent and that of the one in Montreal, except that this was a much larger establishment and it included the G.H.Q. so to speak, of the Order. The Superior-General was Mother Duhamel, a sister of the bishop of the same name: a woman of such gifts in financial matters that she was sometimes consulted by prominent business men in the capital. Not only in the Middle Ages has talent — genius, even, — found quiet shelter between the walls of convent and monastery.

I had fairly frequent visitors here, as several relatives lived in the vicinity. Aunts Alice and Eugénie and cousin Joseph Charbonneau were regular callers. The term 'cousin' always evoked a slight smile from my schoolmates. It was remarkable how many of us had cousins living within visiting distance. After all, were we not about *that* age, convent girls or no?

Here, too, we visited some of the public buildings. The one I remember best is the beautiful Notre Dame Cathedral, where I later would sometimes go on weekdays to listen to the organist. Sitting near one of the side altars — a structure richly encrusted with cleverly set coloured 'gems' enhanced by the soft light coming through the stained-glass window, I would listen to the music. Sometimes it filled the body of the church with swelling harmony, sometimes it receded until it came softly from above the main altar like the clear, pure sound of a distant angel choir. I have wished since that I knew the name of the man whose skill could produce such exquisite spirit-lifting beauty. When I hear the song *The Lost Chord*, I relive the experience.

After having completed the academic year, we were required to take a short course at 'Normal School' in order to obtain a teacher's diploma, third class, for teaching in the schools of Ontario. There were two professors who taught us at 'Normal': one French and one English-speaking and, in addition, an Art instructor from the regular Normal School came once a week. My still rather imperfect command of English (and, for that matter, that of most of us) provided Mr. Edwards with many a hearty chuckle, and our French professor taught me to write French verse during recess. I have an acrostic he wr[illegible] with great skill. No one I eve[illegible] of a piece as he could. One poe[illegible] imagery: *The Legend of the Dis*[illegible] copy that he had given us but [illegible]ther. I never read it without heari[illegible]exible voice. I have a very lively [illegible] at my own expense, but both [illegible]; he was engaged in writing a boo[illegible]*ughter.*[18]

Pro[illegible]ith anyone who could not draw, i[illegible] a couple of afternoon sessions o[illegible] taught. This was a thrill. One da[illegible] the topic of study, I got a stack [illegible] in the following months on a variety of linen articles. Mother's store of such articles was enriched by great numbers of scarves, centrepieces, etc., all featuring vivid designs of fruit and flowers. As a remembrance of Mr. Fleming, I have a framed print of a rather charming charcoal sketch of his: *Winter in Lovers' Walk*, a little path along the side of Parliament Hill.

With one exception, all the people who taught me deserve far more space that I can give them here. All were persons of outstanding talents and merit; all were generous with their time and



18 In the second lot of notes that Mother prepared and left with her original manuscript, I found a further mention of Mr. Edwards. It's too long for a footnote so I have appended it as Note 3. (Lorraine)

*Jeanne Richer in Ottawa, circa 1917–18.*
*Wearing ribbons of scholastic achievement?*

attention, and I remember them all with affection and gratitude. As for the exception, she was soon removed from the classroom, which was the wise and kind thing to do. Perhaps I owe her gratitude for this experience, which may have been, if not agreeable, at least salutary.

Damienne in 1919 for one year attended the convent of the Sisters of Wisdom (*Soeurs de la Sagesse*) in Eastview. Damienne has pleasant enough memories of that convent. One nun particularly was beloved of the students: Sister Madeleine de la Croix, who taught music and art. She was, Damienne says, short and homely, with a florid complexion and a face like a horse. However, she often supervised recreation and was 'more fun,' Damienne says, 'than a barrel of monkeys.' She knew no end of songs and games which she would sing and play with the girls. One of these was an action song called 'The Trembling Old Woman.' The old woman goes through a weekly programme of domestic chores: Monday — washing; Tuesday — ironing; Wednesday — house-cleaning; then, Thursday — she falls ill, and Friday — she dies; Saturday, she is buried and Sunday, she comes back to life, this last to the jubilant jumping up and down of the players. All actions are performed with violent trembling which, Damienne says, provoked great hilarity.





Another pleasant recollection was that of the charming practice of stopping, on the way to the dormitory, before a statue of the virgin which stood in a niche at the turn of the stairs. The girls would pause to sing a good night greeting to her. Around her neck, Mary wore a locket and chain (offering of some devotee). The locket opened on hinges and tiny slips of paper were deposited inside by students with requests for special favours.

Besides music and art, Sister Madeleine taught sewing, pyrography, Hardanger embroidery, and crochet. Sister was a perfectionist, and Damienne must have been a delight to her. Her work aroused admiration, from the nightgown and the large and very beautiful Hardanger tablecloth[19] to the varied articles in burnt wood which Damienne produced: a match holder, pipe-holder, basket, a small plaque, and a handsome picture frame. This nun's teaching, her merry disposition and companionship are Damienne's fondest recollections of that year.[20]

Unfortunately, and certainly through no fault of Damienne's, the Sisters of Wisdom refused to take her back as a *pensionnaire* a second year. They had received orders to that effect from some



19 Auntie Damienne gave the Hardanger tablecloth to Grand'mère and when Grand'mère died, Auntie got it back. One day, she gave it to me. After Auntie Damienne died, I passed it on to Mary-Jo, my cousin, the youngest of Uncle Serge's children and Auntie Damienne's niece. Auntie Damienne had been very fond of Mary-Jo and of her little girls. A couple of years ago, the tablecloth appeared in Calgary at the wedding of Andrea, Mary-Jo's daughter, to Jay Boehm. Auntie Damienne would be pleased. (Lorraine)

20 I can't understand why nobody ever mentions the two books that Auntie Damienne won in that year and which I have in my possession. One is an adventure story about two French citizens in North America, by E. Parès and entitled: *Au Pays du Pétrole*. Auntie won this for her excellence in Catechism (of all things), History of Canada, debating, 'rédaction' (whatever that is — by me it means 'editing' but maybe it is just written composition), and linear drawing. The second one was the English prize. I am fond of this book. It's entitled *A Travers le Midi*; it's a travel book and describes the valley of the Garonne: a trip I shall probably now never take. (Lorraine)

source or authority. Damienne was told this by Tante Amélia, in Mascouche, where she spent a year with the Sisters of Providence.

Tante Amélia was business manager of the convent, and she became very fond of Damienne. She made the mistake of being less than tactful in speaking of our grandmother, of whom we always thought with deep respect. She used the expression '*La bonne femme Côté,*' and in speaking of Mother her praise was faint. That was poor diplomacy and rather defeated her purpose.[21]

Christian was left-handed and may have had some kind of learning problem. Those things were not understood at that time, and Mother thought he was simply stubborn. She despaired of him sometimes and feared he would come to no good. When Christian was thirteen, he wanted to go to work, and he was allowed to join a gang of neighbours doing road repairs. This was usually done by the farmers and counted against their taxes. He exerted himself with such a will that after a while he fainted from sheer exhaustion. The boss brought him home and advised Mother to keep him there because 'he would kill himself,' the man averred, 'trying to do a man's work.'

And now the seeds that had been sown in the hospital in Ottawa in 1911 when Mother, weak and ill, confided in her 'distant relative' — those seeds were about to germinate and to bear fruit.





21 It's funny that Mother should have noted this lack of tact on the part of Aunt Amélia. When Jeff, my husband, and I visited her in Montreal, I noted on her part the same lack of enthusiasm when referring to my grandmother. She characterized her as 'a good sort of woman.' I was nettled; Jeff perceived this and, in order to prevent a sharp retort upon my part, he nudged me with his foot, painfully, in the ankle. That was his way of saying: 'shut up!' (Lorraine)

I was working in Ottawa when Father received the following letter:

Convent of the Dominicans
95, Empress Ave.,
Ottawa, September 12th, 1917

Dear Sir:
My letter will certainly be a surprise to you: to begin with, I am a total stranger to you, and moreover what I have to say to you is somewhat extraordinary.

Although you do not know me, I have been interested in you for quite some time, since Mrs. Richer's operation at St. Luke's hospital, when I was asked by error to call upon her.

What I have to tell you is this: your present situation may be regularized. For fear that this letter may fall into other hands, I will express myself in Latin. *Ob speciales circumstantias casus tui, potes obtinere a sancta sede quasi sanationem quandam in radice, per quam recipi potes ad comnunionem laicalem, et dispensari potes a voto castitatis, ita ut possis contrahere matrimonium validum cum presente uxore tua.*[22]

22 Among my aunt's papers I find the following translation of the Latin phrases: (1) "On account of the special circumstances of your case, you may obtain from the Holy See a release as from the beginning (*sanationem in radice* means *healed in the root,* i.e., made in effect retrospectively effective, referring to the

Yes, my dear friend, and thus you can still *salvare animam tuam et uxoris tuae.*[23]

This would have been incredible fifteen years ago but since, two or three similar cases settled in this way over there may give one hope. Listen to this carefully: one of our Fathers, who is frequently called upon by the Legate as an expert in canonical law, had occasion to present your case to him precisely in connection with the cases I have just mentioned and he (the Legate) displayed all possible willingness to go through the necessary steps in your behalf as soon as you request him to do so.

And, see, now, a providential coincidence. This Father confided in me the foregoing without my having told him anything whatever and about the same time (approximately three months ago) a saintly soul, praying and severely ailing in a convent, told me that God had inspired her to pray for you. She is my penitent and that is how I learned of it. Now none

dispensation from the vow of chastity) by virtue of which you may be received again into the lay communion and relieved from your vow of chastity, thus rendered able to contract a valid marriage with your present spouse." My aunt solicited this translation from a Father Frank Firth of the Basilian Order, then residing at St. Joseph's College at the University of Alberta: her wording (given here) differs in minor detail from that of his letter to her. As made clear in subsequent portions of this manuscript, the vow of chastity was not rescinded on appeal, though the act of excommunication was. (I.A.)

23 "Save your soul and that of your wife." (I.A.)

of us three knew your address, and it just happens that a relative of yours, formerly my penitent and with whom I had been trying unsuccessfully to get in touch, comes of herself to bring it to me.

Dear friend, is there not in all this a sign of the Divine Mercy making your return easier?

Be courageous, and be confident! Come very soon to see me. If I should be absent, ask for Father Rouleau, the canonist referred to above and make yourself known.

Meanwhile, a word telling me that you hope anew and will come would bring great joy to
yours sincerely in Christ,

Father Marc Côté, O.P. [24]





Mother spoke more freely now of her talk with the writer of the letter and of the events that had led to it. In the next chapter, I will discuss these events.

I think we had always felt that Father and Mother were in some way different from the other people we knew. Their educational background explained much of it. Still, we were conscious of a complete absence of that easy familiarity that commonly develops between neighbours of long standing. That was true even as regarded our relatives, who were certainly friendly enough. More

24 This letter and subsequent ones were all carefully preserved by Father.

than once I had envied the light-hearted teasing and the laughter of which we were aware in other households and which was, in our home — at least among the adults, notably absent.

I heard Mother's account without being very much affected — certainly without being shocked or upset. There was a certain academic quality about the whole thing by this time. We knew our parents and their way of life too well for any new light on their past to change our opinion of their worth or our feelings toward them. And so we leave Father pondering over this strange missive while we go back to the beginning of their story.

When you have heard it, you will know why Father and Mother left Quebec and came out west.

# 7

# the why

Consider, my reader, how attitudes changed in the fifty years that followed the First World War. Consider, indeed, how different is the society in which we live today from that slow-moving, formal Victorian world in which my story is set. In order to understand and appreciate Damien and Eliza Richer, we must travel back in time to another era: to a time when the Church wielded real power; when social disapproval could be devastating; when women 'knew their place' and rules were rigid: one broke them at his peril.

Bear with me, then, while I tell their story as I believe it to have happened, without embellishment or excuse.

Man is equally vulnerable through his vices and through his virtues. Mother had such complete faith in the Church and all its representatives that it never entered her mind to question their authority, good faith or wisdom. As a result, she found herself in Coventry through no fault of her own. Added to her confident trust for the clergy in general, there was the special esteem and regard in which Father was held, not only by her but by everyone she knew. She accepted without question the leadership of this man of outstanding piety and integrity. Persons of more experience than she might have done the same.

As for Father, he was not a complex man. His was a world where authority was supreme. The scriptures teach that man is the head of the family as Christ is the head of the Church, and he took that rule quite literally. He sought in a woman the virtues and skills of the wise woman of the Good Book including her acceptance of the rule that the head (i.e., the husband) makes decisions and delivers judgments for both. Milton puts it best: "*Hee for God only, shee for God in him.*"[1]

If God's intent was recorded in the Gospels, it was nevertheless set down by men, and without questioning their good faith I make free to doubt that they were privy to all aspects of the work of creation. Mother may have been trusting and naïve to a degree; she was eighteen and as unworldly as any child can well be, but her allegiance to the Church and her membership in it were her own. When she got ready to go to mass on the first Sunday after her arrival in her new home, she sustained the first severe shock of her life: Father said, no, they would not be going to church. He now explained that their marriage entailed automatic excommunication.

1 *Paradise Lost*, IV, 299.

She never did enlarge on this topic. One can only imagine what she felt, for she had been wronged, and years were to pass before she was given hope of redress.

Mother remained a faithful Catholic all of her life, in the Church's own sense of the term. As to Father, I venture to say that he felt he had done what he had the right to do. I conclude this not only from historical quotations he made but from a statement I found in the manuscript he had pencilled some time before his death:

> An absolute theory, essentially and completely true, is beyond the reach of human grasp. A theory is a personal thing, and has its only entity in the brain and heart of the individual. Absolute truth exists only in God, He only possesses it and grants it to His creatures as it pleases His goodness and His justice, and as it suits His Will (intent, or designs).
>
> Humanly speaking, man finds the truth within himself, provided he does not oppose God's designs on his life but actively seeks this manifestation of the truth. Even from the religious point of view, if he is guided by faith (for faith is a perfect manifestation of his already possessing the truth), he ought not to accept in advance a ready-made theory as absolute. That he must himself seek, with prayer and persistent beseeching to Him who never throws a stone to them that ask for bread.[2]





2 The translation is Mother's. (Lorraine)

The concept of an intimate relationship between man and his God was part of his thinking, and, indeed, St. Augustine's writings are sufficient warrant for this attitude to satisfy the doubts of any thoughtful Catholic. He was unusually well-versed in ecclesiastical history and knew, none better, that disciplinary rules are made by man and by man unmade. His cardinal principles were faith in God and obedience to the law of the land, for all authority derives from God. It is necessary to keep this in mind to understand Father's motivation and his actions.

Here, then, is the story as I had it in part from Mother — some from Father, some from Mother's sisters, and others.

Our grandfather, Joseph Richer, was a baker by trade. He lived in the village of St. André-Avellin in the heart of the country of the Patriots of 1837. His wife Olive (née Grignon) was a schoolteacher. To my great regret, I never knew either of my paternal grandparents. His portrait shows Joseph as a gentle, kindly man, rather like his sons Omer and Oscar. These two, besides their sister, Amélia, the reverend Sister Antoine Marie, were the only ones of the family we knew.

The austere hairstyle of her photograph does nothing to soften the features of Olive. Aunt Amélia once said of herself that she much resembled her mother. There seems little doubt that she had a powerful will. Somewhere Father refers to her as 'my angel mother' with what can only be exquisite irony.

It is difficult to do justice to a woman of powerful character. She needed strength and fortitude to raise a large family, teach school, and more often than occasionally to brave the gloomy hours and

*Joseph Richer*

*Madame Joseph Richer*
*(née Olive Gagnon)*

keep the oven fires going for the morning's baking. Moreover, when modern psychiatrists discuss the Catholic versus the Protestant (puritan) ethic, they forget that the Counter-Reformation produced or enhanced its own brand of puritanism. Grandmother Richer was as narrow a Puritan as any Protestant matron.

Father was a diligent student and gave earnest of a brilliant future. It was clear that he must go to college. I understand by various casual references that Bishop Duhamel was 'interested in him,' but I do not know what role, if any, he played in Father's schooling. The question naturally arose: what profession would the boy choose? He thought he would opt for the Law. The silence that greeted this announcement was audible as a thunderclap. As Mother told it, Olive's reaction was instant, definite, categorical. She would rather see her son dead at her feet than have him embrace such a despicable way of life. All lawyers were liars and crooks. The doors of learning beckoned to young Damien, but there was only one way that he would be allowed to enter them. He must study for the priesthood.

It is useful to remember that at the time of which we speak the religious life not only conferred enviable status upon the individual himself but bestowed upon his fortunate mother special merit in the Great Beyond. The greater the hardship involved (financial or other), the brighter her crown. I do not mean to impute to our grandmother purely selfish motives. She felt strongly about the benefits of education for her children. Indeed, Aunt Amélia said once in a letter to me that "*if grandmother could look down from heaven upon her descendants, she must be happy*" (even though two of those to whom she was referring are lawyers!)[3] And no doubt the way was made easier for students inclined to theology rather than for those seeking secular careers. So Damien (as they called him, though his name was Daniel) went to Rigaud.

He was a very serious boy, shy and with few of the social graces. He calls himself 'a bear.' He did well in his studies, and in his senior years he taught rhetoric. His progress along the path to holy orders is documented in his own hand.[4] Once I asked him about his feelings on receiving ordination. He replied that he had received it "*with mental reservations.*" What these reservations were, he did spell out to Aunt Eugénie: specifically, he pledged to God ten years of his life.

These ten years he gave without stint. He was held in high esteem by members of the higher clergy as well for his scholarship as for his integrity of character, and he was clearly in line for early preferment. He performed his pastoral duties fully and faithfully[5] and was an edifying example to all who knew him. I spoke once to a man who had been a choir boy in his church and used to accompany him when he was called to carry the viaticum to some moribund member of his flock. "*He was,*" said Mr. Murray, "*the best man I have ever known.*"

3 And such have been the changes in the world that both of these are women! One is I, Lorraine, and another is a cousin: granddaughter of, I think, Uncle Oscar. She practices at the Quebec Bar. (Lorraine)

4 I have looked for this document and perhaps one day I shall find it, but I have not found it yet. (Lorraine)

5 There was in our library a manuscript of his addresses to the Ladies of Saint Anne: homilies full of exhortations to Christian duty. It all sounded very familiar.

His personal interests were much the same as when he was a student. History, maps (of which he had a number of valuable old specimens), and books. He had planned, in his student years, to write a History of Canada, and he filled memo books with reference notes for this purpose.

Science was neglected in those days of 'classical' education. Chemistry appealed to him, and it was in the course of an experiment that a fire started in his lodgings in Masson and his maps, among other things, were lost. He loved books and his choice of them showed both his own penchant for serious thought and his concern for the education of the young and for the edification of the people generally. In years to come, we were to benefit greatly from his excellent judgment in matters of this kind.

During the years of his ministry, he not only preached but he taught, and one of the bright youngsters whom he instructed was Eliza Côté, daughter of a family recently come, with a number of others, from the Lac St. Jean country to find work nearer Ottawa. He had by now discharged his pledge, and this child, looking up to him in all innocence as to the fount of all knowledge and wisdom, completely amenable to Christian precepts and to his guidance, must have seemed a predestined life companion to such a man as he.

She studied with the Grey Nuns in Ottawa for a year, obtained an elementary teacher's certificate, and taught for a season in the neighbourhood school. During this time, she boarded with a neighbour, George David, a brother of the Jean-Baptiste discussed earlier. As for Father, in 1896, he purchased the mill and adjoining land, and, in 1897, they were married in Ottawa by a local Presbyterian minister.[6]

I have from Aunt Eugénie an account of the family's reaction. Grandmother Côté and Mother's brothers and sisters were rather honoured than otherwise, so great was the trust and respect in which they held him. Phidime, our maternal grandfather, was less docile: he was also less credulous. His response to the news was to march his daughter from under her husband's roof straight to the convent of the Sisters of the Good Shepherd in Hull, who knew, none better, how to deal with wayward lambs.

Before he let her go, Father assured her that all would be well. He gave her a code through which he could communicate with her when the need should arise. After some weeks, he wrote her that her home was ready for her. She put on her coat and hat and walked out to meet him.

So the bride came home to stay: but, now, on the first Sunday of her conjugal life, her world came crashing down around her. Father announced the fact of their excommunication.

How he coped with her consternation, her outrage at this betrayal, I cannot even guess; yet I am still prepared to assert my

6 This was the Rev. R. E. Knowles, B. A., pastor of Stewarton Presbyterian Church, corner Argyle Ave. and Bank St.
Incidentally, there is a recent book about R. E. Knowles by Jean O'Grady, titled *Famous People Who Have Met Me: The Life and Interviews of R. E. Knowles* (Toronto: Columbo and Co. 1999). Knowles, who was also a novelist, later became the Toronto *Star*'s top celebrity interviewer in the 1930s. My thanks to an anonymous reader for the University of Calgary Press for this information. (I. A.)

I hereby certify that Wilfrid Lowetan, (alias Ricker), of the township of Bowman, in the County of Ottawa, and Marie E Cote, of Poltimore, in the County of Ottawa, were this day united by me in the holy bonds of matrimony. "whom God hath joined together, let not man put asunder"

R R Knowles B.A.
Ottawa Co. Presby. Clergyman
July 12-1897

E. K. Knowles
W Findlay } witnesses



*The marriage certificate.*

belief that he had not intended deceit. Keen intelligence can sometimes be allied with amazing simplicity. He must have taken for granted that she would accept the situation, perhaps on account of the implicit trust which, until then, she had had in him. That trust must have been severely shaken. I cannot think how he managed to persuade her that, in spite of appearances, things were really all right in the sight of God. He may in his own innocence have relied too much on her acceptance of the text about the husband's status as 'head.' The fact remained that she had a head of her own and commitments of her own which could not lightly be brushed aside.

Equally great, in a different fashion, must have been the shock sustained by the family in St. André-Avellin. Father had been their pride.[7] Whatever their reaction, the brothers who lived near us maintained the close relationship that had existed; but news to and from St. André were relayed through them. Amélia continued to write from her convent, but, when in 1913 she asked Father to grant his mother the consolation of a visit in her illness, he sent no answer, as far as I know, and, as I have mentioned, the black-edged letter which arrived some little time later remained unopened. Nevertheless, the family letters which he kept bear witness to a warm concern and affection among the brothers, his sisters, and some of the younger members of the family as well.

7 When Damienne spent a year at school in Mascouche with Tante Amélia, she was told something of the events that had been related to me by Mother, and our reverend Aunt added this reflection: "God no doubt permitted what happened because our mother had taken overweening pride in the fact that two of her children had been dedicated to His service." (The two were, of course, Father and Amélia herself). She also told Damienne that an eternal light was kept burning for his return to the fold.

I was born a little more than a year later, Grandmother Côté assisting. Both she and the good Phidime shared the ban umbrella with their daughter and son-in-law. Perhaps faith made them brave, too, because they seem to have set their own priorities. When I was born, I was taken to the church for baptism and Curé Lortie refused to register me otherwise than with 'father unknown.' Father was not only known, but he was very much present. He appealed to the bishop who induced the curé to see the matter in its proper light.

They say that at first there was great scandal in the diocese. Visiting preachers from the pulpit urged our neighbours to have nothing to do with us: to withhold any and all assistance, including giving or even selling us food and other necessities. The faithful, I suppose, shook a little in their shoes; some in doubt consulted the local pastor who bluntly replied: "Money does not smell." After all, business is business. No one mentioned Christian charity. Father was given to understand that he would be welcome in the church whose minister had officiated at his marriage but he declined.

Father lived by the mill, which he operated, and did a little farming on the few acres included in the property. In an Agreement for Sale of two lots to a George Paquette (September 27th, 1899), he describes himself as a 'farmer and dealer in wood.' How successful he was as a business man I have no idea, but he soon turned to more congenial employment. In 1901, he leased the mill and the carpenter shop, house, and barn to Geo. Paquette and Zénon Courchène and obtained employment with the James McLaren Co. who had large timber limits leased all over that country.

He was now engaged in the outdoor work which he loved best. As a boy he had enjoyed holidays on the family farm and his favourite sport had been shooting the rapids on nearby rivers. The small house which we called *la remise* (storage shed) or *hangar* housed our family until the larger dwelling was built. Eventually, a few more acres were added to the farm when, in 1909, Father bought the Ruet property, a small piece of land adjoining ours. By and by, the garden was developed and cultivated. Mother fetched trees from the forest and set them out on our grounds. Now the place took on a pleasantly tended look. Such are the house and the grounds that we remember.

Mother spoke on a few occasions of the first years after they were married. She had a lot to learn, as there had been older sisters to help with household tasks when she was young and she had often been away at school. She proceeded to learn her household arts, beginning with the baking of bread, straight from the book, except when Grandmother was there to help with her education.

After the first flurry of excitement, the neighbours gradually reverted to something approaching their original regard for Father. They came again for advice, they borrowed books from our library, their manner was extremely courteous to Mother. Those who had been friends were as friendly as before, and, if we had little contact with children our own age, the distance between our homes could well account for it.

Mother's family and Father's brothers held him in high regard and felt for him sincere affection. I was told later that his siblings were well aware that their mother had used arguments tantamount

*Église de Notre-Dame de la Garde, Val-des-Bois, 1908. The church where all the children were baptized.*

to coercion to make him follow the course that he did, and they were, if anything, rather sympathetic. Mother certainly enjoyed the esteem and regard of her own family and some prestige among them as well, as she was the most educated of her generation. There was a particularly close bond of affection between her and the two younger sisters. When we were children, there was nothing to make us doubt that all was well in the best of all possible worlds.

We lived a relatively free, yet orderly, sort of life. We said our prayers without fail in common when Father was at home, said grace before meals, asked Father's blessing on New Years' morning, learned our catechism and absorbed moral teachings from daily living, from the conversations and discussions that we heard, from our daily reading as well as from precepts we were taught. There were various devotional exercises: novenas, the first Friday of the month, and, during the month of May which is specially dedicated to the Virgin Mary, we used to have a little shrine set up in the northwest corner of the parlour. This featured a statuette with candles and what flowers were available for ornaments. On the first of the month, we sang a hymn of which the chorus was

*C'est le mois de Marie*
*C'est le mois le plus beau.*
*A la vierge cherie*
*Offrons un chant nouveau.*[8]

8 "This is the month of Mary/Most beautiful month of May/To our holy beloved Mother/Let us new homage pay." (Lorraine)

and with a different hymn each successive evening to open the family prayers. Mother accompanied us on the piano.

We children attended services regularly. Our parents saw to that, though they themselves could not enter the premises. One memory of church in Val-des-Bois remains with me to this day. I remember the priest coming through the choir; his eye fell upon a local girl about whom there had been some gossip. In full view of the congregation, he gave her a look of such contempt and loathing that I shuddered. This was a lesson — not in Christian charity, but rather in the implacable cruelty of social disapproval.

On Sundays, we often got rides to church with the Dubucs or Lacasses. Sometimes we trudged the two and a half miles, timing ourselves by every landmark along the way: first the corner (*le coin*), then the little bridge over the branch of Pelletier creek which ran in a westerly direction; then came David's house with the outdoor oven, just past the bridge, up a short slope. The next thing was the cranberry bog (*baie des atocas*), a swampy area which extended as far as the road and in which mountain laurel bushes grew, with pretty pink blossoms. If the fields were very dry, we might take a short-cut to reach the main road, cutting across a meadow. Where we went under the fence on the other side to get back onto the road, there was an enormous boulder. This rock was partly covered with a luxurious patch of lichen which I greatly admired: silver grey lining with vivid green top. A strange, fascinating plant.

If we followed the road all the way, we went past the house of Louis David. This house was a vivid yellow with paint made of a locally found ochre mixed with linseed oil. Once (and I digress a little), Mother decided to paint the kitchen floor and purchased from 'big' Charles Morin — our one and only local merchant — the necessary ingredient: that is to say, the linseed oil. The colour we applied was an elegant and emphatic yellow. The next morning, however, when she got ready to move the furniture back into the room, Mother discovered that, alas, she had been sold the wrong kind of oil and the new surface came off with a broom.

The next landmark was a bridge over our creek. There were willows that grew there, leaning gracefully over the water on the left — the far side of the bridge. After that, it was not far to the covered bridge and the church.

Before this bridge was built in 1908, travellers were ferried across the Lièvre River in a flat-bottomed boat (*chaloupe*). The ferryman was a weasely individual who was reputed to have *la main légère* (a light hand) — an expression more elegant than to say he was a thief or that he had sticky fingers. Once we had come to church in the cutter, which, of course, had to be left there while we were across the river, and the buffalo robe which was in it mysteriously disappeared. We returned home without it, not happy. Father looked stern; then he got into the cutter and soon arrived at this ferryman's residence. He knocked, the door opened, and Father said without preamble: "*I have come for my buffalo robe.*" The little man looked at him and without a word went meekly into a back room to fetch it. We were well acquainted with that 'no nonsense' look, though we did not often see it directed at us.

One winter that there was a very thick crust of ice upon the snow, we were permitted to go through the forest beyond Prescott's house to the village. It was a shorter road, and it ran through a swampy area where the trees were very tall: mostly evergreens — spruce, pine, and hemlock. From the branches hung long streamers of that lichen called 'old man's beard.' It was one of the things Christian experimented with to make cigarettes. I recall that forest as a wonderfully mysterious place, all dim light and deep shadows and a little scary. I should have liked to see it again but we never went back.

The little church was of simple structure. One pastor, the reverend Mr. Godin, had it redecorated inside with a star-spangled ceiling: gilt stars on a background of clear summer sky. I thought it somewhat touchingly naïve, but rather pleasing than otherwise.

Christian was a choirboy, and I belonged to the Children of Mary (*Enfants de Marie*) of which I recall little except that I wore, on certain occasions, a wide bandolier and we walked in a group in processions. Not quite everything was sweetness and light, as the boys tell me. I never came up against any expression of disapproval of father's choice, but girls are more or less protected and, besides, we did not attend public school when finally such a one came to be. Christian and Serge, as members of the choir, did associate with boys other than friends and neighbours. "*Faux prêtre*"[9] was an epithet they heard occasionally. I only heard the words once, in Notre-Dame-du-Laus.

There must have been considerable publicity at the time of the marriage since Father did not trouble to go away but remained in his own bailiwick where he was very well known. This circumstance

9 False priest.

caused the clergy great embarrassment and made him at least some enemies. One of them was the *curé* who took his place in Val-des-Bois.



Some services had special features: there was Ash Wednesday, with that pinch of ashes placed on your ear so that it would not get into your hair or your eyes; Good Friday, with long — seemingly interminable — periods of standing (instead of kneeling or sitting) and rich purple funereal trappings; Easter Sunday, with the colourful display of palm leaves, some of them beautifully braided, and the happy, triumphal music. It puzzled me that the Jews were not included in prayers on Good Friday, since Christ had been the first to give an example of forgiveness. I was curious about a number of things, but when no satisfactory answers were forthcoming I tended to draw my own conclusions.



Few sermons left a lasting impression, but there were exceptions: once there had been a discussion on Purgatory, and the priest had enlarged on the severity of the punishment that might be exacted for certain sins — perhaps even hundreds of years in that doleful place! I went home thoughtful. Still musing over the sermon that night, I called to mind some of the heroes of the past who had won our sympathy and admiration. They might have been brave; indeed, completely fearless, and of course invariably they fought on the right side, but most of them were notoriously lacking in the more disarming Christian virtues, such as meekness and — especially — humility. Oh, dear! Suppose Napoleon were there, still yearning for deliverance after all these years! Who would think now to pray for him? Down on my knees I went, reciting my beads with unwonted fervour, weeping silently the while.

Sometimes there were amusing things to relate when we got home. For this sort of thing, Mother was a more likely audience than Father. For instance, there was the Sunday after Easter, when the special Easter offering was publicly acknowledged. Our mayor, 'big' Charles (*le gros Charles*), sat in the front pew with his family. This was the most expensive pew, and he rented it regularly every year. He also faithfully made the most generous offering at Easter. The parish priest would read the names and state, in descending order, the amounts given. It would go like this: "*MR. CHARLES MORIN, FIVE DOLLARS!* Mr. Joseph Côté, three dollars," the volume of his voice decreasing until, when he reached gifts of twenty-five cents, the words were scarcely audible. This little comedy provided the parishioners with considerable amusement, and, as it was performed by the reverend Mr. Godin, a man with an impish sense of humour, it is doubtful that it was done in complete innocence.

Since Charles Morin occupied such an important place in our village life, serving as general merchant, postmaster, keeper of a licensed hotel, and, last but not least, as mayor, he rates a bit of space. From Father's account of him, 'big' Charles had begun his career as lumberjack. He was an unusually hard worker and easily got top wages. In the course of a few years, he had saved the sum of four hundred dollars, which he invested in a stock of general merchandise — groceries, dry goods, and appropriate liquid refreshments. Overnight, he was in business and announced this fact by

*After Council Meeting, 1910. In foreground, L. to R.: Thomas Simard, George Dubuc, Charles Morin, W. D. Richer (in fur), Joseph Côté, Onésime Prescott (far right, cropped).*

putting up a conspicuous sign on the façade of his building. His climb up the ladder was rapid. Within two years, he was elected mayor, though he faced some opposition on the grounds that he was illiterate — not even able to sign his name. This, however, with typical diligence he proceeded to learn.[10] From then on, he presented to the world about him an image of solid worth and financial stability. There were a number of anecdotes told about him — mostly concerning his malapropisms, for he collected long words in a haphazard fashion, never having learned to read, and made up out of these half-understood sounds a vocabulary all his own. On the whole, no one seemed inclined to dispute to him the role of the biggest frog in our municipal pond.

The best day of the year, of course, was Christmas. The decorations gladdened our youthful eyes. The grotto set against the grey hills, the animals, the beautiful wax infant in the manger with Mary and Joseph watching fondly over him in the soft light of many tapers — the smell of burning wax mingling with incense — all this produced a very special atmosphere of solemnity and joy. We arrived at the church already a little bemused by the sleigh ride, covered up to our ears in furs in the well-padded box, lulled by the cheerful jingle of the little bells on the harness. There was a magic about being out in a clear winter's night.

And in church, our hearts stood still as we waited for Uncle Joseph to intone powerfully yet reverently the most beloved hymn





10 Mother does not say whether he learned to read and write or only to sign his name. I wonder. (Lorraine)

of all. That was the moment when the lights, the sounds, and the incense seemed to blend into a fragrant breath of adoration which must surely ascend straight to heaven. Like many another fine hymn, this one cannot be translated so as to render the writer's exact feeling. *O Holy Night* is very lovely, but when we heard it in French as *Minuit Chrétiens* we felt singled out for an intimate, personal privilege of redemption: this must have been a feeling akin to that of the 'chosen people' for their own special deity.[11]

The way home was always short. Our heads were full, our stomachs pleasantly empty of food to make more room for anticipation, and the horses eager to return to the stable and their well-filled mangers. Then there would be the *réveillon,*[12] usually with some guests. *Tourtières*[13] were the *pièce de résistance*[14] and were accompanied by sausages, pies, cake, and other treats which escape my memory, probably because our minds were mostly engaged with what the morning held in store for us of gifts and further goodies.

New Years' Day was graced by candy treats mostly.[15] It was on New Year's Day that we knelt to receive Father's blessing. I wonder

11 These are Mother's words, and I wonder why she laughed when I referred to Québec as 'the Holy Land.' (Lorraine)

12 After midnight mass there is, traditionally, a feast. It is called '*réveillon*' and the English equivalent is, according to Le Robert & Collins, 'Christmas/New Years' Dinner.' I never heard of a *réveillon* at New Year's, but what do I know. (Lorraine)

13 Pork pies. (Lorraine)

14 Oxford gives this unaltered, but it also gives as a translation '*the main dish at a meal.*' (Lorraine)

15 The most memorable of these were large white and red candy canes and delightful animals of red, yellow, and white barley sugar, almost glass-clear and with an agreeable flavour.

if this patriarchal custom is still observed among Canadians in Quebec.

We had been told about the folklore of the Epiphany and once nothing would do but Mother would bake a cake with a button in it to determine who would be king for the occasion. Christian got the token, and we made the most of the day's licence by shouting at his every gesture: "*Le roi boit!*" "*Le roi mange!*" or "*Le roi se lève!*"[16] until the adults put an end to the unaccustomed noisy jollity.

Mr. Godin, the same priest who had the church painted with the heavenly scene on the ceiling also had a new rectory built. It cost all of four thousand dollars. He got into hot water over that (it was thought to be out of proportion to the resources of the parish) and over other things as well. He was fond of telling stories to boys who, on occasion, denied him the tolerance they would certainly have expected for themselves. Mother, in our hearing, repeated the following anecdote: it concerned his housekeeper, a simple soul. It seems that one morning she came to him in considerable distress. The parish had received a visit from the bishop and His Excellency had spent the night in the rectory. Now she wondered: how was she to dispose of the contents of His Excellency's chamber pot: would it be sacrilegious to follow the usual procedure?

When he was transferred from our parish to some locality even more remote, I can only hope it was not on account of the rectory costs. He was a good-hearted fellow with a good deal of horse sense. I heard him chide French-Canadians for their tendency to

16 *"The king drinks!" — "The king eats!" — "The king rises!"* (Lorraine)

envy their more successful compatriots instead of standing loyally behind them.

It was during his pastorate that I, along with the rest of the Children of Mary and other young ladies of the parish, took part in a basket social. As elsewhere, this involved each maiden preparing a lunch for two in an attractive box or basket, these containers to be auctioned off for the benefit of the parish fund to the young bloods of the neighbourhood. In some way, clandestine but effective, each young man seemed to know which basket he was expected to bid on. The competition was quite keen at times, intelligence as to the identity of the owner having been somehow accidentally 'leaked.' This, however, only happened in the case of very popular young ladies and, naturally, all in a good cause. Beginners like myself had to take a chance, and so, for that matter, did those who purchased baskets of unknown origin. After all — something had to be done to keep the shy ones from starving. My creation was nothing as simple as a box adorned with paper flowers such as many others had made. It was a ship in full sail, worthy of riding on the waves of Marie-Antoinette's renowned hair-do. Somehow, like young men who would begin at the top, I often tended to make my early attempts elaborate — only to simplify later, of course.[17]

17 Mother does not tell us what happened to her basket and I am still wondering. (Lorraine)

On occasion, I had happened to see young men of my age, but so far had associated only with my brothers and our cousins. After church, one Sunday, a rather attractive youngster caught my attention and our glances met. He was well dressed, very good-looking and appeared well-mannered. We did not speak, but the following week, as the family was sitting at table, Mother, who had been looking over the mail, handed Father a post card. Father read it, looked at me, and with a brief glance at Mother, shook his head. It was obvious the missive concerned me. I was finally allowed to look at it. The young man respectfully requested permission to write. My heart beat very fast but no matter how I felt, I already had the answer. It did not occur to me to appeal Father's veto. I was only sixteen years old.

If our lives were lacking in frivolity, they were not lacking in interest. True, no talk of money was tolerated in our house and no discussion, either, of fashion or related subjects. I once asked whether I might have a pink ribbon bow on my leghorn hat, and I was clumsy enough to do it in Father's hearing. The sermon this evoked left me — if not repentant — at least determined to be more circumspect in the future. It was well understood, if not expressed, that Mother's views on worldly matters were more flexible than his.

On the other hand, Father did have a genial and pleasant disposition. We loved to hear him talk — whether about his younger days or about his work. Once at college in Rigaud, he had been ill with diphtheria. His chemistry professor found him in the infirmary in a desperate condition. Needless to say, there was little help at the time for this frightening disease.[18] The good Father decided that there was nothing to be lost in any case, and he painted the patient's throat (on the outside) with pure croton oil. In the morning, the whole area was one vast, single blister, but the patient breathed freely.

I suppose that Father's experience may explain the prestige in our house of this medicament as a measure against stubborn cases, be they toothaches or other kinds of internal inflammation. It never failed. I discarded my last vial less than two years ago. The oil in the tiny container was almost dried up.

Another of Father's stories from Rigaud concerned an aspirant to the novitiate. In an interview with his spiritual counsellor, he was quite prepared to promise anything at all that would get him the coveted admittance. The counsellor stressed the austerity of the monastic life and the need for self-denial. He wound up the lecture with the admonition: "*… but above all, my son, you must practice the virtue of humility.*" "*Oh, that's all right then, Father,*" responded the hopeful one, brightly: ""*L'humilité, c'est mon fort!*" (Humility is my long suit!)

Father held all social pretension in the greatest contempt. He told how one of his college classmates was a little ashamed of his parents' country clothes and manners. The father of one student had come to visit, carrying his belongings in a bag tied and flung over his shoulder. As he was walking away from the college, the

18 I was told by a woman that when her child was about to suffocate on the white matter that filled his throat, she took a button hook and managed to dislodge enough of it to allow him to breathe: he recovered.

son, wishing to recall him yet not eager to reveal their relationship, leaned out of a window and called out: "*Hé, l'homme à la poche, voulez-vous revenir un moment?*" (Hey, you with the sack, will you come back a moment?)

We loved to hear about Father's travels in the north of the province, especially when they involved something really exciting like wolves, or Indians. One time he had been delayed in reaching camp. He had to walk several miles after nightfall through the forest alone, armed only with his pocket knife and accompanied a good part of the way by a pack of wolves who followed at a short distance in a parallel path until he reached the cabin.

There was an Indian whom he knew well: a fellow of unusually powerful physique who accompanied him on many of his canoe trips. This chap could carry more than twice the load of any average man and was invaluable on long portages. Once, however, he added a little extra excitement to one journey. He imbibed too freely of fire water, and in that state he presented a problem. It took all of Father's considerable powers of persuasion to calm him down and to keep the heavy-laden canoe from foundering.

We understood the problem involved. We had a birch bark canoe that Father's Indian friends had made for the boys. On one occasion, Father allowed me to come with him to 'Green Lake' (now called 'Clear Lake'), to take up a fish net. The ride in that fragile, precarious vessel confirmed my admiration for the natives who handled them in such masterful fashion.

Serge recalls going fishing with Christian in the canoe on 'Green Lake.' On the way back, they got thoroughly lost. After wandering awhile, they climbed on the nearest high point to try to get their bearings. They saw a farmstead below. Hoping to obtain directions for getting home, they climbed down, went to the door and knocked. The door was opened by Mother, who greeted them with profound relief. Serge says (and I remember Mother telling it) that it took the boys some moments to realize who she was and where they were, so completely disoriented had they been.

Sometimes Father told of the men in lumber camps he visited. Long, lonely evenings were the bane of the lumberjacks' existence. Some knitted socks for themselves to pass the time; some told stories. Long before spring, boredom and small irritations made tempers short and ragged. There were stringent rules about fighting in camp. One little story Father told amused me particularly: one fellow after what had been a trying season was at the end of his patience with a campmate. One day, unable to hold out any longer, his pent-up resentment and frustration burst out in a flood of invective, the variety and richness of which only a seasoned lumberjack could equal. At length he stopped, out of breath and out of words. The object of this tirade calmly looked up and asked: "*And how am I to take this?*" — "*Take it any way you damn' please!*" retorted the angry one. "*Well, then,*" — was the serene reply: "*I'll take it as a joke!*" (*J'vas le prendre pour rire!*)

I have said that sometimes Father also served as game warden. He had no patience with sportsmen who would catch large numbers of fine fish and then leave them on the shore to rot. He would report such activities but would overlook the odd breach of regulations by Indians who, he said, never killed game except to make use of every part of it, including the hide.

Father had a quiet manner, was not given to small talk, and we were not encouraged to indulge in persiflage. My memory picture of him is serene. I like especially the recollection of him in his smoking cap and jacket, with a little smile on his face, slowly filling the bowl of his pipe in preparation for a period of relaxation. He was, I think, very shy, and that made him appear even more reserved than he may have meant to be. He was particularly fond of us as small children. He would play with Serge, sing for him, and dandle him endlessly on his knee until he was tired and Mother called halt to the game. He often took a short nap after a meal, lying flat on the floor. He liked a bed-time snack at night — usually tea and toast with jam. As I was the only one who shared that predilection, I had the privilege of preparing the refreshments. I also sometimes was permitted to fill his pipe with the pungent Canadian tobacco he favoured.





His health must have been very good. The only time I remember him ill was once when he suffered from meningitis. He was lying on the sofa in his office and telling Mother in his delirium to be hopeful, their ship would surely come home — only it seems that it was a star, rather than a ship.

Like many men, he disliked dressing up. The silk hat and Prince Albert suit which we discovered in an attic trunk were never used after he was married. As I have said, he was hospitable and not only acquaintances but any passing stranger found a seat by our fire: in winter there was a little glass of brandy to warm up a shivering night traveller, and, in the daytime, there was always a meal at our table.

Mother was as provident in the matter of food as she was in everything else. Dried fruit was purchased by the box, not by the pound, and stores of all kinds were kept replenished without fail. Besides preserves in plenty, she also made such drinks as raspberry vinegar — a soda drink which was sweet and fizzy, ginger beer, root beer, sarsaparilla wine, spruce beer, kept cool in the cellar and foaming like whipped cream when it came out of the tap, and barley beer.

I well remember the last barrel of barley beer at our house. Father had placed it on the kitchen porch, and, as he inclined it to position it for drawing some from the tap, a sound rang out like a cannon shot; the porch floor was drenched with beer and foam was splattered all over the walls. Fortunately the barrel had been at such an angle that, instead of going through the wall, the bottom of it had disappeared somewhere in the direction of the hill. Father laughed, as did we, but no more barley beer was ever made. On hot days, ice cream was safer and just as refreshing, though it cost more work to produce.

Summer holidays were good times. The outdoor freedom which we enjoyed and the truly exceptional richness and variety of our literary fare kept us from feeling too much the lack of companions of our own age. On one occasion, though, our isolation was brought home to us: Christian and I accompanied Father to La Salette to do some haying on a farm he had just sold, reserving the hay crop for himself. Uncle Omer and his sons Antonio and Nilphas were helping with the haying, and I did the cooking while the men worked in the field. The boys had picked some black currants earlier, and this provided an opportunity to display my skill at making jelly.

While we were there, the neighbours happened to have a party: there was music and dancing — the usual country entertainment. Christian and I did not know how to dance and so we were mere observers. It seemed to me such innocent fun that I felt resentful that we would certainly never be allowed to join in this frivolous sort of activity. It was the first time that the narrow boundaries of our puritanical way of life stood revealed, and I resolved that I would, some day, be free of meaningless restrictions.

This was not truly rebellion, because we did not reject what we were taught. Parents were figures of authority, but we respected them without any reservations, and we embraced the principles they professed.

Observance of rules was, however, tempered with common sense. One Sunday, it looked like imminent rain and as Father started out to get the hay in I asked him if he was not going to ask permission from the parish priest as we had in catechism class been instructed to do. He simply replied that God expects people to use their own good judgment. On another occasion, he told me that if my prayers were not answered, I should persist. "God likes to be coerced," always provided, of course, that one's demands do not run counter to His laws.

Mother always observed fasts prescribed by the Church, but she saw to it that we never lacked the full measure of nourishing food needed by growing children; so our God was an eminently sensible God, who expected good faith and was disposed to respond in kind: just and righteous, but approachable.

I have said that we gathered moral teachings from our readings. Many had a built-in moral, such as the fables of Lafontaine and Aesop and as did other stories. There was *Le Brin de Cerfeuil* (The Sprig of Chervil), a little fairy tale which extolled the virtues of plain food,[19] and there was one about a ewe and her lamb which taught not to return violence for violence: "It is better to suffer evil than to inflict it"; then there was one that taught a lesson in sharing — "when there's enough for two there's enough for three." Gradually we passed on to longer works of fiction and of history which provided topics for discussion.

There was a long story about an old retired Zouave of the French army who had more or less adopted a young orphan boy. In the course of a long, eventful career, the old man had met most of the experiences which make human life meaningful; he would relate these to the boy when the lad's path was beset by difficulties, discoursing at length on the principles of honour and of service due to king and country. These ideas were all the more effectively set out, I suppose, because they were addressed to a youngster our own age. The two became so real we dreamed about them. Many historical personages there were whom we admired: for instance, Napoleon: not only for his remarkable military and administrative genius but because of his firm stand vis-à-vis the Pope. We were also impressed by the captains who were part of Joan of Arc's entourage when she drove the French to a supreme effort to rid

19 Mother left this one in her notes and I have reproduced it as Note 4. (Lorraine)

the soil of France of the foreign invader. DuGuesclin particularly became a favourite with us.[20] In his youth, he rebelled against the routine of lessons, and he drove away his tutors, one after another. Still, as Christian gleefully pointed out, he attained both fame and greatness. We loved Frontenac. His defiant stance as he gave his memorable answer to the Yankees made our hearts swell with pride, but along with this we realized the moral courage needed for him to fulfil his mandate as Governor against the opposition of the clergy, who tended to treat New France as a possession of the Church rather than as a French colony. Obviously, our judgments were simplistic and lacking in maturity: valour against great — even impossible — odds; loyalty to chief and country; obligation on the part of the strong to protect the weak; division of power between Church and State, and allied to that was the fact that all discussions over such topics took place between Christian and myself. No wonder Mother was to say to me later that I thought 'like a man.'



Most of the novels we had which dealt with the period of the French Revolution were pro-Church and King, and it was easy and pleasant to identify with the charming and cultured 'aristos' and the gentle, if ineffective, king, rather than with the shouting republican rabble. But there was also history: the stirring speeches of Robespierre and the others. Once we read a French translation of Dickens' *Tale of Two Cities*. The episode that really did the trick

20 I was delighted to meet this old friend again in Conan Doyle's fine historical novel, *The White Companies*.

for me was the bit where the peasants are compelled to beat the ponds all night in order to silence the frogs, that the fine people in the castle may enjoy their sleep undisturbed. Whatever the reason, this affront to human dignity struck me like a thunderbolt. I went to bed that night then and forever a sympathizer with all revolutionary causes. Much later, Father was to express a tinge of disapproval at my partiality for the new C.C.F. party. Had he but known it, the seed had been sown in his own library. There may be a lesson in that.

Father did not make it a practice to give us religious instruction as such, but he taught us a kind of ethics. He warned us not to be impressed by wealth or worldly prestige. Character was the only important thing that mattered. Discrimination against any group on any ground whatsoever was anathema. Race and creed were God's affair, and only He had the intimate knowledge necessary to judge of the worth of any man. Politics? The law allowed freedom of conscience, freedom of association and freedom of speech. It was to be expected that people might avail themselves of these privileges.

Concerning women, he always treated Mother with the utmost respect and courtesy, lifted his hat to any female and praised virtue, competence, and common sense in the fair sex, but his more general view of their place was expressed most exactly in a book I was reading today: "*The best reputation a [Maya] woman could have was not to be spoken of among men for either good or evil.*" Father's own words were: "*The best thing that can be said of a woman is that there has never been anything said about her.*"

I did not object to this dictum. Neither did I allow it to disturb me. The women I knew and those I had read about were hardly such nonentities, and if they had been I should not have wished to emulate them.

In business dealings with others, he was so scrupulous — not to say so fastidious — that he nearly drove Mother to distraction. There was one incident she used to relate as a sample of his performance as a man of business. It was (it would be!) a horse deal. A neighbour was buying a mare from Father. There was no flaw, be it ever so slight, that Father did not reveal in minutest detail. Listening to him from a discreet distance, Mother thought that surely anyone who did not know him would decline the animal as a gift. She held her breath in suspense as his description of the mare drew to a close. He paused and then added: "*— Ah, yes; and a couple of years ago she broke a leg!*"





I think that the documents drawn by him, contracts and so on, demonstrate his concern for thoroughness and accuracy. He was also incapable of pettiness.

After teaching at Notre-Dame du Laus for a year, I went to work in Ottawa as secretary-typist and bookkeeper. That was in 1917–18. Damienne was in convent in Eastview.[21] It was then that Mother read an advertisement for French-speaking teachers for the West and suggested that I go to Saskatchewan to seek my fortune.

21 I am having a problem with these dates. Auntie Damienne's prize books are dated 1919: Mother's dates show Auntie Damienne in convent with the Sisters of Wisdom in 1917–18. Maybe the answer will come. (Lorraine)

The year I came to Zenon Park, the Orangemen were waging a campaign on the slogan of '*One flag, one language, one religion. Down with the Catholics and the French Canadians.*' On my way from Ottawa, my first stop was Vonda, Saskatchewan. There, I came across a news sheet published by a former Irish priest, name of Maloney. It was full of hysterical accusations against the Catholic clergy: wild stories of corruption and abuses of all kinds. On the front page was a photo of a Spanish torture chamber with an a lurid article describing the rack and various other instruments of torture used under the direction of the Holy Inquisition. The article actually suggested that these practices were current, and not part of a distant past. But how many readers were ignorant enough to accept this as recent events, one does not like to think.

As for me, I was all ready for the fray, if fray there was to be. When I got to my school, there was no crucifix on the wall, so a neighbour made a cross for me, which I painted in black enamel and further adorned with a Sacred Heart. The inspector offered no comment and neither did anybody else.

This brings to mind an incident of which I was reminded years later by a former pupil: while teaching at Zenon Park, I agreed to include catechism if I might do it outside school hours, i.e., at 8:30 A.M. There was, to the best of my knowledge, no objection on the part of students or the parents. Once in a while, the local curé would come to the school and examine the children on their proficiency. He liked to ad lib a little and to challenge them with questions of his own. One day, he asked if a man might be married and later become a priest: short silence, a timid "*no,*" a few tentative murmurs of "*yes.*" The priest shook his head in negation. At that, a bright sixth grader from the back row stood up and said firmly: "*Yes sir, a man may marry, and if a widower he may be ordained as a priest.*" "*How do you know?*" was the startled rejoinder. "*Because Miss Richer says so.*" The priest looked at me, I looked at him. He demurred: "*We-e-eeell, it could happen of course, but it is not the usual thing.*"

After the children were dismissed, I asked him why he had tried to deny what anyone knew to be so, as history has abundantly demonstrated. Why contradict the facts? — "*Well,*" he replied, "*it can be and has been done, but we don't like to tell them.*"

During the time I was in the West in 1918–19, Damienne was in the Providence Convent in Mascouche, where Aunt Amélia (Father's sister) was in charge of the business affairs of the community.[22]



While I was in Ottawa Father had received another letter from Father Côté inquiring as to our names and ages. Mother gave him, in a letter, the data required by church authorities. No reason for this request was given at the time, but as Mother told me later, every aspect of our collective and individual lives was the object of a scrutiny which would have done credit to the Holy Inquisition. There simply was not an iota of reproach which could be levelled at Father or Mother, and we, of course, were hardly out of the nest except for Damienne and I, who had spent much of our time thus far within convent walls.

22 Maybe it was at Mascouche that Auntie Damienne got the prizes. (Lorraine)

It was while I was in Saskatchewan that the decision was finally arrived at to 'regularize,' as Father Côté had expressed it, 'their position.' Our parents, after having gone through a new marriage ceremony, were to leave their home and go to a place where their past would be unknown. Some pioneer region was suggested, for land was then being opened for settlement in various parts of Canada. Though it must have been a frightful wrench to him to leave his beloved *Lièvre* country, Father agreed to emigrate. As to the marriage ceremony, he simply refused to go through a perfectly meaningless procedure since he was already legally married. To do so would have been to invalidate his stand in the sight of all those who knew him, and, more important still, to deny his own convictions. His belief in the law was as firm as — and even part of — his belief in God. Authority was one, indivisible. On that point, he refused to budge. For the sake of Mother, Father accepted to leave Val-des-Bois and seek another home. The ban was to be lifted under conditions laid down specifically in correspondence with Father Rouleau, binding Father to silence except with his spiritual guide under the seal of confession.[23]

So the house was sold, and most of the household goods. Mother saw with bitterness their long-cared-for (some treasured) possessions being auctioned off for a pittance. Even if Father had

23 Mother, for some reason, does not in this text make reference to the requirement of strict chastity thereafter which was now imposed upon her parents. I wonder if Mother was, deep down, also a bit of a prude: but I think this was unconscionable and ought to be mentioned here. They kept the rule, too, and this was not the least of the punishments which were heaped upon the innocent head of my grandmother. (Lorraine)

had the skill (which he did not possess) to attempt getting for them anything like what they were worth, I am sure he did not have the heart, nor the will. They left with little more than some books, clothing, and a few objects of sentimental value.[24]

Their destination was Timmins in the north of Ontario.

After the house was sold, Mother and Serge went to Hull while Father was looking for a place to live. Aunt Eugénie was then working at Pharand's ready-to-wear emporium and they stayed with her and Grandmother. Serge attended school at Notre Dame college, a school operated by the Brothers of Christian Schools. He enjoyed his classes very much.

One day, Serge was sent to the store with a message for Aunt Eugénie. On returning home, he fainted dead away on the front porch. The doctor was called and diagnosed typhoid fever. The fever in due time abated, but complications set in: he suffered a relapse and phlebitis; a clot formed in an arterial vessel of the right leg. Liquid diet was continued, the leg painted with iodine. Days passed. No change was apparent except the limb kept swelling more and more until it seemed likely to split from the pressure. Mother was getting little sleep. The doctor said one day: "*If you want to save your boy, we will have to amputate this leg.*"

— "*I had rather,*" said Mother, "*see him dead than crippled!,*" and Serge was inclined to agree. So Mother sat by his bedside day and night, bathing his leg and cooling it with compresses.

24 Among these were the two guns referred to in his tale "*Il y a cent ans*" (One Hundred Years Ago), to be found among his papers. See also p. 15.

An old aunt (Serge thought she was more than a hundred years old) came every day to pray by his bed. One evening, she told Mother: "*Your son will be all right*" and she gave Mother a tube of capsolin which she had brought. From knee to toes they applied the capsolin to skin now flimsy as tissue paper, and loosely but carefully they bandaged the leg. The next morning, the doctor came. He removed the bandages. "*Who has been treating my patient?*" he asked. The swelling had gone down and Serge was declared out of danger.

His illness had lasted several months, and Serge was still using a cane when they rejoined father in Timmins. Chris was working in Ontario at the time, and he bought Serge a fine bicycle during the end of the stay in Hull. When he began to get about, Serge learned to ride his bicycle with one leg, the cane held in front of the bike in lieu of a brake.

Incidentally, the Old Aunt was "Aunt" Anna (see p. 127), and, though she looked older, she died in 1923, three months short of her eighty-eighth year.

Damienne came to Timmins from Mascouche in June 1919. Father obtained work there similar in nature to the work he had been doing for McLarens. But, oh! The difference in the forest! Here was not the glorious mixture of hardwoods and evergreens of the Laurentian country with clean, firm footing underneath. Here was the northern black spruce growing in wet, mossy bogs. He hated it. "*This damned country,*" he exclaimed once in my presence — he who never swore. Mother, on the other hand, was quite ready to make the best of things, as she had always done. To go away from Val-des-Bois had long been her dearest wish.

The place had associations that were too painful. Father could weather the fulgurations of the clergy and the suspicions of the docile devout, standing firm and straight in his belief that he had done no wrong, but it would be idle to pretend that Mother could feel similarly secure. To begin with, her loyalty to the Church was immediate and unequivocal. Unlike Father, she had no faith that could enable her to appeal directly to the Throne over the head, so to speak, of the establishment. Also, a woman's social position is too vulnerable to warrant defiance of custom. I repeat: she had entered into this union in complete innocence. To remain in what could never be anything but a false position in the eyes of the community and her own was intolerable. For her, Ontario was not exile, but a long-hoped-for second chance.

In the winter of 1919, influenza struck Canada for the first time. In Zenon Park, Saskatchewan, where I was teaching, people died as in the medieval plagues of Europe. Those who remained on their feet performed miracles of endurance and devotion. Cattle were fed, the needs of the sick were somehow attended to, and though many were the graves added to the local cemetery, a lot of us pulled through and greeted the spring with drawn, pallid faces.



I had been one of the victims of the flu, nursed like a number of others by faithful Marie-Louise, wife of Auguste Hudon, but my strength was slow coming back. I dragged myself along with great effort, and I was glad when Mother wrote and asked me to come home. I joined the others in Timmins. Mother had been ill and felt very weak. When I got there, wan and tired, she braced herself to find fortitude for both of us.

I got employment as secretary-bookkeeper for a local grocery merchant: a Pole. The office was a sort of corner balcony which overlooked the store. The work was easy enough (except for computing accounts, which I never learned to enjoy). My typing was not modern in technique but adequate to the needs of the business. I had acquired some bookkeeping experience in Ottawa in my job with a wholesale tobacconist's firm.

We had little in the way of diversion, but we were permitted outings such as picnics with friends. Damienne and I were courted by two sons of a French-Canadian family; some old acquaintances turned up from time to time: Phidime Lemieux, brother of Charles and Nazaire Lemieux, who did not conceal his admiring regard for Mother, and Edmond Lemieux, a cousin of my age earlier referred to. Edmond, Emmanuel, as well as Christian were young men on their own, now, out in a wider world.[25]

The Prince of Wales, later Edward VIII, came through Timmins. The local girls made such a fuss over his visit that I was disgusted and stayed home.

Then, one fine day, Chris Olsen came to visit. We had been corresponding since our meeting in Prince Albert the year before. His stay was not very long, but it was pleasant. He had come to meet my family. He always claimed thereafter that it was the cream of tomato soup my mother served at dinner which caused him to propose.

Life here was not too unlike our previous existence: it was made up of work, religious observances, quiet, unfrivolous recreation

25 Christian had gone at fourteen to join a spring drive for McLarens, and at fifteen he worked with these two cousins in Gissis' Saw Mill.

— except that father had lost his former serenity. At one point, Mother tried to help along by establishing a small corner grocery in one room of our house. Neighbours came to purchase bread and small supplies.

Among her customers was a recent immigrant from somewhere near the Baltic who would have liked a woman to help raise chickens and generally look after a small acreage he had on the edge of town. He did reluctantly admit that he had a wife in the Old Country but, since Europe was so far away, he reckoned that this far-away wife should constitute no impediment to another relationship. He had his eye on either or both of us. Damienne was getting to be a very attractive young lady, but, being older and likely to be more knowledgeable in practical matters, I emerged as the more likely candidate. This caused considerable merriment among us — merriment which we discreetly did not share with Father.





Mother's little enterprise came to an untimely end when Father decided to sell the house and rent lodgings instead. When Father sold the house on Maple Avenue and Cedar the family moved into the Larose house on Fourth Avenue in Moneta, a suburb. This was where Mother engaged in the only illegal activity of her life.

According to the somewhat confusing regulations governing the handling of liquor during the days of Prohibition, its sale was forbidden except through government outlets. However, citizens might order a maximum of a case a month for their private use. Upon eloquent urging by Mr. Larose whose family occupied one half of the house while we had the other unit, Mother sent for her quota of gin (twenty dollars a case) every month, and, when notification of delivery came from the railway, Serge would sally forth with his little sleigh and fetch it home from the station. Then Mother would knock three times on the door of the Larose quarters, the door would open, Mr. Larose would hand over four ten-dollar bills and take charge of the package. This, of course, never came to Father's ears and I have often wondered what he might have said, had he known.

Serge, whose memory (and that of Christian) I envy, has various amusing recollections of Timmins. He tells of an incident concerning a would-be suitor of Damienne's. There was at the house an old chair with a webbed seat. Father had replaced the webbing with new strips and painted the whole thing a cheerful red, then placed it in a corner of the parlour, out of the way, to dry. Young Bergeron, perhaps out of shyness, selected this seat when he came to call. No one dared to say anything, it was too late anyhow. We watched with bated breath as the young man, the visit ended, rose and slowly walked away, a perfect red checkered pattern indelibly printed on the seat of his fine, light grey suit. He never returned.

Father's reaction to the general community in Timmins was much the same as his feeling for the northern Ontario forest. This was alien corn; it was bitter exile. Timmins is a mining town and has always had a large population of immigrant workers. We did not, of course, come into contact with the rougher side of such a society as he did, but Father was much concerned with the effect upon us of such an environment as this. The 'blinkers' of our sheltered home life bade fair to be rudely torn off our youthful eyes in the midst of this urban mixture of races, religions, and social classes: Father felt that our very salvation was jeopardized. It did not help when he asked me, after Chris's visit and departure, whether I intended to marry him. I answered that I might do so if he should ask me. Father continued gravely: "*Is there anything I can say that might deter you?*" Perhaps more resolutely than necessary, I answered, "*No.*" It was the first time that I had pitted my will against his. He turned away, and I walked quickly upstairs.

The objection was two-fold: Chris was a foreigner and he was not a Catholic. The abyss was yawning before our generation, and one of us was already teetering on the brink.

One can imagine the thoughts that passed through Father's mind, and what was the relative weight of any one factor, only he knew. Be that as it may, he decided one fine day that he had had enough of the new life and we would all return to Val-des-Bois. I do not know what he thought we would do there. Our old home had been sold; there was, just as before, a complete lack of opportunity for growing youngsters. Mother was in despair. As we left him at the railroad station on the way back to our old home, her farewell words to him were: "*I will never, never forgive you!*"





It was a gloomy journey. Grimly wondering, we looked furtively at one another while Mother sat rigid in her seat and wept. About half way to our destination, a railway official came to her, bearing a telegram. It read: "*Change of plans; news from West; return at once.*" Mother dried her tears. Puzzled but relieved, we got off at the next station and took the first train back to Timmins.

There had, in fact, been talk of the West before: I had had some correspondence with the people I knew in Zenon Park, and after Chris's visit to Timmins, Father had travelled as far as Winnipeg to survey the prospects. He met Chris (Olsen) for dinner there, and what he heard could not have been of a nature to discourage him. The prairies, however, seemed a world away from everything that had been familiar and dear. His courage failed him, and he came back to Timmins. Not for him was the Far West (as he called it) God's Country.

Mother learned later about what it was that changed his mind. A friend of hers had been present at our doleful departure. After we were gone, that friend took Father severely to task: she taxed him so eloquently with selfishness and utter disregard for Mother's unhappiness that she shamed him into sending the fateful telegram.

Christian, meanwhile, came home from Sault Ste. Marie where he had with gratifying success been working in the lumber camps. He loved that work, too. However, Mother said to him, "*If you go west and buy land, I'll help you pay for it.*" When Father realized that Christian really meant to go west, he decided to go along.

There had been letters from Zenon Park. Louis-Philippe Hudon had found for sale a farm not far from his own. The land was bought, and Father and Christian decided to break it in part and rent it to Philippe on crop shares, then go back East to their respective occupations. Before they could accomplish this, however, Mother had packed all of our belongings in Timmins and landed, with the rest of us, in Tisdale, bag and baggage.

The house in Ditton Park was put up rather in a hurry as winter was approaching; a team of horses and wagon were purchased and, after a few months, Christian went back to the Great Lakes lumber forests, where he remained for seven years. The farm was the one on which now live Christian and Muriel and their son Wilfrid with his family. Christian's savings went into the clearing of the original acres, which more have since been added.[26]

Shortly after our arrival, Chris Olsen came to call and corroborated his proposal of marriage which he had made by letter of some months before. I went to Saskatoon and we were married in August 1920 in the rectory of St. Paul's Catholic church.

At the age of 42, Mother settled down to be a pioneer wife and Father went to work for the Forestry department.

Looking back, it seems very likely that even if she and Father had not come west, the rest of us would have done. Though I had not yet 'drunk of slough water,' as the saying goes, this country would inevitably have drawn me back, and it was the natural focus of interest for enterprising youth looking for a more varied choice of opportunity than the Old Province could offer. Once married, what could be more natural than that I should invite my only sister to find a home with us while considering her future course? Yes, I believe we would very likely have come here, thanks to Mother's initiative in suggesting that I answer the advertisement for French-speaking teachers. Even so far back, bilingualism was A Good Thing.

Now I can pause in my story for the time being, for I think I have explained why the family came west.

26 "Ditton Park," as such, seems to have disappeared from most contemporary maps of Saskatchewan. Family members of the region inform me it was little more than a post office north-west of the Francophone community of Zenon Park. Sometime around 1926, Christian took over the farm and the elder Richers moved to Hudson Bay Junction (now Hudson Bay) where they had built a house. They also had a homestead outside of town, eventually abandoned (I.A.).

# 8

# the last chapter

... though perhaps there is no such thing, really, as the last chapter of any life story.

We left in Val-des-Bois two little graves. I spoke of them, briefly, in this account: two children of our parents died in Val-des-Bois: Marie Damienne Albertine Eva, aged ten months, of whooping cough, and Joseph Oscar Daniel, when the doctor found no way of saving Mother's life but to deliver him with forceps, crushing his skull. There is, among Father's papers, a poem in which he says goodbye to the two 'angels' he leaves behind as he accepts his exile from his home.[1]

1 This chapter is cobbled together from bits that Mother left and as much as possible I am retaining her voice. The poem is in French. Mother translated it for my cousin, Christian's son, Barry, and he gave me a copy. It is very moving and shows a little of the anguish that Grandfather felt as he turned from his beloved Quebec to seek a home in the West where Grandmother might find peace. In this, the English version, I have added the poem as Note 5 in case the reader cares to read the original; Mother's translation appears as Note 5a. (Lorraine)

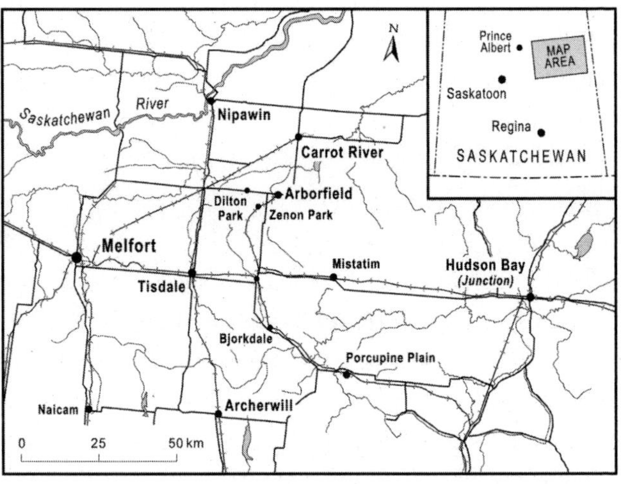


*Map of East-Central Saskatchewan, Nipawin area.*

Ditton Park, unlike Zenon Park, was not a particularly welcoming place. The settlers were almost all English speakers and the conditions were primitive.

Mother had brought very little from the East: except for a few books and our piano, we left in Val-des-Bois our furniture and most of our chattels. We were urgently in need of a house in which to live, and Father and Christian set to work at once to provide it. They quickly put together a simple structure with two rooms on each floor. There was no furnace. The kitchen stove alone provided heat. I don't believe the house was ever really finished, and it has since been replaced by a much more modern structure. Wilfred, Christian's youngest son, lives there still.

Mother set to work and built her own furniture, and, using the wood from the shipping crates, she fashioned tables, shelves, chests, even beds.



For some months, the four of us were there, at home. Christian helped with the building. We had visitors, sometimes, from Zenon Park where I had taught the year before. We had our books, and sometimes we had music. Father would have approved us girls marrying farmers, toiling with them, submissive to the church and all bound by family duties. I think he would have expected us to be happy with little of intellectual interest in our lives — he who so nearly sold his soul for the privilege of education; but I had already decided to marry outside of the French-Canadian community, and Damienne found the local swains too boring to bother with. Few of them had read many books or, anyhow, you would not suspect them of it from their conversation.

This is not to say that they were lacking in worth. I imagine that both of us might enjoy talking with them now, but the trouble was with us, too; we had much to learn about the real world of every day: especially about this pioneer existence.

I rode to the post office for the mail on a smallish mare that Father had bought. That animal looked like a horse, but no mule was ever more contrary than she. If there were a special need for speed that was when she decided to slow down or even stop. She had me buffaloed and she knew it. One night in the fall, I was late coming home, the crops on the field had attracted gophers, and game birds and coyotes were making the most of their luck. Night fell as I was riding along a fence, and from just a few stooks away came a chorus of yapping. I started nervously, and, of course, the mare stopped dead in her tracks. It was quite dark when I finally reached home, cursing the stubborn beast. I knew that coyotes are not likely to harm human beings, but I was not yet inured to their barking, and, besides, in childhood we had read blood-curdling tales about the wild dingoes of Australia.

The following year, Damienne went to Regina to enrol in a nursing course.

Father, warmly recommended by his employers in the East, quickly found a job as a scaler with the Forestry Department. There was an assistant scaler to Father who did not relish the subordinate position. He did, however, assist in getting Serge a job on the crew.

At LePas on the Carrot River some fifteen miles south of town, there was an Indian reserve. A dispute arose over timber rights belonging to the Reserve Indians. The timber had been cut and sawn by the Government of Manitoba and the Department of Indian Affairs claimed that the amount paid to the Indians was short by several millions of feet of lumber. Father was asked by the Forestry Department to investigate. There was a real difficulty: only the stumps were left.

Neither the Scribner Rule used in the West or the Doyle Rule commonly employed in Quebec and Ontario can be applied when only the butt or stump is available for measurement. Father went to work: sheets piled on top of sheets of figures and intricate calculations. When he had finished, he had developed a new rule for this special case, applied it, and submitted his report. The report was accepted, and the money was paid to the Indians. The Government of Manitoba paid Father the compliment of retaining his rule: without compensation, of course. I don't suppose he offered any objection; that was the sort of thing that drove Mother to despair.





Two young Swedish engineers were staying at the same camp. They were university students and had been doing timber cruising — estimating and mapping. One night, they seemed to have encountered some difficulty and had a longish discussion. Father, as usual, was quiet, smoking his pipe and reading a book: a very unimpressive figure in the disreputable clothes he affected for working. After listening a while, he offered, "*Sirs, would you mind some help with your problem?*" A sneer appeared on the assistant's face, but the young Swedes were eager indeed for any help. It took Father five or six minutes to find a solution. They were most grateful and expressed their pleasure at meeting a man like him. Serge looked at the scoffer. Somehow the sneer seemed to have disappeared.

A great many moons have waxed and waned since we came to the west country.

To our children, and to us as well, this is home; the home we made, with the help of our spouses.

We learned to find beauty in what seemed, at first, an almost featureless landscape. The character of prairie land emerges gradually. Aspen took on more dignity and importance in the absence of oak, elm, pine and cedar. But there were new types, like Jack Pine. There were Saskatoon bushes and our old acquaintances, choke-cherry, pin-cherry, the white birch, spruce. It was some time before we became familiar with the 'bald prairie': that region where man's ignorance and greed transformed the buffalo pastures into a dust bowl: a land which dearth of rain could turn into a nightmare of desolation. The country where Father's farm was located was parkland, much like that around Prince Albert and the farm that we, Chris and I, had nearby Canwood where both our daughters were born.

There was so much to do that none of us had time — or, truth to tell — inclination — for nostalgia: except, of course, Father who had not chosen the move.

I never heard Mother express regret for our old home or for the province we had left. The land was certainly of better productive quality than that on most of the small farms in the Laurentians. Only, Mother was 42 and Father 56 when they set out to become settlers on a piece of land which had to be cleared and brought under cultivation. Father had never done arduous physical work, and in those days the powerful machines which today demolish forest and building with equal ease were not as yet familiar. Bulldozers; juggernauts; they no doubt spare men a great deal of back-breaking effort, but I never see one pushing relentlessly through obstacles without a shudder: they are such blind, mindless monsters.

This country had its songs too: *Little Grey Home in the West*; *Springtime in the Rockies*; *Tumbleweed*; *Where the West Begins*; not to mention *Don't Fence Me In* and *Home on the Range* and scores of more recent ones. This, too, we gradually discovered, has its charm and its beauty: its moods of enchantment.

Indeed, '*the West has everything*' as Eynar, my brother-in-law, once said: '*only*' he added, '*It's so far between!*'



That was what we had to get used to; the distances. I had already learned about this in Zenon Park. If two settlers wanted to be close together, it would be at least a mile to the next one. The one thing which would dictate arbitrarily the location of one's habitation was (and is) the availability of water; and on flat land, with no lakes or streams to speak of, there is no guarantee of a suitable or adequate water supply, as many found to their cost.

Water for washing was often hauled from the nearest sloughs, those odoriferous temporary lakes tinged a little with brown from dead grass but preferable to hard water in the wells. These nevertheless had their uses, providing drink for cattle during a part of the season, besides water to float a raft — a poor substitute, I thought, for our little boat on the pretty Lac Pelletier; but it would be exaggeration to say that we looked back with nostalgia: except possibly — even probably — Father.

At twenty, there is everything to be done, and the present, with the future, is all that counts. But it was not the case with Father.

It would be pleasant to relate that the Church, having banished them, forgave and forgot, leaving us all to live happily ever after or, anyhow, free to cope with purely human problems. What follows I write "for the record" and not in a spirit of resentment. For some time now, such things have lost much of their relevance and are pretty well only of academic interest.

Father and Mother remained faithful, of course, but three of us at least were rather relieved to be in 'Protestant country,' where, as Voltaire points out in his *Lettres Anglaises*, the sects are so absorbed in their differences that one may easily enough escape their attention.

After a few months had passed, I went to Saskatoon, where Chris and I were married (August 24th, 1920). The ceremony took place in the rectory of St. Paul's church, the Rev. Chevigny, O.M.I., officiating. Little was said except to point out the usual condition: that no opposition will be offered to children being raised in the Church.[2] We lived in the city for a few months, Chris being engaged with a couple of partners in a small real estate business. One fine day, he came home and told me of meeting a

2 Chris, at first, was a little dubious, but I pointed out to him that I had made no promise!

local Father on the train and that, quite gratuitously, that reverend gentleman had confided to him that I was an illegitimate child. Chris did not seem particularly impressed by this intelligence, but I was, needless to say, highly incensed. On our first visit to Ditton Park, I asked Mother for the marriage certificate I knew she had in her possession, and I showed it to Chris. He noted with some amusement that, although I had asked him to be married in the Church in order to spare their feelings, my parents, themselves, had been married by a Protestant clergyman.

The correspondence with Rome's representatives specifies that Father was bound never, except under the seal of confession, to refer to the conditions of their reinstatement in the fold. No such injunction, of course, had been laid upon anyone else and human nature being what, alas, it too often is, what wonder that malice was not restrained by Christian charity when it could be given rein without fear of opposition or resistance.





Some time after my brother Christian's return from the Great Lakes country, he became engaged to a young woman from the neighbouring French-speaking community of Zenon Park. All was well until they applied to the local *curé* and asked him to publish their bans. To their stupefaction, the priest refused to perform the ceremony on the grounds that Christian was illegitimate; he even went so far as to claim that his certificate of baptism and other papers were forged, and he created a public scandal. From the correspondence that ensued, it would appear that he even went so far as to refuse the sacraments (communion) to Father and Mother. Consternation!

Father and Mother hastened to Prince Albert to appeal to the bishop. That worthy, under the impression that they wanted to sue the parish priest,[3] received them with such scant courtesy that they were aghast. The bishop would not listen to what they had to say and ended his dismissal with a threat: "*We'll be watching you!*" Mother told me of that interview. "*We were,*" she said indignantly, "*treated like criminals.*"

Christian was first surprised, then puzzled, then angry. The engagement was broken, and he swore never more to have anything to do with the Church. Father immediately wrote the bishop a letter which contains what he had intended to say, had this dignitary been willing to listen (see Note 6). His Excellency's reply is probably as much of an apology as he could expect (see Note 6a). The *curé*, an ignoramus as well as a fool, was reprimanded, but it was another priest, one whom I had known slightly while in Zenon Park before, a truly good man and a person of sound common sense, now retired and enjoying a regard akin to veneration in his former parish, who gave the people a talking to which helped to clear up the confusion.

Damienne, when a student nurse in Regina, applied to join the Grey Nuns. She was refused entry on the grounds (a) that she was illegitimate, and (b) that history might repeat itself and that she might behave as her mother had done! Damienne was a very attractive young woman, and one of the discoveries she made rather early was that young priests are no more immune than other

3 In fact, following this trip to Prince Albert, Mother consulted a lawyer on this very question, but, as the man of law pointed out, who could testify? Only Father could, and he had been sworn to silence.

men to what Victorian writers so prettily call "the tender passion." A young priest tried to kiss her. To a girl raised as we had been, that was a shock of some magnitude.

When Damienne had finished her training in Regina (1923) she worked for a while at the Sanatorium at Fort Qu'Appelle. She was in Cabri when she met Dr. Adam, a young dentist who had recently set up practice in that little Prairie town, about fifty miles from Swift Current. They became engaged. Stuart's father was a Presbyterian minister, and he offered to perform the marriage ceremony.

When Father heard that news, he wrote a long letter to Damienne to dissuade her from such a course, pointing out that it might well lead to 'eternal perdition'; "*and,*" he added, "*remember that such a marriage is not valid.*"[4] Damienne, however, had made up her mind, and the letter was not likely to frighten or influence her. The marriage took place at the parsonage in Gull Lake, Saskatchewan, on the 29th of June, 1929.

4 My aunt seems not to have had before her the original of this June 9, 1929 letter, now in my possession. Its exact wording: "... for some years now a marriage between a Catholic and a non-Catholic before a Protestant minister has been granted no legitimacy. There is no marriage. At one time it was considered a serious offence but at least there was a marriage. Today that is not the case." (*... depuis quelques années, le mariage d'un catholique et d'un non-catholique par devant un ministre protestant est nul. Il n'y a pas de mariage. Auparavant c'était bien consideré comme un offense grave mais au moins il y avait un mariage. Aujourd'hui, non.*) The phrase "eternal perdition" does not appear, but its equivalents do: he later speaks of fears that Damienne will be "dead to God and daily living in sin" (*morte à Dieu et vivant chaque jour dans la péché*). There are certainly ironies here, but it is clear that my grandfather believed his own 1897 marriage (between Catholics) to be valid in every sense, whatever its status in the eyes of Church authorities. (I.A.)

Shortly afterwards, Christian married Rachel Wilson, a teacher in Ditton Park, without the benefit of clerical blessing. To Christian as well as to Rachel, Father appealed not to follow a course so disastrous for the salvation of the soul of his son. I cannot at times but wonder whether he really spoke from conviction or from loyalty to his given word. But then, this is part of the mystery which surrounds questions of faith.

So three of us were clear of the old bondage. We had long understood that these ties could exist only as long as we were willing to accept them, and the break had brought only relief.

Serge, so far, had remained unswervingly loyal, but, for all that, he did not escape harassment. Sara, his wife, says that, when they decided to marry, she and her family were warned that such an alliance might prejudice the chances of relatives who might wish to enter religious orders. The shadow of papal disfavour still brooded.

It still brooded long years after Father's death, when Mother was living with us in Edmonton. Rodolphe, Christian's first child, had been in Mother's care since his birth, as phlebitis had taken his mother Rachel before she could leave the hospital. Rodolphe was attending school at the College Saint-Jean (an Oblate institution), in Bonnie Doon in the southern part of Edmonton. One day, Mother received from the College — out of the blue, so to speak, a letter addressed to "Miss Eliza Côté." Had someone just caught up with a bit of ancient gossip, or was it just to remind her that the Hounds of Heaven never sleep?

# *epilogue*

*by G. Lorraine Ouellette, née Olsen*

*Memory fades; must the remembered*
*Perishing be?*
*(Walter de la Mare, "Farewell")*

**Introduction**

Perhaps this is more of a sequel: a sequel to a book that Mama wrote to explain her parents to their progeny. It was an exercise in loyalty, and it does her credit. Whether I deserve commensurate approval for this undertaking of mine is a question. That judgment will be made in due course by those who read it. I know that Mother often refrained, out of courteous discretion, from telling tales that might hurt or offend. She did add some notes later, after the dissemination of the first printing, and I have added those notes in this re-edited text. I found, in fact, the whole of Chapter 8 scattered through several files, and I put it together keeping her voice as much as possible and suppressing my own. Now, however, I am adding this piece, and it is I, Lorraine Ouellette, who speaks.

I am trying to strike a balance between truth and tact, but I conclude that my story will suffer if I fail to tell it as I saw it then and as I see it today. My reader can allow for what he may believe to be my bias: for from partiality, whether or not perceived, no one is ever free.

G. Lorraine Ouellette
Edmonton, April 1999

*"Happy the people whose annals are tiresome"*
*(Montesquieu)*

## Epilogue

In a trip to Québec, cousin Barry came upon a little history of the parish of Notre-Dame de la Garde de Val-des-Bois, by one Marc-Claude LaRocque (1983).[1] This interesting tome contains a number of references to Grand'père: indeed, an entire chapter is allotted to his story as the author believed it to be. Here we have a signal instance of the unreliability of the 'oral tradition' of which, these days, we hear so much laudatory nonsense. With the best will in the world, memory being notably unreliable, we tell our stories as we recall them, and our hearers re-tell them with embel-

1 This work, evidently of limited circulation, bears no ISBN number. Upon its cover are letters in gold: "1908–1983" and the title page reads: "NOTRE-DAME DE LA GARDE / DE / VAL-DES-BOIS (1908–1983) / par / Marc-Claude LaRocque / Comité Socio-Culturel, Val-des-Bois Bowman Inc. / 1983."

lishments and deletions. The notable thing about Mr. LaRocque's book is that Grand'père should be remembered at all: and — given the nature of his story — that he should be so kindly portrayed.

His essential goodness impressed all who knew him. He was probity and justice personified. He was never deterred from the path of virtue, though he tried manfully to temper justice with mercy and was never unnecessarily judgmental. My mother's fulsome characterization of him was fully justified.[2]

Mr LaRocque's book is in French, and so I went through it for those who are not fluent, peeling out and translating references to Grand'père and adding, in footnote form, comments that correct some of his factual errors. I find his report surprisingly perceptive.. Mr. LaRocque does not downplay the persecution of Grand'père by the church. Indeed, he stresses it. Times have changed in *la belle province.*





**Page 10**

(The second paragraph deals with the Vicarage at Notre-Dame-de-la-Salette, which Vicarage had charge of the sub-parish of Val-des-Bois, and with its first priest, one Father Louis Clerc) then —

**Page 10, third paragraph:**

His successor, the reverend Daniel[3] Richer, also would serve the mission of Notre-Dame de la Garde. In 1890, he acquired the

2 See Note 7; quotation from Mama's letter to her sister, my Auntie Damienne.

3 His name may have been Daniel, but he was called Damien. Auntie Damienne, of course, was named for him; she was the only person I have ever encountered who bears that name.

ancient bell of the church of St-André Avellin. In 1891, he constructed a little wooden parsonage for the missionary, and, in October of the same year, he organized a retreat which was preached by the reverend father Ladislas, a Capucin. Upon this same occasion, a great cross was planted on the summit of the mountain which dominates the chapel.



**Page 65, Chapter Seven**

W. D. Richer, Parish Priest

Popular memory is short and when we think of the generations which have preceded us, we have a tendency to believe them to be wise or severe, as they appear to us upon the photographs in our albums.

However, these people lived lives which resembled ours: most of the time ordinary lives and sometimes lives marked by incidents out of the common.

Thus, Val-des-Bois saw, at the end of the last century, an unusual love story. Here are the broad outlines of that story. Daniel W. Richer, a brilliant young man who wished to become a doctor,[4] was pushed by his family to become a priest. About 1896, while he was still quite a young cleric, he was sent to be Vicar[5] of our region. He was a good priest: a just man, and sincerely concerned with the

4 I believe he wanted to be a lawyer and that his mother, the lantern-jawed lady depicted on p. 176 of Mother's book, made the not-very-original statement that 'she would rather see him dead at her feet,' etc.

5 'Vicar' in English equals '*curé*' in French; don't ask me why. I didn't do it.

well-being of our population. As was the custom, the priest taught catechism to the children of Notre-Dame de la Salette and also to those of the missions of Notre-Dame de la Garde and St-Louis de France at Poltimore. Among the young persons who attended classes in catechism was a young woman in whom the young priest developed a particular interest. This was an intelligent young girl but not very rich. The parish priest decided to have her placed in a convent to receive further instruction. Two years later, she returned to the region.[6]

Love then became stronger than all of the Reverend Richer's preceding vows. It is thus that, one Sunday morning, the parishioners found the doors of their church locked and barred. Having until this point never found any fault with their parish priest, they were worried: they sought him. They soon discovered that he had deserted his post for the beautiful eyes of the young woman.[7]





The Archdiocese of Ottawa did not regard the situation with favour. A delegation of priests visited the young couple in order to bring the young parson back into line. In vain. However, the clergy did not give up; it omitted no occasion thereafter of harassing D. W. Richer and attempting to drive him from the region.

Upon their side, the love of the young couple was strong and sincere. They had four children. D. W. Richer was of the view that

6 This is garbled. It has always been my understanding that she attended upon him for the purpose of learning some Latin which she had not had the opportunity of learning in school, and I think Mother's account clears up the story.

7 I cringe as I quote this twaddle. Grand'mère would purse her lips and tap her foot.

he should stay in the region. By remaining in that place, exposed to constant reproof for his desertion, he hoped to expiate his fault.[8]

By staying in that place, he placed himself at the disposal of the populace, and he became an important resource person for his area. He was Municipal Secretary, municipal auditor, assistant scaler for the McLaren Company. He acted as a dentist and medical assistant when required. He was also a notary and did any necessary conveyancing when requested.

He lived honourably with his family. He remained a believer. He was always very devoted to our population, and the people of the area, in response, always retained a high esteem for Mr. Richer. Our people accepted the situation and no one made life difficult for him or for his.

In spite of the understanding vouchsafed him by the people of the district, Mr. Richer did suffer certain afflictions. He was never permitted to enter the sanctuary of the parish church, and, at the funeral services of his infant daughter Marie Damienne, he was obliged to kneel upon the steps of the church porch.

Later still, his house burned down. A fellow citizen, Mr. Georges Dubuc, extended the hospitality of his home to Mr. Richer and to his family. To mark its displeasure, the church refused to Louis Dubuc, son of that same Georges, the privilege of making his first communion during that time.

8 This is arrant nonsense. The author did not know my grandfather. Grand'père never did anything that he thought was wrong: he was incapable of being 'pushed by passion' into any action whatever, and the reason he stayed where he was is that he felt no guilt of any kind.

Later, Mr. Richer left the parish of Val-des-Bois to join his daughter who was teaching in Cochrane, in Ontario.[9] Afterwards he moved to Edmonton in Alberta[10] where he occupied the post of janitor in a school. He died of a heart attack. [11]

Page 133 of Mr. LaRocque's book gives a short account of the mill. Mama, in her manuscript, cites an article in *Le Bulletin de Buckingham* which article bears the date September 3, 1970, and I have reproduced her translation of it as Note 8. It indicates that Grandfather built the mill with a partner, a Monsieur Leblanc, in or about the year 1892. Mama writes: "*The above was confirmation of what Mrs. Thom had told me some time before when I called on her. She said that father had discussed the suitability of the site with J. B.*

9 I can't imagine where he gets this. It's quite inaccurate; but, considering the time lapse, it's surprising that the story should be as well reported as it was.

10 Grand'père never lived in Edmonton. He lived first in Ditton Park, then in Hudson Bay Junction. He worked for the Forestry Department for much of his time out here. It's true that for a little time he did janitor the school in Hudson Bay Junction. I remember when he was janitor and wore overalls to work it made no difference to his 'standing' in the community. Everyone called him 'Sir,' from the principal of the school to the loafers in front of the pool hall. One did not ever even think of calling Grand'père anything else. He had Presence....

11 He died of bone cancer in Hudson Bay Junction. Grand'mère nursed him through his illness. When she came to us, she was completely exhausted. There was a story current among the local clergy that he had died in horrible agony as a punishment for his misdeeds (i.e., leaving the priesthood to marry). He certainly died in pain as bone cancer patients do and did, especially in those times when pain management was not as well developed as it is today. I do not believe that he ever 'repented' his sin, for he was not conscious of having committed one.

*David, her father, when he drove through that district on his pastoral visits. Therefore, from 1892 until 1910, father owned the mill for 18 years.*" In 1904, the mill burned down. Mama writes: "*Father was away when it happened and was informed by a neighbour who was travelling that way. He promptly came home and a careful examination of the premises revealed a sizable bundle of birch bark, partly burned, fallen under the mill into the water before being entirely consumed. There was little doubt that it was a case of arson.*"[12]

Grand'père rebuilt the mill. Père Georges Dubuc, Arthur Paquette and Edouard Plante all operated the mill: it seems to have been a kind of lease arrangement. When he left the country, Grand'père sold the mill to Edouard Plante.

Some dates are important to set out here:

- Grand'mère was born in 1878, on the 25th of May. She died in 1954 at the age of 77.
- Grand'père was born in 1863, on the 2nd of September. He died in 1941 at the age of 78.
- When they were married in 1897, on the 12th of July, Grand'mère was 18; he was 33.
- Mother was born in 1899, on the 21st of December.

12 I have dealt with this story by putting in (see Note 8a) the tale as I had it from Uncle Christian.

- Grand'père — His father was Joseph Richer (*dît* Louveteau) and his mother was Olive Grignon. They were married at St. Jérôme Terrebonne on the 26th of May, 1851.
- Grand'mère — Her father was Phidime Côté and her mother was Marie Côté (née Tremblay). They were married at Hébertville, January 25th, 1869.

I don't personally know very much about Grand'mère's childhood, and I don't know very much about the rest of her family. Grand'mère was educated to be a teacher. It was conceded in her family that she was unusually intelligent, and in those days the only possible career for an intelligent girl was in the teaching profession: until she married.





Mother has told about why they came west, and how they came west. She remembers this part of the story, and I have no reason to differ with her recollection. The Church — at Grand'mère's urging — had lifted the ban of excommunication on three conditions, which conditions were communicated to Grand'père:

(1) he was to leave the Province of Québec where he was, clearly, a source of embarrassment to the hierarchy. It was particularly embarrassing for the local priest and the bishop that people of the district continued to consult him at every turn. He had a little office in their house, and there he received people who came seeking

every imaginable kind of advice: medical (!) dental (!) (he even, *au besoin*, extracted their teeth); legal (he served as a kind of local notary and prepared documents for them). He never, of course, charged money for any of these services; he just performed them as a matter of course. The English would say, 'noblesse oblige'; there was no formal 'noblesse' at play here; but his character spoke for itself.

(2) they were to live, thenceforth, as brother and sister; there would be no more marital relations between Grand'père and his wife. They would live celibate; this was part of their imposed sentence. I believe that this was no particular hardship on Grand'père, but in retrospect I know that Grand'mère suffered cruelly. She embraced her pen ance, however, as a condign punishment dictated by her beloved Church. She would not and could not admit that it mattered for that would have been immodest. She bit her lip and endured it.

(3) But he would not accept the third condition of his pardon. The bishop directed the two of them to appear before a priest and have their 'marriage' blest. "*No.*" said Grand'père, with quiet finality. "*I would be stating that my marriage was not valid and that my children are illegitimate. I will make no such assertion.*" I guess he told them that they could pardon him on the basis of (1) and (2), and that, if they were not satisfied with that extent of compliance, they could do the other thing.

Grand'mère, as much as she could, hewed to the line set by the church. They went to live on a farm in Saskatchewan in a district in which there were some immigrants from the East. There's a whole story here to which I was not privy: nay, not one, but several stories. Indeed, when I first penned this sequel I had not yet found Mother's additional notes which gave me the material I needed for Chapter 8. Uncle Christian was bitter about the Catholic church, and now I understand why that was. And by now you, my reader, will understand it too because you will have read Chapter 8.

Because Grand'père kept copies of his letters, I have in my possession a handwritten rough copy of a letter from Grand'père to Rachel Wilson, she who became my Uncle Christian's first wife. In this letter, Grand'père attempts once more to keep Christian in the fold by pleading with his fiancée to accept a marriage blessed by Mother Church. It did not work. Even before Rachel came into their lives, the long arm of the clergy had reached even into far-away Saskatchewan to harass and embarrass Grandfather and his family.

L. P. Hudon, father of Philippe (friend of Mother's — whom at one time she had thought of marrying) — was travelling on a train to Armley, Saskatchewan. In conversation with a Reverend Father Robveil, he (Hudon) learned that a local priest had affirmed that the documents of Christian Richer: certificates of baptism and communion, were false and had been falsified or forged.

There is a letter to Grand'mère from VanBlaricom & Hamilton, Barristers and Solicitors of Tisdale on file, in which these solicitors affirm that, in their view, my grandparents have good grounds for action for slander. The action was not seriously contemplated, but they were anxious to stop the scandal that these falsehoods had stirred up.

The details of attempts to counteract such rumours are set out in Chapter 8. That chapter alludes to Notes 6 and 6a, which give the text of relevant correspondence between Father and the bishop. I think Father's letter itself is valuable because it so clearly mirrors the character of the writer. It sounds so much like him that I believe I would recognize the author, even if I did not otherwise know who had written it. It's vintage Grand'père: courteous, respectful but never flinching. He looked straight across at his interlocutor, incapable as he was of dropping the dignity that was so much a part of him.

Uncle Christian married again after the death of his first wife, Rachel; this time he married another beautiful Irish girl, my Auntie Muriel. I doubt if there was any question of churchly blessings upon this occasion.

But that is not to say that the church's denunciations were at an end. Auntie Damienne suffered the 'illegitimate' label when she applied to enter the Grey Nuns (see Chapter 8, p. 230).

I believe that Auntie Sara hesitated to accept Uncle Serge's proposal of marriage, being reluctant to share in the scandal of his birth and parentage. Mother Church may be a loving parent, but from her displeasure there is no quick respite. The sins of the fathers, verily, are routinely visited upon their progeny as far ahead as memory can extend. It is not surprising that, of all their children, Uncle Serge was the only one to remain a faithful Catholic.

*The farm house, Ditton Park.*

I suppose that some of this constancy may be credited to Auntie Sara, but it was also his nature to be forgiving, and certainly Grand'mère did all that in her lay to foster and strengthen his belief.

Grand'père, too, remained a devout Catholic. I suppose he was able, in his own mind, to insulate from the Church itself the petty malice of her clergy.

They lived on the farm when I first knew them. I do have a picture of the big square house, but the one I have reproduced here is a snapshot that Auntie Damienne had: it's better than mine (see p. 245). I lived in that house with my uncles and grand'père and grand'mère for much of my early childhood, and I remember the inside of that house very clearly. I think when they built that house they were remembering the home they left in Val-des-Bois; it appears to me to be much the same kind of house that appears in Mother's text (p. 12) a big, square house that radiates hospitality. From such a house, one could properly expect help of any and every kind.

There was a big kitchen. The floor was painted grey, and on it were braided rugs and strips of *catalogne*. On one wall was a little blackboard in the kitchen. Grand'mère would stand at her ironing board, and I would write on that little blackboard. That is how, at age four, I learned to read and to write. The memory of those lessons is a happy one. I loved that little blackboard, and I loved having all of Grand'mère's attention. I never felt pushed or constrained. She was a wonderful caregiver, and her patience never failed.

Grand'mère even used pillow-shams; starched and ironed ones. I never saw pillow-shams anywhere else except in convent. It seemed that this was just one of the ways that she refused to let the side down. Her house was always spotless and everything was done; on time and perfectly. Uncles Chris and Serge went to a neighbour's (M's) at threshing time once, and when they came back they said how good the boiled beef was! (Mrs. M had just cooked a quarter in a big pot, outside)! They had never had boiled beef. Well, I guess not. Grand'mère didn't say anything, but she pursed her lips.

This story is not supposed to be about me; but I can't resist adding another bit of gossip about the luckless Mrs. M. Grand'mère did not seek out her company but sometimes she was forced to do the neighbourly thing and pay the lady a call. She took me with her, having, presumably, no one with whom I might be left. I can't imagine that she considered me a social asset. Mrs. M was delighted to welcome us and set immediately about mixing up a cake for tea. As she beat in the ingredients she complained of a cold, or a touch of hay fever. And as I watched, a drop fell from the tip of her nose into the batter!

— "*Grand'mère,*" I said, in a pig's whisper and in French: "*Please let us go home; now.*"

Grand'mère was understandably reluctant, but I began to cry. And cry. And between sobs (still in French), I told Grand'mère the reason for my distress.

We went home.

The living-room (in which we seldom sat) housed shelves of Grand'père's books and also the piano. In accordance with the custom of the time, there was a vase of dried grasses and 'immortelles' on the top of the piano. I was allowed to play on the piano.

No one ever discouraged me, and I soon discovered that one could make sounds on this instrument: sounds that made sense. Sometimes I only romped with my hands on the keys with no attempt to produce anything but noise. The motion was in imitation of Uncle Serge, who sometimes sat there to play. One day I was sitting on the piano bench, plinking at random, when Philippe Hudon came to call. Now, Philippe Hudon had at one time been my mother's beau, and someone had misguidedly mentioned that 'he might have been your father.' As a result, I conceived for that same Philippe Hudon a deep and undying hatred. As he came in, thinking to be pleasant, he said to me: "*That's my favourite piece; play it again!*" I ran to Grand'mère, outraged that this man had had the temerity to trifle with me. I was furious. But I was not even reproved. Grand'mère's patience was limitless.

There was an ice-house in the back yard: a wonderful structure lined with great blocks of ice all around the walls, and sawdust on the floor. There were barrels filled with comestibles of one kind and another. I visited the ice-house on a regular basis because one of those barrels was always full of *beignes* (cake doughnuts), and I indulged in these fairly frequently. No one ever said that I might not. Indeed, I was very seldom told that I might not do this, or that; I wandered at will through the house and grounds, though never far from Grand'mère.

There was a hired man: Tom T. He never did any work, but for some reason Grand'père kept him on. There were hilarious stories about his laziness and the extravagant lengths to which he would go to make Grand'mère think he was busy.

*Grand' père as I remember him.*

In my recollection, all of the work that was done in my line of vision was done by Grand'mère. Grand'père would frequently disappear into 'the bush' to do wonderful and mysterious things. Uncle Christian would go to the lumber camp and come back with wild stories that he would tell me and which made me open my eyes very wide, until Grand'mère put a stop to his tales. He told about hanging the cook at the lumber camp because the beans were not up to par. But Grand'mère said it wasn't true.

When the pigs were slaughtered, it was just a bit scary, but I held the pan to catch the blood; Grand'mère made the best blood sausage in all the world.

I was anything but brave. I would not even consider riding a horse. Once Grand'père sat me up on the back of our mule (named Jean-Paul for some reason that I can't recall); but I cried until I was taken off.

Grand'mère tended the animals, and also the turkeys and chickens, with the help of Mickey, the collie dog. If two tom turkeys fought, as they did sometimes, Mickey would go calmly out to the yard and place his paw gently on the back of one of the combatants to make them stop.

In the winter, if he were home, Grand'père would get up early to light the fire. I slept with Grand'mère so I would not be cold.

Often in the night there would be urgent knocks at the door and Grand'mère would get up quietly, make a bun of her braided hair, take her medical bag (which was always ready and packed) and go off into the night. But I never remember her staying in bed in the morning, even if she had been out until dawn. She brought more than one hundred babies into the world, and never lost a one. In this as in other ways, Grand'père and Grand'mère continued the tradition of gratuitous service to their community that they had established in Val-des-Bois.

Recently, I was privileged to enjoy a visit from Marilyn Hérié, a daughter of my cousin Ellen.[13] Marilyn made a remark that stuck in my memory. She thinks that the women in the family have been largely neglected in our home-grown family histories in favour of the accounts we have given of the men. There is truth in this, and it was a similar impulse that made me protest to Mama when I typed *As I Remember Them*. I certainly revered Grand'père as we all did, but I was acutely conscious of the fact that life went on in their house even when he was not there and that the hand which guided that life — the hand which wrought our comfort and well-being was the hand of Grand'mère, bless her heart.





My recollections of life on the farm are, obviously, the recollections of a small child. Grand'mère kept no diary that I am aware of. Uncle Christian is a heroic figure in my mind, a kind of knight-errant who came and went. Uncle Serge was kind and gentle and (Grand'mère told me later) he would 'spell' her if I were suffering an earache or some other painful affliction that kept me awake and made me cry. I was never suffered to cry uncomforted. The only thing that I regretted sometimes was that I had no children with whom to play, and I longed to remedy this by visiting the

13 Uncle Serge and Auntie Sara's eldest child. She has written an admirable account of the life of her father.

*Grand' père and Grand' mère.*

neighbours who were, in this matter, exceedingly well-endowed. They had troops of children. But Grand'mère pursed her lips and resisted my entreaties. Their French was not of a standard that Grand'mère wished for me and, as I found out the one time I was allowed to go there to play, they were afflicted with head lice. Now, we had neither bedbugs nor head lice in our house, and that fact, in itself, is remarkable, because those were common tribulations on farmsteads in those times.

On p. 252 is a copy of an old snapshot of Grand'père and Grand'mère sitting in front of our house. I wish I had pictures of the yard into which it opened. There was the ice-house; there was the *balançoire*; there was the poultry yard. Sometimes I can shut my eyes and see it. It was so safe, so comfortable; every child ought to have such a house in which he is the centre of attention of some wonderful woman who knows everything, can do everything, and is always there for him. Such a person was my grand'mère, may her descendants honour her memory forever.

My cousin Ellen, of late, has taken on the rôle of 'grand'mère.' I know that she does this in the same spirit as actuated Eliza Richer in the twenties; I know that the little girls who blossom under her care today will one day bless her as I do the lady in this picture. For Grand'père was away a lot. For much of the time he worked 'in the bush'; he made maps, he surveyed — he spent a great deal of time alone with his thoughts. He never needed anybody, I believe. I remember one day — he was setting out on one of his trips and, as he walked down the road, he turned to Grand'mère and said, kindly: "*Travaille pas trop fort, Liza!*"[14] Even as a child I thought that admonition ridiculous. There was no time when she didn't work too hard.

Barry and Willie (Uncle Christian's boys) have discovered that, at one time while he was living in Hudson Bay, Grand'père organized a school for foresters. Unfortunately, nobody remembers much about that school and our efforts to learn about it have come too late: time passes, and people pass with it.

When they lived in Hudson Bay Junction, Grand'père took out a homestead. This was a quarter section ten miles from the town. I absolutely refused to ride a horse, and so poor Grand'mère had to walk with me. She did so, always, without complaint. Sometimes it was just Grand'père and Grand'mère, and sometimes Mama and Auntie Damienne would come as well. I did not enjoy our trips nearly as much when they were along because I thought they seemed always to be complaining about their respective husbands, and I resented criticism of Papa. Also what I knew of Uncle Stuart I very much liked. Besides, when the two of them were there, I could not call upon all of Grand'mère's attention, and I was accustomed to no less.



The garden was wonderful; it grew unbelievable fruit and vegetables, and Grand'père grew his own pipe tobacco there, too, and we picked blueberries and cranberries in the forest. The ferns grew as high as a man's head. The moss was so thick and deep that I could sit back on a moss bank and create a deep, soft chair. This was fun, but I soon tired of it. I hated the mosquitoes that surrounded us as we picked berries, and I whined rather a lot.

14 "Don't work too hard, Liza!"

*Cabin on the homestead, Hudson Bay Junction.*

There is an old snapshot of the cabin that Grand'père built on the homestead on p. 255. It was a wonderful cabin, but I was not only afraid of horses, I was also afraid of the wolves who howled at night, and I frequently complained to Grand'mère that I wanted to go home.

Grand'mère was trained as a teacher. It was a 'given' among those who knew her that she was unusually intelligent. She possessed, however, many exceptional talents in addition to her quick mind and deft hands. She did not allow those talents to atrophy for lack of cultivation. She did what there was to do and what she did not know, she learned. She could read, and she read to some purpose, although I can't imagine when she managed to do this reading.

When they came west, all of her children could communicate in English: and this in spite of the fact that she, herself, had never been instructed in that language. As I understand the story, Grand'mère simply got a book, taught herself enough English to manage basic communication, and proceeded to teach it to her children. This, in my view, is a feat for which she has never received the recognition that she deserves. Her students retained some peculiarities of pronunciation, which for the most part soon disappeared. (Not entirely; my mother, when I was very young, spoke of the 'Mediterraneen' sea), But they all spoke fluent English, though Christian and Damienne retained their accents all their lives.

Her home was a model. She worked slowly, steadily, carefully; everything she did was thought out and planned. One day in the forties when my husband, a veteran, was at university and I was trying to cope with an active child and 'roomers,' she came into my house on a rare visit. I was looking dejectedly at an enormous pile of ironing. She said: "*You can attack this in two ways: you can hurry it — in which event you will be very tired at the end of the day; or you can carefully dampen each piece, roll it meticulously, and proceed without thinking of the time. When you have finished you will not be nearly so tired and you will have a good feeling about your day.*"

She was a nurse of extraordinary ability. Once, when I was living away from home with a friend (to exercise my independence) I developed 'pink-eye' and the infection was so severe that I went to hospital. Here the doctor instructed that my eyes be bound shut; but because there was an abrasion on one of the eyeballs I could not bear the pain. I signed myself out of the hospital and went home to Grand'mère. As always, she knew what to do; as she knew what to do when I had measles. I can still hear her gentle voice as she came into the dark room at just the right time with just the right thing for me to eat.



She could comfort in a trice a sick child, screaming with the pain of colic. It seemed that she could heal with a touch of her patient hands. Auntie Damienne, a wonderful nurse, inherited this power.

Grand'mère was a modiste with unfailing fashion sense (though she did not trouble to exercise this talent upon her own behalf). When she first came to live with us, before I went into the army, she made some of my clothes. They were 'smashing.' I was far and away the best-dressed stenographer at Burns & Co. as I swanked around in her productions. She taught me that for real chic one ought never to wear one's clothes skin-tight; an easy fit was her aim. She could do anything with fabric.

She kept on learning and she became expert in every field of clothing manufacture. Indeed, she taught me, actually over the phone, how to cut out and position a lining in a tailored coat. It's a never-fail system, and I use it to this day.

She has been cruelly undervalued even by many of those of us who owe her an enormous debt of gratitude for her unfailing care and concern. There are very few pictures of her smiling. Perhaps she did not have a lot to smile about.

Certainly I would not presume to criticize Grand'père. He was always courteous to her, and I suppose he thought that he was kind and supportive. I guess she thought so, too, but he did set at naught her more practical values in favour of his rigid sense of righteousness. I have an example to set beside Mother's account of the horse.

This is the story of the ten dollars. Mama used to get upset with me when I told this story but it is true, and it's one reason why I agree with Mama that I ought to 'write my own book.' This happened during the Great Depression while they were living in Hudson Bay. Now, largely because of the good sense of my Papa and of Grand'mère (who could make a tent comfortable, I believe), I never really felt the bite of poverty, but Grand'mère was very concerned about a shortage of funds. She was not miserly certainly, but she did not feel comfortable unless she could rely on little reserve. She set about accumulating a sum for emergencies.

There was a barber in Hudson Bay, commonly called 'Frenchy.' Grand'mère approached Frenchy with an offer to launder his barber towels. I remember how she used to comb out the fringes on those towels with a stiff brush. What her rates were I don't know, but I do know that as a result of her efforts she managed to accumulate the impressive sum of ten dollars. This money she deposited in a sugar-bowl in the kitchen cupboard.

Now, the Depression was deep; I was not suffered to go outside the yard by myself, for Hudson Bay Junction was the end of steel and every day a horde of unemployed men would descend upon the town, looking for work, or just for food. They mostly camped in a kind of hobo city just outside the town limits. I went walking once with Grand'père and saw the 'hobo jungle.' The 'jungle' was not occupied when we were there, but there were the remains of campfires and blackened tins. It was interesting, I thought, for I did not realize the tragedy that those fires revealed.





Every morning after prayers and before any other task, Grand'mère would busy herself and make up a loaf of sandwiches. These were individually wrapped in waxed paper and stored beside the front door. All day long they came, and to the inevitable question: "*Do you have work for me? I would work for a meal....*" The answer was: "*I have no work, but here is a sandwich. Bless you, and good luck.*" One hobo was more inventive than the others. Grand'père was at home, and he answered the door. The man got right to the point: "*My mother is dying, sir, and I need to go to be with her. Can you spare me the money for my fare?*"

As I watched him hand over Grand'mère's ten dollars, I found it difficult to comprehend Grand'père's lack of scepticism. My mind flew to my own Papa, and I could not, somehow, see *him* complying so readily with what, even as a child, I recognized as a scam. Grand'mère did not scold, but she questioned.

And his answer was: "I do not doubt my fellow-man."

Well, 'la-de-dah,' I thought to myself: 'it was *her* ten dollars!' In this one instance, I did not admire Grand'père.

It was while they lived in Hudson Bay Junction that Grand'mère adopted Christian's first-born, Rodolphe.

When Rodolphe's mother (Aunt Rachel) died, Uncle Christian was trying to farm the family farm. He had no money and no help. He could certainly not take care of a small child. Grand'mère took the baby.

After a time, Uncle Christian married again. This time, he married another beautiful Irish girl, a local teacher, Muriel Hanna. Aunt Muriel offered to take Rodolphe home to the farm. Aunt Muriel was a very kind woman and would certainly have been very good to Rodolphe, but Grand'mère would have none of it, on two grounds: (1) Aunt Muriel was a Protestant, and (2) Grand'mère said that a step-mother is never as fond, etc. etc.

Rodolphe has sometimes questioned his having been 'left' with Grand'mère — and I, who was also 'left with Grand'mère,' am here to tell you that this was no sad fate: indeed, if you want an ideal childhood in which you are coddled and made much of — in which you are the centre of the world — in which your welfare is at the top of somebody's list, then have yourself left with Grand'mère.

When Grand'père died in 1941, Grand'mère moved to Edmonton, where she lived with us. Directly her health permitted her to seek work, she found a job with T. J. LaFlèche, custom tailors, and she remained at that job until she retired. She carefully saved her wages for Rodolphe. She never thought of herself. Mother did what in her lay to provide her, not only with necessities, but also with suitable comforts so she was not permitted to deny herself essentials, but her concern was never for herself and always for Rodolphe.

She insisted on sending him to a Catholic boarding school, partly because our house was not a Catholic environment, and also, to be fair, because Papa wasn't all that thrilled with having him around. This was half the fault of Papa and the other half of Rodolphe. Papa was not used to boys (having had two daughters), and Rodolphe didn't seem to like him much either. Papa tried a little, but he just could not understand the boy. They never communicated. Grand'mère was pretty cool to Papa. She also did not like him much.

Grand'mère and Mother were not that close, either, if the truth were known. She never said so, but she could not conceal her feelings entirely. They were very different. There were, I believe, resentments that went way back, and these resentments found expression in curious ways. Mother, for example, would not speak French to Grand'mère. Her motives may have been more elevated than I thought: it's possible that Mother thought that Papa would take exception to being left out of their conversations, and, who knows: he might have, if the conversations had been daily, in his presence. But there was something else, too, because Mother would not speak French to me, even when Papa was not present.

Grand'mère really only craved one thing: to be independent: especially of Papa; and, in any event, if she had to live with family, she would have vastly preferred the hospitality of either Damienne or Serge and Sarah, but neither Damienne nor Serge could afford it, and Papa could, and that is probably why Grand'père, on his death-bed, did that patriarchal, traditional thing. Addressing Mother he said, "*Jeanne, je te laisse ta mère*" (Jeanne, I leave you your mother.). Much as she loved him, Grand'mère must have wanted to kick him.

I need to say as I set down her unusual virtues and pay homage to her infinite kindness to me — I need to say how much I regret the fact that I, of all the beneficiaries of her care, came to hurt her the most. I did not remain a Catholic; I was married outside the pale of the Church, and there came a time when I disappointed her most bitterly because I appeared to 'take sides' in a controversy which has nothing to do with this story. In retrospect, I don't know how I could have prevented any of these happenings. Still, if she were here today, I hope she would comprehend and forgive me, for she was truly my refuge and my strength until I went to school and, indeed, upon many occasions thereafter. I cannot recall a time when she rebuffed me or failed to understand.

I hope that Mama would understand why I added this sequel to her book. I wanted to finish the story. She, evidently, wanted to finish it as well, for as I have noted Chapter 8 comes from bits of writing of hers that I found and cobbled together after she had printed and distributed her original composition.[15] Sometimes, during the process of putting this book together, I have had a strange feeling of communication with Mama: a feeling that I have experienced sometimes when I am reading a book of hers or when I remember her and something that she may have said. Since I am not Scots, nor do I have among my ancestors any Highlanders, I can only ascribe these fancies to the strong and deep enduring affection that I feel and shall always feel for those dear people whose story Mama began to tell and to which I have tried to bring an appropriate conclusion.

Dear Mama; this is for you.





15 See also Note 9, from her diary of several volumes. This BLUEPRINT FOR CONTENTMENT was discovered therein by Heather Simpson, her grand-niece, as she consulted Mama's diaries for a short biography, a project for a history course at the University of Calgary. Heather was not born when Mama died, and I often thought that she was just exactly the little girl of whom Mama dreamed when she herself was young. Indeed Heather was the little girl of whom anyone might dream. I teased her once, calling her a "little brat," and she replied, her big eyes wide and her little mouth pursed: "I am NOT a brat! I am a pretty little girl with curly hair." She was a most loveable child, and she became a loveable woman. Mama would have rejoiced in her, as did her parents, Ed and Mary-Jo Simpson, and her grandparents and other relations and friends. In November 2001 she was tragically drowned in a white-water rafting accident in Peru. Although she had never known Mama, she seemed to be instinctively drawn to her and her choice of Mama as a subject pleased me very much.

# notes

# 1

# connétable



The French use the word *Suisse*. The functions, uniform, and bearing of this personage make it plausible that he represents upon a modest scale the equivalent of the Swiss Guard at the Vatican and bears the name by analogy.

Our man came in quite a different way by the title *connétable*. The word derives from the Latin *Comes Stabuli* or Count of the Stable, once the chief officer of the household, Court administrator and head of military forces. In France, he rose to be commander-in-chief of the King's armies. There existed in England a corresponding title: 'Lord High Constable' which was forfeited in 1521. The office was abolished by Cardinal Richelieu in France in 1627, but in England it remained in use for lesser grades of authority.

We had in England and in Canada police 'constables' as they are familiar to us in cities and villages but also petty or parish constables who were conservators of the peace in parishes or townships.

I asked a professor of History in Ottawa for some clue to the local phenomenon, and this is the answer I received: "In my native parish we always called this man Constable (pronounced in French)." Now, did someone, wishing to avoid the obviously foreign term, substitute for it the literal dictionary translation, thus going back to other times and other customs? If so, it is surely one of those ironical little jests in which life seems to delight.

# 2

# country mice in the city



In those days the city was as alien to many as is the natural world to many urban dwellers today. One of our neighbours had never been away from the parish in which they lived, but they had a daughter who lived in Montreal. She had married a young man of that city. Once they decided to pay her a visit. Mother made a suit for the old man and a dress and hat for his wife so that they would be suitably clad for such an important outing.

Mother and Serge (also wearing a sailor suit and hat of her making) travelled with the pair as far as Masson, by one boat to High Falls and another to Buckingham and Masson, where they were to take the train — the neighbours to Montreal and the others to Hull.

The travellers arrived at the station after dark. Out of the distance, suddenly a monstrous ball of light appeared, accompanied by a thunderous roar, the clanging of metal and the ringing of bells. The old couple had not been prepared for such a sight. Blinded by the powerful headlights and persuaded that the train was coming straight for her, the wife, ran in wild panic into a barbed wire fence whence she was finally extricated, clothing torn and face and hands deeply scratched.

They nevertheless reached their destination. The wonders of the big city were for a long time to come a source of fascinating recollection. One marvel was a bridge recently erected to span the St. Lawrence. The pair speculated on the likely cost of such a structure. the old woman ventured a possible fifty dollars.

— "*Ah, ma vieille,* " objected her spouse, "*Ça doit coûter plus que ça. J'pense que ça coûte ben cent piasses.*"[1]

The son-in-law was employed by the Montreal transit system. He made the old man a present of a pair of used hip boots. Such contraptions had until then been outside of his experience. He was so enamoured of them that he wore them all the way home.

Father was at the mill with Serge the next day when they saw our neighbour coming toward them, limping badly. To their courteous enquiries he replied crossly: "*Mes maudites jambes sont enflées; j'peux quasiment pas marcher.*"[2] Father bade him sit down and by dint of much agonizing pulling (the feet were badly swollen) managed to

1 "Oh, my dear old thing, it must cost as much as a hundred dollars."

2 "My damn' legs are swollen. I can hardly walk."

remove the boots. Their proud owner had not only worn them all during his trip, but had slept in them as well.

# 3

# c. h. edwards



He lent me a book, during that normal school course, about an angel who had been shot down by an enthusiastic hunter who had mistaken him for a large white bird. While his wing was mending, he learned much about the planet and its inhabitants and the latter's way with one another. As all this burst upon his consciousness without any preparation, inconsistencies and irrational behaviour gave rise to protest, to questions, and to philosophical observations. The angel found himself bewildered and sometimes shocked by what he saw. His parting words, as he prepared to take flight, were: "What I cannot understand about you human beings is the zest with which you inflict pain."

I have often felt like echoing this sentiment.

Mr. Edwards derived a good deal of amusement from the ingenuousness of our class and from our French accents. One song we learned for elementary grades I sang to my babies:

> Pretty little bluebird, where do you go?
> Come back, come back to me.
> I go, said the bird, as he flew on high
> To see if my colour matches the sky.

(Some said 'collar,' which would make Mr. Edwards chuckle).

While I was teaching school, he came to Notre-Dame-du-Laus for a week's hunting. Damienne was with me, although she says she does not remember. She may not remember but I do, for I was happy to have her as a sort of chaperone. My good professor's notions of young country schoolteachers did not quite jibe with those with which I had been brought up. I am glad there was no opportunity for me to lose my pleasant impression of summer school. I may have disappointed him — perhaps, by my all-too-obvious lack of interest and curiosity. Shades of Casanova!

# 4
# le brin de cerfeuil (the sprig of chervil)

In English, it comes out more elegantly if we say the Sprig of Parsley. It doesn't matter, either way —

In a beautiful garden where the fairies loved to walk grew a little chervil plant (*un brin de cerfeuil*).

This plant had very ambitious dreams: it longed to be a human being, and it begged a kind-looking fairy to perform this metamorphosis. Every time the fairy passed by the herb patch, the little plant would plead again. One fine day, the fairy said: "*If you will do exactly as I say, I will grant your desire.*" The eager sprig promised to do anything and everything necessary to obtain the fulfilment of his wish. So, duly instructed and transformed into a fine-looking youngster of fifteen or so, *Brin de Cerfeuil* departed to seek his fortune.

Now the king of that country had for a long time suffered from dyspepsia, a term used then to cover any and all digestive troubles. A succession of palace cooks had tried to alleviate the King's distress. They did their best, calling upon all of their most exotic spices and condiments, but to no avail. They lost their heads. A call went out to all points of the Kingdom. Several new chefs now attempted to produce a dish that the King could digest, but the royal stomach could find no relief; they, too, lost their heads. Needless to say, all these highly-trained cuisiniers were masters of the most elaborate recipes.

Now our young hero presented himself at the palace to offer his services as a cook, and great was the astonishment of the king and his entourage. The courtiers scoffed, the ladies wiped a tear at the sight of the candid, engaging youth daring to challenge a certain merciless fate. The king said: "*Do you realize what awaits you if you fail?*" "To be sure, your Majesty," replied the boy lightheartedly, and since no other candidates were in sight, he was there and then given the freedom of the royal kitchens.

The first meal was served: Dishes so simple that they were, in this place, an unheard-of novelty. The king tasted, he tasted again. "How were these prepared?" he asked. "*A la croque au sel,*[3] *may it please your Majesty.*" The king and court ate and marvelled. Not a burp, not a qualm. The ladies (and the new cook) breathed a deep sigh of relief. Days followed, and more dishes, all prepared according to the magic formula given by the good fairy. King

3 "With salt and pepper."

and Courtiers recovered the health and keen appetite of their first youth. *Brin de Cerfeuil* was appointed Royal Cook for the rest of his long life.

# 5
# adieu à nos deux anges dans le cimetière de val-des-bois.



Ici chers anges nous vous quittons.
Le coeur débordant d'une amère tristesse,
Ici nous vous disons adieu !

Navrés, nous vous laissons à la terre chérie
Qui plus de vingt ans fut notre coin de patrie.
Comme des exilés nous partons.
Et vous, anges aimées, pour un temps vous restez.

Restez, Eve et Joseph, roses trop tôt fauchées.
Embaumez d'alentour les tombes ignorées.
Ici dormez en paix votre dernier sommeil.
Mais lorsque sonnera l'heure du grand réveil

De vos restes menus rassemblant la poussière
Légère,
Pour le Bord éternel
D'ou vient toute lumière
A la terre du Val, aussi dites adieu !

Sur vos ailes de flamme ah! franchissez l'espace
Montez — montez vers Lui.
Et le front rayonnant d'innocente allegresse
Devant Lui célébrez
Avec les choeurs des anges,
Sa gloire, Ses louanges.

Et là vous souvenant toujours des exiles
Pour eux demandez grâce,
Qu'il les appelle à Lui de leurs bords reculés
Pour ensemble goûter au ciel la douce ivresse
De voir enfin Sa Face
Et de s'aimer en Dieu !

W. D. Richer
Timmins, 1918.

# 5a
# farewell to our two angels in the cemetery of val-des-bois



(This is Mother's translation of the poem quoted as Note 5. She sent it to cousin Barry, and Barry sent it to me so that I might include it in this book.)

Here, dear Angels do we leave you.
Our hearts brimming over with bitter sadness,
Here we bid you farewell.

Deeply grieving we leave you to the cherished sod
For more than twenty years our corner of the Homeland.
Like exiles we depart.
And you, beloved ones, for a time you abide.

Remain, Eve and Joseph, flowers too soon cut down.
Spread your fragrance among forgotten graves.
Sleep here in peace your last slumber.
But when the hour of awakening comes,
Gathering the light dust of your slender remains
        For the eternal Shore
        Whence ever dawns the Light
To the land of the Vale, do also bid adieu!

On your shining pinions ah! fly through space
        Fly up, fly up to Him.
And your brow all abeam with innocent gladness
        Before Him sing out with
        The choirs of the angels
        His glory and His praise.

And there ever mindful of the distant exiles,
        Beg for them Divine Mercy
That He may call them to him from afar,
And we may enjoy there the sweet rapture
        Of beholding His face
        And loving one another in God.

W. D. Richer
Timmins, 1918.

# 6

# letter from w. d. richer to the bishop of prince albert

What follows is Mother's translation of the letter. I have just copied it as it stands in her file. (Lorraine)

> My Lord Joseph H. Prudhomme,
> Bishop of Prince Albert and Saskatoon.
>
> As I may not, under the circumstances, solicit the favour of an interview, I can nevertheless not bring myself to leave Prince Albert without a last word of explanation on the subject which was the motive of my trip and on certain words exchanged in the courses of our somewhat animated conversation of the other evening.

I see very well that nothing will remain of it but an extremely unfavourable impression on both sides. I realize it is a little late, as I do many things, but I see all the better for that the duty incumbent upon me to try to correct this impression in so far as it concerns the sentiments that Your Grace [sic] may have attributed to me as I was departing.

Far from me, Your Grace, has ever been the thought of dragging before civil tribunals a member of the clergy and to attempt to obtain a decision from others than his Ordinary (diocesan bishop) on questions that concern his ministry directly or indirectly. Even though my rights as a Catholic are supremely violated I do not wish, and my Catholic conscience absolutely refuses to recognize in others than religious authorities any competence in the matter. I only meant to convey, Your Grace, that your words did not augur well for my hopes of this interview, and that the only recourse left me was against those who, following the example of M. le Curé's conduct toward my family and on the strength of it, might spread rumours and reports that I would prove to be falsehoods and lies, recourse necessarily painful, because it may involve developments anything but edifying.

If Your Grace perchance understood anything else I beg Her to believe in my profound sincerity when I say that She ascribes to me sentiments and intentions that I have not and never have had.

Whatever happens, and even in the sad condition in which we are placed by the unwarrantable action of the parish priest, given the impossibility for myself, my wife and my children to fulfil our outward religious duties in accordance with a pact consisting of certain concessions on the part of our mother the Church, and on my part, the sacrifice of a well earned decent and comfortable situation, — even in this melancholy condition I do not claim the privilege of making my just complaint heard by any but by my ecclesiastical superiors.

I will add that in appealing to Your Grace, against the conduct of M. le Curé towards my family, action which brought about consequences so disastrous and so undeserved, I hoped to be able to avoid the other recourse in question: and in order to enable Her (Y. G.) to better arrive at a judgment, I wished to confide in Her as to my confessor without the least doubt that you would receive my confidence in that light. However Your Grace closed my mouth at the very first words and did not allow me to finish.

My means are exhausted, Your Grace, and it is impossible for me to make any further financial sacrifices and to resume my existence of Wandering

Jew. But if Your Grace is pleased to suggest some possible steps which might lead to this result which is at the present time the chief object of my life — that is, keeping my children within the bosom of the Catholic Church which, even when separated from Her, I have never ceased to love and respect with all my heart, I will be sincerely grateful to Your Grace, leaving it entirely at your convenience.

And in these sentiments of profound regret, but also of deep respect, I inscribe myself, &c.

October 16th, 1926.

# note 6a
# the bishop's reply

Bishopric of Prince Albert, Saskatchewan
October 21st, 1926
Mr. W. D. Richer
Arborfield, Sask.



Sir,

Your letter of the 16th corrects an unfortunate impression that I had retained from the interview. My bishop's heart feels compassion for your misfortune and I understand to what degree your situation causes you to feel apprehensions that are only too justified. Hence I am writing this very day to M. le Curé.

May God help and guide you.
(signed) Joseph H. Prudhomme
Bishop of Prince Albert and Saskatoon

# note 7
# jeanne's letter to her sister damienne



As to her views on religion: when I knew her best she was almost violently anti-Catholic, but it's clear from her letters to her sister that Mama was at one time exceedingly devout. Certainly her anti-religious fervour had its roots in the treatment suffered by Grand'père at the hands of the Church hierarchy. I think that only some time later in her life did she become a 'free-thinker.' Her letter to her sister Damienne in December 1920 voices her indignation at the manner in which the Catholic church harassed her father:

> *Mienne, l'homme que toi et moi révérons le plus — qui jusqu'à ce moment a toujours été pour moi le plus frappant exemple de droiture et de probité, plus que cela, de scrupuleuse fidélité à la loi divine, de*

*respect envers l'Église, cet homme a été sous le coup de l'excommunication pendant 20 ans. Et laisse-moi te dire que, malgré que cet homme ait été en butte aux persécutions, aux basses intrigues à la jalousie du clergé (du même clergé qui prêche la charité au peuple, qui ôse, du haut de la chaire de vérité, nous répéter les paroles du Christ — "que celui qui n'a jamas péché lui jette la première pierre" — du clergé qui oublie hélas trop souvent qu'ils sont la lumière du troupeau confié à leur soin et que pour éclairer la lumière doit être pure. Malgré que pendant 20 longues années cet homme a été traité comme un criminel hors la loi par ses voisins, par des catholiques et que pour gagner de quoi faire subsister sa famille et lui-même il dut avoir recours à des héritiques — à des protestants — Mienne, pour ma part du Ciel — sur les droits que Jésus Christ a acquis pour moi quant il est mort sur la croix, si cet homme n'est pas sauvé, il n'y a pas un seul catholique, prêtre ou autre, qui ne le précedra pas en enfer.*

For those who have trouble with the French, I have inserted the English equivalent although, I have to say, it lacks some of the flavour of the original:

Mienne; the man whom you and I most revere;
who until this moment has always been for me the
most outstanding example of integrity and probity;

more than that, of scrupulous fidelity to divine law, of respect to the church, this man was under the scourge of excommunication for twenty years. And let me tell you that, in spite of this man's having been the butt of persecution: of base intrigues instigated by the clergy — that same clergy which preaches charity to the people, which dares, from the height of the pulpit, to repeat to us the words of Christ: "Let he who has not sinned cast the first stone" — from the clergy which forgets, alas, too often that they are the light of the flock entrusted to them and that to enlighten, light must be pure. In spite of the fact that during twenty long years this man was treated like a criminal by his neighbours — by Catholics — and that in order to earn a subsistence for himself and his family he was forced to have recourse to heretics, to Protestants.
— Mienne, for my part of heaven; for my part of the rights that Jesus Christ won for me when he died on the cross: if this man is not saved there is not one Catholic, priest or other, who will not precede him into Hell.

(The translation is mine. [Lorraine])

# note 8
# the mill



Throughout this text, there have been many references to Father's mill, occupied during most of the time we remembered by a succession of tenants. Sometime in 1973, I received from Aunt Eugénie a news clipping which had been given to her for me by Mrs. Thom, née Emerence David, a daughter of Jean-Baptiste, our old neighbour.

Here is the article in question.

> The Buckingham Bulletin
> September 3, 1970
> Val-des-Bois — The Old Mill is Being Demolished
>
> The oldest remaining saw mill in Val-des-Bois is in the process of being torn down. This saw mill,

the property of M. René Plante, was constructed in 1904 on the site of the first mill which had been built by Messrs. Richer and Leblanc in 1892 and which had been destroyed by fire in the course of that year (1904).

The partnership Richer and Leblanc became Richer and Thibault, and in 1910 Messrs. Edouard Plante and George Dubuc Sr. purchased the business and became partners. In 1921, the partnership became Plante and Geo. Dubuc Jr. and about twenty years later Geo. Dubuc's share passed to M. Pierre Sarazin.

Finally, about 1950, after forty years of activity with various partners, M. Edouard Plante retired and his son, the present proprietor, replaced him with M. Aurèle Proulx for some time, then ran the business by himself.

The mill was operated by means of water power and in 1910 and for a number of years after that supplied services for a population spreading some twenty miles around, a considerable distance at a time when lumber was hauled by means of horses. Lumber was sawn and planed, shingles were made and grain was also ground. Sawing was done for a fee of $2.50 per thousand feet of lumber, and the grinding of grain was paid in kind, at a rate of ten pounds for a hundred pounds ... but there were no taxes in those days.

For some years, the old mill has no longer been operating and even though the frame was still solid, the piles forming its base that were built in the water showed signs of impending collapse.

The crew occupied in taking the building apart will no doubt find antique objects of interest and a few planks of old structure will surely find a new lease of life in some modern walls.

***

The above was confirmation of what Mrs. Thom had told me some time before when I had called on her. She said that father had discussed the suitability of the site with J. B. David, her father, when he drove through that district on his pastoral visits. Therefore, from 1892 until 1910, Father owned the mill for eighteen years.

It seems likely that the partnership with Mr. Thibault came to an end when a lease was signed with Paquette and Courchène in 1901.

***

And that is all very interesting, I guess: but it pales before the story of the mill as told by Uncle Christian. I have set this out in full as Note 8a. I took down the story on my little tape recorder as Uncle Christian told it to me from his bed in the nursing home in Nipawin. He told me other stories, too, and they are worth repeating, though this one I add here because it should have formed part of Mother's book. (Lorraine)

# note 8a
# the story of the burning of the mill

*(added by G. Lorraine Ouellette)*



My Uncle Christian told me this story, and he knows it to be the truth about how the mill was burned.

> 'Grandfather, having found work with the James McLaren Lumber company, quickly advanced until he was placed in charge of all of the scalers. A scaler is the official who receives a shipment of logs as it comes from the river and stamps the base of each log with a scaler's stamp. This is a steel hammer something like a branding iron which marks the end of the log and indicates that the log has been counted. Grandfather went from one scaler to the other and checked their operations. It seems that one of the scalers was involved in a scam. After his logs had

been scaled, that is, marked with the hammer, he sawed off the end of the log which bore the stamp and had the logs re-scaled. Thus he managed to get paid at least twice for every log.

Grandfather discovered this; he found a cache of *roulettes* (slices from the ends of the logs). He confronted the scaler and told him that he must make restitution, otherwise he would be reported. The scaler swore that he would replace the logs, and there the matter rested, until Grandfather returned for his next check. Once again, he discovered a fresh cache of roulettes. Now he reported his findings, and the man in the result served two years in jail for his misdeed.

Grandfather owned a mill at Val-des-Bois, hard by his house, and while he was away on his job at McLaren's, he had a man who took care of this mill. The day the scaler got out of jail, the mill burned down. The caretaker drove him to the station, whereupon he disappeared and was never seen again.

The caretaker was not too bright, and he was jealous of Grandfather who was, he thought, doing rather too well; but, although he was not a particular friend, he was a community member. Grandfather said nothing to him about his relationship with the scaler or the roulettes.

Some time later, this man, who was well stricken in years, decided to hand over his farm to his son. This was usual procedure in rural Quebec. It was called *la donaison*; (the gift). Farms were too small, generally, to be divided among sons and so the custom was that the father entered into an agreement, usually with the eldest, whereby he handed over the farm to the boy with the proviso that he and his wife should reside in peace on the premises for the balance of their lives. The son made himself responsible for an honourable burial. I presume that safeguards were written into the agreement, for the deal was usually done before a notary.

Now, Grandfather used generally to act as notary for the people of the district, and he had done many of these agreements, but when it came time for the family to enter into theirs, they decided to go to another: a lawyer in Buckingham. There was an intended insult here; father and son were saying that Grandfather's services (always given free) were not good enough for them. Not too long after the agreement, the son simply ejected his father from the premises. He and his wife were out on the street. What to do?

At the suggestion of another neighbour and finding himself in desperate straits, the father consulted Grandfather. After reading the lawyer's agreement,

Grandfather opined that there was nothing that could be done. No safeguard existed for the tenancy. The father, of course, was stricken. He faced a very sad old age.

Grandfather sent for the son. No one knows what he said to him, but in the result it seems that he had handed over his copy of the agreement to Grandfather and agreed to return the farm to his father.

Handing the document to the father, Grandfather said, quietly, "*Here, Monsieur, is your farm.*"

— "I don't deserve it," was the weeping reply. "I don't deserve this from you."

— "*And why is that?*" asked Grandfather.

— "I am the one who helped that man burn your mill," he said, "You didn't know that."

— "*Of course I knew it,*" said Grandfather.

— "Then why did YOU not come after me?"

— "What good would that do? You are a poor man, as I am; you could not make restitution."'

Trusting his own judgment and walking by his own light. That was Grandfather.

# note 9
# blueprint for contentment



1. Thou shalt not demand of anything more than thy share AND thou shalt not claim any special privilege.
2. Thou shalt in nothing take thy incapacity for granted AND thou shalt make reasonable efforts to develop thy talents.
3. Thou shalt respect those who provide services, however humble AND thou shalt not be impressed by self-importance nor be guilty of it.
4. Thou shalt be willing to serve in any honourable capacity BUT thou shalt be no man's lackey.
5.[4] Thou shalt strive so to live as to maintain thy self-esteem AND thou shalt avoid injuring that of others, even at some

4 The hardest because it contains all the law. Will try to define it next year.

cost to thine own vanity.

6. Thou shalt rejoice at all good fortune — thine own and that of others.
7. Thou shalt have compassion for the misfortunes of others AND thou shalt endeavour to bear thine own trials with equanimity.
8. Thou shalt not judge persons, for no man knows another's motives BUT to evaluate deeds is both thy right and thy duty.
9. Above all things shalt thou seek knowledge and understanding for therein lie strength and peace of mind.
10. Think often on all things good and all things lovely that thy soul may be serene in the midst of confusion.
11. Remember to keep the windows of thy mind open to winds of change for TODAY is the day for living.

[Written in my 70th year (1969)] — J. E. Olsen

# appendices

I

Wilfrid Damien Richer

Ottawa, Ontario. 12 juillet, 1897

II

Joseph Richer — Olive Grignon

St. Jérôme Terrebonne 26 mai, 1851

III

Joseph Richer — Marie Louise Brunet

St. Eustache 11 février, 1828

IV

Joseph Richer — Suzanne Paiement

St. Eustache 23 juillet, 1798

V

Paul Eriché — Cecile Brisebois

St. Laurent 22 mai 1758

VI

François-Jacques Eriché — M.-Anne Brunet-Letang

St. Laurent 18 octobre 1723

VII

Jacques Eriché — Marie Joffrion

Montréal 7 avril 1698

VIII

Jacques Eriché — Catherine Pin

de Louveteau - diocèse de Rouen

Normandie, France



*Appendix I*

*Genealogy of Joseph Richer and Olive Grignon*

I

Eliza Côté

Ottawa, Ontario, 12 juillet, 1897

II

Phidime-Alexandre Charles Côté – Marie Tremblay

Hébertville 25 janvier 1869

III

Simon-Jules Côté Eulalie Dessin

Baie St. Paul 13 novembre 1838

IV

Moyse Côté Olive Gauthier

Baie St. Paul 25 janvier 1803

V

Joseph Côté Dorothée Tremblay

Petite Rivière 20 février 1759

VI

Thomas Côté Geneviève Gagnon

Les Éboulements 2 mai 1735

VII

Jean Côté Geneviève Verdon

Québec 25 février 1686

VIII

Jean Côté Anne Martin

Québec 17 novembre 1635

de Mortagne, Perche

France



*Appendix II*

*Genealogy of Phidime Côté and Marie Tremblay*

# legacies shared series

1. *Looking for Country: A Nowegian Immigrant's Alberta Memoir*
   Ellenor Ranghild Merriken

2. *The Last Illusion: Letters from Dutch Immigrants in the "Land of Opportunity" 1924–1930*
   Edited and translated by Herman Ganzevoort

3. *With Heart and Soul: Calgary's Italian Community*
   Antonella Fanella

4. *A History of the Edmonton City Market, 1900–2000: Urban Values and Urban Culture*
   Kathryn Chase Merrett

5. *No One Awaiting Me: Two Brothers Defy Death during the Holocaust in Romania*
   Joil Alpern

6. *Unifarm: A Story of Conflict and Change*
   Carrol Jaques